The Future of Policing

The Future of Policing

200 Recommendations to Enhance Policing and Community Safety

Scott A. Cunningham

ROWMAN & LITTLEFIELD
Lanham • Boulder • New York • London

Published by Rowman & Littlefield
An imprint of The Rowman & Littlefield Publishing Group, Inc.
4501 Forbes Boulevard, Suite 200, Lanham, Maryland 20706
www.rowman.com

86-90 Paul Street, London EC2A 4NE, United Kingdom

British Library Cataloguing in Publication Information Available

Library of Congress Cataloging-in-Publication Data

Names: Cunningham, Scott A., author.
Title: The future of policing : 200 recommendations to enhance policing and community
    safety / Scott A. Cunningham.
Description: Lanham : Rowman & Littlefield, [2022] | Includes bibliographical
    references and index. | Summary: "America is challenging everything about
    policing—its equipment, tactics, role, tasks, and even its very existence. This book
    guides those conversations by providing 200 specific recommendations that cover all
    aspects of policing, even the most controversial and important issues"—Provided by
    publisher.
Identifiers: LCCN 2021047733 (print) | LCCN 2021047734 (ebook) | ISBN
    9781538163047 (cloth) | ISBN 9781538163061 (paperback) | ISBN 9781538163054
    (epub)
Subjects: LCSH: Police administration. | Law enforcement.
Classification: LCC HV7935 .C86 2022 (print) | LCC HV7935 (ebook) | DDC
    363.2—dc23
LC record available at https://lccn.loc.gov/2021047733
LC ebook record available at https://lccn.loc.gov/2021047734

This work is dedicated to the following groups and people:

To all those police officers who do the job the right way for the right reasons. You are the vast majority of police officers who have chosen a difficult profession. You strive to serve legally, ethically, professionally, fairly, and impartially. You strive to protect individuals and the community and do so with great tact and minimal force. The vast majority of police-citizen interactions are without incident, and most are positive. This is because of you. You are there to answer the calls for help. Whether it be a traffic crash, an assault, a burglary, a disturbance that people can't settle among themselves, or an active shooter, you are the ones that respond to stabilize the situation, and to return order, calm, and peace to a home, business, park, or society. You see things, and make decisions, sometimes critical decisions in split seconds, that no one should have to experience. You put yourself in harm's way to protect people you don't even know. It is because of you that society overall and individual citizens enjoy the high quality of life that exists. Some of you have suffered permanent injuries or even sacrificed your lives to protect others. To you, and your families, an unpayable debt is forever owed.

To those citizens who have been harmed by police officers who inappropriately handled a situation or used force unnecessarily, even illegally in some cases. Your pain may be long-lasting, and the pain of your loved ones might be forever. You deserved better.

To my family, who has stood beside me and walked along with me during a thirty-eight-year career in policing. You have seen, heard, and endured a lot. More than families should have to. Without your love and support, I could not have served as I did. I owe you everything. I love each of you tremendously.

Contents

Introduction

The years 2020 and 2021 were years of struggle. The pandemic caused by the coronavirus COVID-19 wreaked havoc throughout the world. During 2020, the world saw over 81 million sick, with over 1.8 million people dead.[1] The United States alone experienced over 20 million sick and more than 350,000 dead.[2] The year 2021 saw the virus continue but slow due to several vaccines that became available. But then, the delta variant appeared and created a second wave of death. The pandemic resulted in severe economic impacts as society tried to stem the spread of the virus. However, differing viewpoints about wearing masks, limited social gatherings, and closing or limiting business operations all were part of how American society responded to the pandemic. Even disagreements about a vaccine existed, including who was responsible for developing the vaccine, what order should it be provided to people, should it be taken, and even should it be mandated?

The year 2020 was also a presidential election year in which the usual political commentaries, claims, and attacks rose (or sunk) to new levels. Misinformation, claims of "fake news," outright lies, and personal attacks by some candidates became the norm. Unfounded claims of improprieties in the election process, voting, and ballot counting exceeded all previous election year concerns. The country became very divided, vocal, and, in some cases, violent, often in the name of politics and democracy.

These events are important when considering the significant issues that surrounded American policing in 2020 and 2021. Policing does not happen in a vacuum. The mood, viewpoints, and stresses of society impact how policing occurs and how it is perceived. The pandemic and the election brought added pressures on policing. In some cases, the police were tasked with enforcing governmental efforts to deal with the pandemic. This included forcing businesses to regulate the numbers of customers or even close. The police were also tasked with enforcing mandates to wear masks which included issuing citations in some situations. This was not a popular activity for police. The election and resulting political campaigning placed additional demands on the police. Besides providing protection and crowd and traffic control at various rallies and protests, the police were called upon to stop protests when opposing groups could not voice their opinions and views civilly. The police were viewed by many participants as favoring one group over the other, using too much force, or not taking sufficient actions. It was virtually a no-win situation for police.

Combined, these and other issues also lead to an increase in serious crime. Depending on which source and how measured, homicides increased between 15 percent and 42 percent when comparing various time segments in 2020 to the same time frames in 2019.[3] Aggravated assaults also increased, but, in general, property crimes dropped. Most of the increases occurred in larger, more urban, and densely populated communities. Several reasons and opinions have been offered for the 2020 jump in crime. Some of the more likely include: impacts of COVID-19 overall, "de-policing," increased lack of trust in police, increased availability of firearms, overloaded hospitals, and a poor economy generally caused by the pandemic.[4] A rising crime rate always brings into question the ability of the police to impact crime and leads to discussions regarding the role of police.

Against this backdrop of societal turmoil and stress, various incidents directly involving the police occurred. Starting in June and July 2020, the nation saw weeks of protests, civil disturbances, and riots that were specifically directed against the police. The spark that ignited this most recent round of public unrest was the senseless, needless, and improper death of George Floyd, a black man, at the hands of a white Minneapolis police officer. Some may question why race is mentioned, but unfortunately it is an important part of the issues facing America and policing. After being arrested, the officer put Mr. Floyd face down on the roadway, and placed a weight-bearing knee on his neck and upper shoulder area. Despite Mr. Floyd stating he could not breathe, the officer kept Mr. Floyd pinned to the ground for an excessive and unnecessary length of time. Other officers on the scene suggested medical attention for, and the repositioning of, Mr. Floyd. However, this did not happen. Eventually, medical aid was called for a now-unresponsive and possibly deceased Mr. Floyd. At some point, George Floyd died. The officer was charged, convicted, and sentenced to twenty-two years in prison.

Having seen similar deaths of black males while involved with police officers, the nation had had enough. Protests started immediately in Minneapolis, and then spread quickly around the country. Many protests were peaceful and called for justice. Justice for George Floyd, and many others who had died while interacting with police. Familiar and prevalent cries included

Black Lives Matter, end police brutality, and for the officer involved to be immediately criminally charged. People were angry, and justifiably so. Some protests turned violent and destructive with buildings burned, officers assaulted, and citizens hurt. Protests even occurred around the globe.

This time something was different, and positively so. The anger and demands for something to be done were far-reaching and involved more than just the black community or a few protestors. An all-encompassing variety of people either joined the protests or supported them. People of all demographic backgrounds, economic levels, and professions resoundingly condemned the actions of the officers in the Floyd incident. Even police officers and police leaders condemned the actions that resulted in George Floyd's death. This was a new, massive groundswell of support. It was the beginning of a sea change in American policing. These protests called for changes in policing. Some suggestions were minor while others were significant in scope. Some suggestions and demands were reasonable (policy changes regarding use of force), some were not (defund or abolish police agencies). One thing was certain. Policing in America needed to change. And this should be good for everyone.

As we begin this effort to improve the future of policing, a few words about how the book is organized, its limitations, and its potential benefits. This work is not intended to be an in-depth history of American policing, nor to cover all aspects of policing. There are numerous other works that can provide more in-depth information about these and various other topics related to policing. It is not intended to cover each topic discussed here in a definitive manner, as that would be quite a voluminous work and other existing sources can provide a more focused discussion of the individual topics. Plus, other sources can supplement this work, and, more importantly, can supplement the discussion that needs to happen.

Rather, it is intended to discuss a variety of important topics and make recommendations that can have significant implications that should lead to meaningful change. This work intentionally goes beyond a mere discussion of various concepts by presenting specific recommendations that should be considered. While having a general discussion can be beneficial, there has already been considerable discussion. What is needed now is focused discussion centered around specific recommendations that can be implemented. By identifying numerous recommendations focused on specific actions, the discussion can move into real-world impact. It moves the concerns from discussion to action, from reimagining to realizing the future.

This work and its chapters are organized based on topics that are common to policing, and in many cases any organization. There is room, and in some cases sizable room, for improving and enhancing the delivery of police services. Understanding this, these discussions and recommendations are offered with the intent that, individually and collectively, they could enhance policing and improve the quality of life for everyone. These recommendations should be considered, discussed, and implemented as appropriate. There should not be a mad, unthinking, emotional rush to implementing these or other suggestions. But those recommendations that are beneficial should be implemented with deliberate speed. Unnecessary delay can result in bad outcomes that can have devastating impacts on individuals and communities.

This work is broken down into parts and then chapters. Each part groups topics together that are generally related to each other. Each chapter includes a discussion of the general topic, and then moves into specific discussions and recommendations for enhancement. There is some overlap in topics and recommendations. This is because many topics share common concerns and issues. Many issues are interrelated and impact other issues or concerns.

It should be remembered that policing is one aspect of an overall criminal justice system. Many issues that impact policing are part of larger issues and concerns within the criminal justice system. This includes the prosecutors, courts, corrections, and all of their components. Even legislative issues impact policing as it is the legislatures that create the laws that police officers are expected to enforce. When an unpopular law exists, it is usually the police that bear the brunt of citizen dissatisfaction. This further negatively impacts how police are perceived, even though they are tasked with enforcing an unpopular law. Decisions made by prosecutors, judges, and juries impact the police and the perceptions of the criminal justice system. While the entire criminal justice system should be reviewed, this work focuses predominantly on policing.

Police professionals, academics, elected and appointed officials, and most importantly citizens should consider these thoughts and recommendations. Agencies and citizens should engage in civil dialogue to identify common ground and discuss what changes should be made, and how policing can be enhanced. All stakeholders should have calm, professional, courteous discussions and conversations regarding these recommendations. Everyone should fully listen to the views of other stakeholders as the views of others might not be fully understood by everyone. Everyone has life experiences with either government, policing, or the criminal justice system. Some of these experiences may be personal, or have involved relatives or friends, or may just have been experienced through the media.

And these experiences influence how policing is perceived. By police officers, officials, and citizens. Through meaningful and civil discourse, society as a whole should be able to reengineer policing so that all of society is safer, more just, and has a better quality of life for everyone.

Part I

GLOBAL POLICING CONCEPTS

Chapter 1

Role and History of Policing

Policing is not a new concept. Versions of policing existed in ancient China, Babylonia, Egypt, Greece, and the Roman Empire.[1] It has continued throughout history until modern times. Policing began with the intent to keep groups of people (communities) safe. Safe from animals, fires, people outside the community, from community members. This also included maintaining public order and preventing disturbances and disorder. As communities grew in size and density, the focus of police activity became the regulation of human behavior. Outsiders were viewed suspiciously and generated increased citizen and police attention. But eventually a significant amount of attention shifted to people within the community. This included people with a history of causing problems for other citizens, and then those who were perceived as likely to cause problems.

Most American policing grew out of the need for safety and followed the English model. The primary focus of early policing centered on preventing crimes and disorder issues, and not so much on serious crime.[2] Policing in America was originally both formal and informal. Most communities utilized a "watch" or "watchman" system wherein citizens took turns standing watch, primarily during night hours. Later, this watch was extended to daytime hours. Formalized policing in North America began in 1626 when the New York City Sheriff's Office was created.[3] As communities grew, the desire and need for policing also grew. Between 1751 and 1838, many communities implemented various versions of day and night watches. Some of these were volunteers, while others used a variety of methods as compensation including a pay-per-case method. It is generally agreed that the first centralized municipal police force in America was organized in Boston in 1838.[4] Between 1789 and 1792, several federal agencies (U.S. Marshals Service, Park Police, and Mint Police) were created for specific purposes related to the operation of

3

the federal government. American policing, while responding to the needs of American society, did not develop in a vacuum. It was heavily influenced by the history of policing in other parts of the world, and the views and perceptions American citizens held regarding government control and power.

The culture, conditions, and activities of society shaped the way police evolved. How a society lives and the values it possesses determine the nature of its police, and how police act and respond. From a culture where it was the civic duty of people to act as watchmen, to volunteer watchmen, to officers who were paid for property recovery, to today's full-service police professional, law enforcement has evolved considerably. And policing continues, and must continue, to evolve and change with shifts in technology, knowledge, laws, and, most importantly, with the expectations of society. Policing exists to the extent that society cannot or will not conform to the norms of that society. When people have a common viewpoint or perception of how society should be, there is less need for a formal police force. Societies that have a more diverse viewpoint of life, regulation, freedoms, government, and generally how to live, require a more formal and active police force.

Policing has always been expected to protect and maintain the status quo in society. Some attribute this to protecting the powerful or wealthy, but the reality is that policing is intended to protect the current order, calm, and views of society. Policing must enforce the laws as they exist (and have been upheld or interpreted by the courts) at the time. While agencies can choose to put more or less emphasis on certain issues or laws, they generally do so based upon the support, if not the direction of the community and governmental parent (mayor, manager, council, etc.). Historically, the public never wanted the police to be leaders in social change as this would be viewed as the government mandating societal change through force. Also, in most cases, those advocating change are generally those with either a minority viewpoint or minority voice (minority here meaning numbers). If those advocating for certain changes were in the majority, applicable laws and societal norms and expectations would have been changed. In most cases, the majority of the public have wanted the police to maintain the status quo.

However, many times throughout our history, the police have been called upon to maintain social order, even when the minority voice or viewpoint was right in calling for the change it advocated. And since the police were tasked with maintaining social order, it sometimes seemed (and in some cases actually was) as if the police were opposed to the changes. In most cases, the police were trying to maintain calm, social order, and enforce existing laws, without regard for the actual issues involved. And in many ways, that is what the public expects—enforce the law and maintain social order regardless of the views of the officers or agencies. But this has led to the perception (and in some cases, the reality) that the police were opposed to the changes being advocated.

Examples of these situations include enforcement of sundown laws, drug and morals laws, and stopping protests (peaceful and violent) involving issues like women's voting, civil rights, and police and community reforms. This has harmed the perception of and influenced the history of the policing profession.

Throughout history, there have been examples of individual officers and, in some cases, whole agencies, acting inappropriately and, occasionally, illegally. Some people argue that policing originated from slave patrols and therefore all policing efforts are designed, intended, and/or founded upon the concept of treating persons of color inappropriately. While the historical connection has some accuracy, the viewpoint that all current policing is controlled or at least influenced by the history is inaccurate. Policing, including American policing, existed prior to slave patrols.[5] Most police agencies, especially those in the north and west, were not influenced by slavery. However, in some southern states, slave patrols did exist, some as early as 1704.[6] Some argue that these slave patrols then evolved into police agencies with some of the intent and focus on controlling recently freed slaves. It is without question that some early southern police agencies put a lot of effort into regulating the actions and behaviors of blacks. This should have been expected given the views of many southern citizens and communities, and the changes in society regarding slavery. Laws can change and can take effect quickly. Unfortunately, changing the views, perceptions, and beliefs of people, individually and collectively, usually takes a much longer time frame, with many resisting changes. And some of the attitudes regarding blacks were strongly held by some who resisted these changes, even to the point of using governmental powers, aka the police, to hinder the desired and appropriate changes. It is true that slavery and slave patrols influenced some agencies, specifically in the south. But the belief that all American police departments, and American policing in general, was born of or grew out of slave patrols is not supported by historical evidence. However, this perception lingers and negatively impacts policing even today.

The historical actions of some police officers and some agencies have impacted people's perceptions of police, in mostly a negative manner. Some of the issues surround how the police handled these issues and the protests related to them. In many circumstances, there has been or is concern regarding how much force was used by police in controlling the protests or making arrests for the underlying issues. And these issues still exist today as there are concerns about police tactics and techniques in the various protests, disturbances, and riots of 2020. Past societies and current societies shape, define, and influence the perception and role of policing. This has been good and bad, but hopefully will be better going forward.

Recommendation 1: The history of American policing, including local issues and history, should be taught to agency personnel.

Because of the history of policing (real and perceived), all agency personnel should learn the issues, concerns, and history of policing. This education should begin in the police academy during basic recruit training so there is perspective on how policing might be perceived by various citizens or groups of citizens. While this should include historically accurate information about worldwide policing, it must focus on American policing and various perceptions and beliefs. Information relative to the specific agency should also be discussed, as it can be especially pertinent to the community and its perceptions of that agency. Different police agencies have different histories that might be due to where the agency exists (northern versus southern), or what specific incidents the agency may have been involved in throughout its own specific history. Understanding the history of and perceptions regarding policing (global, national, and local) can improve the knowledge, compassion, and understanding of officers as they provide services to citizens in various communities. This knowledge and understanding of local history becomes more important when fewer officers were born and raised in the specific community. Realizing that policing plays a role in society, various movements and issues can put the role of policing into perspective and context. It can also remind people that certain actions such as order maintenance can be viewed as oppressive or as being against issues or changes in society. It can also lead to more compassionate tactics and techniques when groups engage in lawful protests regarding societal issues and concerns.

ENGLISH IMPACTS ON AMERICAN POLICING

As is often the case, history impacts organizational structures, practices, and philosophies. Oftentimes these impacts last centuries. America's historical connection to England has impacted much of American law, government, and policing. Because of various British attitudes and actions toward the American colonies (and the colonist's perceptions of those actions), American society has evolved with certain views and limitations regarding government and policing. Many of these views are reflected in the U.S. Constitution and Bill of Rights. Many of the limitations placed on the government can be directly traced to colonial times. This is especially true when considering the Bill of Rights, which contains the first ten amendments to the Constitution. These specifically prohibit certain governmental actions and reserve specific rights as belonging to the people. This sets the foundation for how American policing evolved over the course of time. In fact, it can be very easily argued that five of the first ten amendments directly relate to the functions of the criminal justice system and policing. These five amendments[7] are:

Amendment I:

Congress shall make no law respecting an establishment of religion, or prohibiting the free exercise thereof; or abridging the freedom of speech, or of the press; or the right of the people peaceably to assembly, and to petition the Government for a redress of grievances.

Amendment IV:

The right of the people to be secure in their persons, houses, papers, and effects, against unreasonable searches and seizures, shall not be violated, and no Warrants shall issue, but upon probable cause, supported by oath or affirmation, and particularly describing the place to be searched, and the persons or things to be seized.

Amendment V:

No person shall be held to answer for a capital, or otherwise infamous crime, unless on a presentment or indictment of a Grand Jury, except in cases arising in the land or naval forces, or in the Militia, when in actual service in time of War or public danger; nor shall any person be subject for the same offence to be twice put in jeopardy of life or limb; nor shall be compelled in any criminal case to be a witness against himself, nor be deprived of life, liberty, or property, without due process of law; nor shall private property be taken for public use, without just compensation.

Amendment VI:

In all criminal prosecutions, the accused shall enjoy the right to a speedy and public trial, by an impartial jury of the State and district wherein the crime shall have been committed, which district shall have been previously ascertained by law, and to be informed of the nature and cause of the accusation; to be confronted with the witnesses against him; to have compulsory process for obtaining witnesses in his favor, and to have the Assistance of Counsel for his defence.

Amendment VIII:

Excessive bail shall not be required, nor excessive fines imposed, nor cruel and unusual punishments inflicted.

Certain other core concepts act as foundational principles and beliefs for American policing. Each of these can and should provide guidance to communities and agencies in ensuring that police agencies perform the desired tasks in a manner that is acceptable to and desired by the citizens. Some concepts have been practiced and are still practiced, while others were abandoned for various reasons. It is imperative that each and every police agency in America adopt, maintain, and focus on those core foundational principles and beliefs that support quality policing in America.

THE PEELIAN PRINCIPLES

In the early 1800s, London was a large city with a population of over 1.5 million residents. Protection services were provided by 450 constables and over 4,500 watchmen. But this large number was generally ineffective because they worked for several different organizations that competed with each other and did not work together for the good of the community. Efforts to create a city-wide police force were greatly resisted for several reasons.

As home secretary, Sir Robert Peel was focused on resolving the crime issues. The Metropolitan Police Act of 1829[8] created a Metropolitan Police Force that served areas around London, but not the core city itself. The mayor and city of London refused to participate believing that it was the role of the local government to control the police, not the central national government. People also opposed a large, centrally controlled, and possibly armed force in the belief that it could inhibit protests or could become a military dictatorship. These views impacted how American policing developed and still influence policing today.

In creating the Metropolitan Police Force, Peel wanted to avoid many of the citizen concerns that existed at the time. This is why the Metropolitan Police Force avoided a militaristic appearance and were unarmed. Peel and his commissioners created a set of principles by which the officers would be guided. Even though at the time, Paris had a paid, well-trained, and professional police force, Peel became known as the father of modern policing. The principles have generally been accredited to him and these principles were used as the foundation of many American police agencies, and in some cases still are. In fact, a version of these principles is displayed prominently on the main staircase of the New York City Police Department's Training Academy. These principles have stood the test of time.

Recommendation 2: The Peelian Principles of Policing (nine principles and three core ideas) should be a core foundation of every American police agency.

These principles have been rewritten and adjusted with different language over the years and by different entities. This version is from the Law Enforcement Action Partnership.[9]

1. To prevent crime and disorder, as an alternative to their repression by military force and severity of legal punishment.
2. To recognize always that the power of the police to fulfill their functions and duties is dependent on public approval of their existence, actions, and behavior, and on their ability to secure and maintain public respect.

3. To recognize always that to secure and maintain the respect and approval of the public means also the securing of the willing cooperation of the public in the task of securing observation of laws.

4. To recognize always that the extent to which cooperation of the public can be secured diminishes proportionately the necessity of the use of physical force and compulsion for achieving police objectives.

5. To seek and preserve public favor, not by pandering to public opinion, but by constantly demonstrating absolute impartial service to the law, in complete independence of policy, and without regard to the justice or injustice of the substance of individual laws, by ready offering of individual friendship to all members of the public without regard to their wealth or social standing, by ready exercise of courtesy and friendly good humor, and by ready offering of individual sacrifice in protecting and preserving life.

6. To use physical force only when the exercise of persuasion, advice, and warning is found to be insufficient to obtain public cooperation to an extent necessary to secure observance of law or to restore order, and to use only the minimum degree of physical force which is necessary on any particular occasion for achieving a police objective.

7. To maintain at all times a relationship with the public that gives reality to the historic tradition that the police are the public and that the public are the police, the police being only members of the public who are paid to give full-time attention to duties which are incumbent on every citizen in the interests of community welfare and existence.

8. To recognize always the need for strict adherence to police-executive functions, and to refrain from even seeming to usurp the powers of the judiciary of avenging individuals or the state, and of authoritatively judging guilt and punishing the guilty.

9. To recognize always the test of police efficiency is the absence of crime and disorder, and not the visible evidence of police action in dealing with them.

Peel's three core ideas are:

1. The goal is preventing crime, not catching criminals. If the police stop crime before it happens, we don't have to punish citizens or suppress their rights. An effective police department doesn't have high arrest stats: its community has low crime rates.

2. The key to preventing crime is earning public support. Every community member must share the responsibility of preventing crime, as if they were all volunteers of the force. They will only accept this responsibility if the community supports and trust the police.

3. The police can earn public support by respecting community principles.
   Winning public approval requires hard work to build reputation: enforcing the laws impartially, hiring officers who represent and understand the
   community, and using force as a last resort.

As is obvious, several key concepts exist here that have great impact
in today's society. These include voluntary compliance with laws and the
responsibility of citizens to participate in community safety; policing must
build trust and gain the support of the citizens; the prevention of crime is the
main priority of police, and if done effectively there will be low crime and
low arrest numbers; force should be only when necessary and then only the
minimum amount used to accomplish the lawful objectives of the police; de-
escalation should be used; and to enforce the laws fairly and impartially. Each
of these is critical, and if fully embraced by citizens, agencies, and officers,
could reduce negative police-citizen interactions and could result in a safer
community with a higher quality of life for all.

Chapter 2

Redefining the Tasks for Which Police Are Responsible

Over the course of time, the police have been tasked with many responsibilities. Many of these were not sought out by the police but rather were dropped on them. When most other governmental entities or services closed for the workday or week, police became the default governmental service provider twenty-four hours a day seven days a week. Ironically, when full-time Fire Departments began to appear in many communities, they were not called upon for tasks beyond fire response, some rescues, medical issues, and the periodic "cat up a tree." Today, some advocate changing the role of police. The primary role hasn't changed and should not change. The role of policing remains to preserve the peace, enhance the quality of life for everyone, and to do so while protecting the constitutional rights of every citizen. However, there are strong and logical reasons to change some of the tasks that police are currently expected to perform.

Over time, the number and variety of tasks assigned to police increased. In many cases, staffing, training, and policy did not keep up with these new demands for service. One of the biggest additions was the expectation of police to handle calls involving persons with mental illnesses and/or those citizens suffering a mental or emotional crisis. Decades ago, many mental health facilities were closed for various reasons. Known as deinstitutionalization, most large, dedicated mental health facilities (variously known as psychiatric hospitals, mental wards, or insane asylums) were closed. The 1962 book, and 1975 film *One Flew Over the Cuckoo's Nest* heavily impacted how these facilities were perceived. The burden of dealing with persons who had varying degrees of mental illnesses was being shifted to local communities through community health centers. In some cases, the facilities had become associated with poor and sometimes inhumane treatment of patients. Society also believed persons with mental health issues should not be warehoused and

11

could be treated better if out in society. The perception that costs could be reduced if the patients were treated locally also played into these decisions. This all resulted in facilities closing and persons with mental health issues being put out into society, sometimes literally dumped on city streets, without any type of support mechanisms.

When issues arose, or society became concerned about these individuals, they called the police to remove them from sight. When the police did respond, they did not have significant special training to deal with people in crisis. They only had the tools and techniques with which they had been trained and given. This included some degree of verbalization but generally involved officers providing direction or commands to the subject. When these commands were not complied with (for many reasons), many officers resorted to the physical skills to coerce compliance with the applicable laws. This sometimes resulted in using various levels of force to remove the subject from the area, and often times resulted in criminal charges (disorderly conduct, failure to comply with lawful orders, resist arrest, etc.). Without a good understanding of mental health issues, most officers simply did not realize that many of these citizens could not understand or comply with directions for various reasons associated with their particular situations and conditions. This did not help the citizen in crisis and began to overcrowd jails, which subjected the person in crisis to new and additional conditions and horrors. In fact, jails and prisons have become the primary provider of mental health services, and actually house up to ten times more persons with serious mental illnesses (SMI) than state hospitals.[1]

Another topic closely related to the mental health issue is homelessness. The number of homeless and the resulting numbers of calls to police for dealing with the homeless increased dramatically during this same time period. Many people in crisis or with mental health issues could not get or hold a job, which meant they could not afford a place to live. Homeless camps grew in prevalence and size. Some citizens called police about these camps and persons. Some of the calls were founded in a genuine concern for their well-being, but most calls occurred because people wanted these less fortunate citizens removed from sight. There was no one else to call about the homeless and sometimes the homeless had behavioral problems due to mental illness. So the police were called to handle the issues.

Other tasks have long been the responsibility of the police but in many cases didn't need to be. The police took responsibility for the tasks because oftentimes disputes would occur and the police were viewed as the only reasonable and available resource to maintain public order and safety. One such task involves vehicular traffic crashes. In most cases, a fully armed and sworn police officer is not technically needed to investigate many of the crashes that occur. But there are numerous reasons why virtually all crash investigations have become the purview of police. One of the primary reasons crashes are handled by the police is that involved citizens do not comply with reporting requirements or the involved parties become involved in disputes that often times become physical. Other reasons for police involvement include no other options existed, injuries, significant property damage, verbal and some-times physical confrontations, order maintenance, traffic control/direction, insurance expectations, and the likelihood of civil suits.

But if citizens are reasonable, other viable options do exist. In Canada,[2] the operators of vehicles in minor crashes drive to a nearby "collision center" where trained adjusters evaluate the damages and conduct the process of documenting the crash and damage, and begin the repair process. Police are only involved when the vehicles can't be driven, or there are injuries, vio-lence, or other laws and circumstances involved. This has resulted in clearing roadways faster, reducing confrontations, reducing traffic impacts, and free-ing up police to handle other issues. But this requires citizen cooperation and compliance with relevant expectations.

Another option is to hire civilian (not armed and non-sworn) personnel to handle a variety of tasks such as crashes. Some agencies have experimented with this concept and some called them public safety officers (PSO) or com-munity service officers (CSO). Many agencies, like the Tampa, Florida Police Department, still use versions of these programs. Tampa Police experimented with civilians responding to crashes but discontinued the program due to citizens demanding a "real" police officer and, in some cases, verbally or physically attacking the other driver or the PSO. Cost was also a factor in stopping the program as many citizens thought that the cost savings (roughly 30 percent) was not significant enough, and desired more officers for a rela-tively small amount of additional cost.

Today, the concept of shifting some calls away from sworn police response does exist in various formats. Many agencies have components that take police reports over the phone, via walk-in, or online. This is one way in which Tampa PD still utilizes its CSO program. In most of these programs, the people handling the calls and reports are trained civilian personnel. These programs still operate under the control of the police agency as the reports are still part of larger investigations, may serve as the entire report of the incident, and do require investigative skills to elicit the full and necessary information. The personnel that handle these reports are also trained by the police agency. So there is valid benefit to having the operation within the oversight of the police agency.

Recommendation 3: The tasks for which policing and police agencies are responsible should be revisited by the community and policing professionals.

Meaningful discussion should be held to decide what tasks are best suited for police agencies and sworn police personnel. These tasks should consider those that require or are best performed by sworn and armed personnel and which can be effectively and efficiently performed by non-sworn personnel but within the employment and oversight of a police agency. The responsibility for some tasks should be shifted to other groups or entities that can provide better service by way of being more efficient or effective. Care should be taken in making these decisions to ensure that community order and safety are maintained. For example, as mentioned previously, traffic law enforcement should remain a police function and task. This is due to citizens being upset about being stopped, being cited, probably not complying with non-sworn personnel, and the great number of injuries and deaths that occur in traffic crashes. There is little reason to believe that failing to stop for police, resistance to being cited, and assaults on personnel will lessen simply because the enforcement person is non-sworn. In reality, there is an expectation that these and other problems will increase if traffic enforcement is conducted by non-sworn, unarmed personnel who cannot effect an arrest when necessary.

But there should be discussion regarding these issues. The discussion should include enhanced uses of technology. For traffic law enforcement, cameras can be used. Many agencies and communities have used traffic cameras to assist with speed enforcement and red light violations. There has been good success with these programs from an enforcement, violation reduction, and crash severity standpoint.[3,4] Public perception and reaction to these tools and efforts appear to be the primary reasons these programs are either implemented or prohibited. Some opponents argue that the programs are purely for revenue generation, while others argue the accused (driver) cannot confront their accuser. Depending on the jurisdiction, these arguments have been found to be legitimate or to be flawed. Proponents of the technology argue that it increases enforcement activities without the cost of stationing an officer at the location around the clock, and does act as a deterrent to committing the violations. The reality is that technologies can be useful in reducing enforcement costs and direct human interactions, while decreasing violations, crashes, deaths, injuries, and property damage.

There are several possibilities that can be considered to adjust what tasks the police are directly involved with. Discussions by society that include all stakeholders can provide a variety of viewpoints and options to at least consider. It depends on the willingness of everyone to have the discussions and to also comply with the laws as set out by society.

Recommendation 4: Mental health providers should have primary responsibility for handling mental health incidents.

Nonviolent mental health calls should be handled by certified mental health practitioners or other appropriately trained individuals. In its purest form, it might be preferred that these personnel work for an agency other than the police department so there is clear distinction about the different mission and focus of mental health responders. This could be a stand-alone agency or attached to emergency medical services (EMS). The responders could work under the guidance of a certified medical provider just as paramedics do within the EMS environment.

This entity must be fully funded and staffed, with a proper number of qualified personnel, who are deployed in such a way as to make them useful and capable of responding to relevant calls 24/7. If they cannot be available at all times, then program effectiveness would be seriously compromised. They should be equipped with radios to summon additional resources, including police if needed, and have cameras activated to record the encounters.

There are, however, significant issues and concerns associated with having another entity take over responsibility for handling mental health-related calls. First, there is the issue of knowing what calls are mental health-related and, therefore, having that entity respond. In many situations, it is unknown if there are mental health-related issues involved. Even upon arrival of police personnel, in many cases, it is not obvious or even discernable that mental health issues exist until after the situation is handled and completed. In some cases, the caller/complainant may have specific knowledge of the individual and can, therefore, provide reasonable information regarding the existence of a mental health concern. But, unfortunately, in most cases, this information is simply not available or provided. Related to this concern is determining in advance what calls would be considered mental health calls which would thereby initiate the mental health response protocol.

A second concern centers around having mental health practitioners that are willing to serve in the environment that would exist. Most mental health professionals perform their services in a somewhat controlled environment and setting. It is either a facility of some type (medical or mental health), or in an office setting. These environments provide various degrees of calm, comfort, and safety. Rarely are practitioners out in the open world with limited safety nets, interacting with citizens who are in acute crisis. It is a low probability that there will be a sufficient number of practitioners available who are willing to respond to calls involving actively aggravated, angry, or violent persons in an acute crisis situation.

Third, there is the issue of availability and response to such calls. Any other entity that is expected to handle mental health calls must be available at all times. This service cannot operate Monday through Friday during normal business hours. There also must be sufficient resources available to handle the amount of calls for service at any given time. Depending on the community and the extent of mental health calls, most likely several or even dozens of mental health practitioners/responders might be needed at all times. Only a full analysis of prior calls would provide the number of personnel needed. The analysis would have to be more than just the number of calls, but also involve the projected length of a response to deliver full services. Also, there must be a viable mechanism for the practitioners to be able to respond to the location of the call. If EMS becomes the provider, then additional vehicles will be needed as most likely it will not be possible to tie up an ambulance for such calls. In many communities, EMS crews and resources are already spread thinly and response times can become unreasonably long. Adding another service and responsibility to EMS could either seriously and adversely impact base EMS services or require significant investments to create the required response resources and capabilities.

Fourth is the issue of the sporadic nature of the calls for service involving mental health issues. In some communities, a mental health practitioner/ responder could be kept quite busy. It is possible that the practitioners may respond immediately from one call to another. The number of pending calls could impact the ability of the practitioner to deliver a full response to any single call. This is especially true since many of these calls take considerable time to stabilize. In other communities, the calls might be very few. This brings up the issue of what would the practitioner/responder do between calls. Paying someone to be available for immediate response and possibly responding to only one call or possibly none during their shift might not be a desirable cost for a community.

A fifth concern directly involves funding. It is fully believed and understood that the government should bear the cost of providing this critical service. But part of the reason police were tasked with handling these situations was directly due to the closing of other mental health service options and the cost-effectiveness of having the police respond. Since the police were typically available at all times in all areas of the community, it was viewed as cost effective to have the police handle these calls. The sporadic nature of the calls provided further incentive to add this to the responsibilities of the police. If society is going to provide such services, then the funding needs to be provided before the responsibility is shifted. Also, at least initially, the funding cannot be taken from the police. Since the calls are sporadic, they are currently handled as one of many calls an officer or agency might handle that day. It is simply not practical to cut police funding to provide the funding to another entity or service. The number of officers on the street at any given time is based on the workload of the agency and the community. Each individual beat or patrol area is designed to provide roughly equal workloads with other beats. This enables each officer to have time to respond to the calls for service in their beat; to allow for investigative, proactive patrol, and community-oriented activities; and to allow for various administrative tasks which are required. Since mental health calls are not the majority of calls for any beat, they are only a small part of the officer's overall workload. Taking away the responsibility for such calls does not alleviate the need for the beat officer to handle all other required tasks. It also does not allow the number or size of beats to be adjusted, thus possibly reducing the number of officers needed.

After an alternative mental health response resource has been put into place and is operating for at least one full year (two is preferable), then an analysis would produce useful information. It might be possible then to slightly reconfigure beats, or even possibly reduce the number of officers needed to handle all other expected tasks. And then it might be possible to reduce the number of officers through attrition to better reflect the new, possibly reduced, workload. But practical experience and careful analysis are needed before such action is taken.

It might also not be feasible to shift the responsibility completely away from police. In such a situation, trained mental health practitioners should be assigned to the police department. This would resolve many concerns involving logistical issues such as transportation, communications, need for protection, and cost-effectiveness. By assigning the mental health practitioners to the police agency, several benefits can be realized. First, the support logistics for call response already exists. Police would also be aware of any calls and could either "stage" (position themselves nearby for quick response if needed) nearby or respond with the practitioner. In most cases, the practitioner would be riding with an officer and both would respond. In other formats, the practitioner would respond in their own vehicle, with police also responding. In either situation, the practitioner would take the lead and the officer would be available only if needed to provide support such as ensuring the safety of the practitioner, making any arrests if needed, and requesting additional resources as might be beneficial.

One program structure that has seen promising results is the co-responder model. Developed in Colorado Springs, this model combines police, fire/ EMS, and a mental health provider into a single response vehicle that responds to calls involving persons in crisis. They jointly handle the call and it has proven successful. The Tulsa Police Department has used this model since 2017, and recently enhanced its availability to forty hours per week. They have the goal of stabilizing the immediate situation, providing long-term services to the citizen, and eliminating future, repeat calls for service. Tulsa also has a mental health clinician within its communications center. These efforts have been found to be quite successful.

This format is easy to implement and also offers the added benefit of enhancing the interaction with and skills of the officers and the agency. It results in only minor incremental additional costs (practitioner salary and personal equipment) and allows for enhanced services that can be fully evaluated for continuous enhancements.

Recommendation 5: Citizens should not call the police for issues that should be handled by the involved citizens.

Many times, the police are called to respond to issues and situations that the involved citizens should be able to resolve among themselves. This includes minor neighbor disputes, a child not respecting a parent or refusing to go to school, and various other disagreements such as most civil matters. The police can respond and ensure that there is no violence and destruction but in many situations, the police cannot resolve the core issue. There are options such as mediation that are more appropriate to handle and settle such disputes. Some issues, especially issues involving children and family members, should be resolved peacefully, through discussion.

Involving the police in such matters oftentimes results in an escalation or exacerbation of the core issues. One party inevitably feels that it was unreasonable to call the police, which leads to additional stress in the relationship. And the reality is, in many of these situations, there is little the police can do since no laws were broken. The police can act as a mediator or independent third party that can make recommendations, but oftentimes they cannot force or implement a decision that ends the issues or situation. Such calls for service place the officer in an untenable position as they can't resolve the concerns, or if they do, then at least one party is unhappy with the outcome. It can also serve to create animosity, disrespect, or fear of the police. The citizens should act with understanding, logic, and reasonableness to find a middle ground that allows all involved parties to peacefully move forward. Should the property be damaged or the interaction is out of control and there is the possibility of violence, then by all means, the police should be summoned. But for those situations where reasonable people should be able to resolve their concerns, they should do so.

Chapter 3

Role and Responsibility of the Federal Government

Since most American policing and police activity is a local matter, the federal government has had a sporadic role in policing. At times, the federal government's presence and impact in policing have been virtually nonexistent. At other times, the federal government, through its various entities, has been quite active even to the point of virtually controlling local police agencies. In reality, the federal government is the one resource and entity that can bring consistency to all of policing.

It is understood that there will be a lot of resentment to expanded federal involvement in policing, which has been, and still is, largely viewed as a local issue, almost a state's rights issue. For numerous reasons, it is not suggested that a national police force be created. But it is suggested that the federal government should play a more active role in the broader topics that affect the core foundations of policing, and in those areas that relate to the rights of all persons as protected by the U.S. Constitution. Retired Seattle Police Chief Norm Stamper recognized the value of federal involvement through six of his proposals to fundamentally reform policing.[1] There can be a balance that improves policing, enhances the quality of life for everyone, maintains states' rights, and protect the rights and lives of citizens.

This will be a controversial topic as policing in American is predominately a local function. Most police agencies in America are municipality (town, city, township) or county-based. Virtually every city and town has their own police agency, and every county (or parish) has a sheriff, with some also having county police, marshals, and constables. Citizens and governments have favored local police agencies over centralized, federal agencies throughout American history. State agencies exist with varying levels and degrees of powers, but American policing is predominantly local. One of the primary reasons for favoring local policing centers on control. Citizens and governmental entities want to have a strong say in their police agencies, and how they are run. On its face this is not a bad concept, as different cities have different resources and desire different levels and focus of police service. But this can cause problems when police professionalism is supplanted by political goals or the desires of wealthy influences.

American policing can and should remain predominately a local governmental responsibility and task. However, there are reasons and benefits to (and recent events point out the need for) having some federal involvement in policing. Some of these include consistency on basic fundamental issues like the use of deadly force, legal protections, and the ability of citizens to know they will be treated fairly and impartially regardless of what community they are in. Historically, the federal government has been involved in policing through programs such as the Law Enforcement Assistance Administration (LEAA) and the Law Enforcement Education Program (LEEP). Other federal involvement exists through U.S. Supreme Court decisions regarding the use of deadly force, and the protection of constitutional rights. Additional federal involvement is needed to standardize certain basic protections and police actions for the benefit of all citizens, including the police.

Recommendation 6: The laws, regulations, and guidelines regarding the use of force, especially deadly force, should be consistent across all jurisdictions and agencies. The federal government should take the lead by (1) adopting the National Consensus Policy on Use of Force, making it mandatory for all American police agencies; (2) mandating participation in the National Use of Force Database which would be administered by the U.S. DOJ or the National Institute of Justice; and (3) the federal courts must assist in building a viable use of force policy that can apply to all jurisdictions and agencies.

In October 2017, the International Association of Chiefs of Police (IACP) published the National Consensus Policy on Use of Force. It also published a companion Discussion Paper, both of which were revised in 2020.[2] It was the product of the IACP and the Fraternal Order of Police (FOP) bringing together eleven of the primary police leadership and labor organizations in a collaborative effort to build a template for agencies to consider when creating or revising their use of force policies. This suggestive policy covers an extensive array of topics, many of which are the subject of much public concern and are currently under discussion. These include de-escalation, force models, shooting at or from moving vehicles, neck restraints, using deadly force, intervening when force is excessive, and training. Agencies should utilize this policy as a reference point in reviewing their individual use of force policies. Communities should also be involved in relevant discussions regarding their agency's Use of Force policies. This consensus policy should be reviewed periodically to determine if revisions are warranted.

On January 1, 2019, the Federal Bureau of Investigation (FBI) implemented the National Use of Force database[3] based on the request of the major organizations in policing. The database does not examine individual incidents, but rather is intended to provide information and insight regarding national trends involving the use of force. Currently, participation is voluntary. However, compliance is very low. Only 27 percent of American police agencies provided data in 2019, and preliminary data for 2020 indicates only 27 percent of all agencies participated and covered 42 percent of police officers.[4] In order to provide comprehensive data so competent decisions can be made, it is imperative that all agencies report the full data in a timely manner. This database should remain in the federal government so everyone has access to the information. This information can be used to enhance police training and policy, provide overview information regarding the use of force, and be used by agencies, citizens, and decision-makers to make more informed decisions to improve the quality of life for everyone.

Due to the variety of jurisdictions at the federal and state level, and the significant number of police agencies in the United States, there are also hundreds of different use of force policies in place. While many share common aspects, there are nuances that exist regarding what weapons, tools, and techniques are authorized, and when each can be used. Some agencies can use certain techniques while that same technique may be prohibited in the very next jurisdiction. This is not fair to citizens or officers and causes great concern when understanding what is authorized or appropriate.

Even though state and local authorities can create laws and build policies to govern within their respective jurisdictions, to preserve fundamental fairness to all citizens, there should be a high degree of consistency in the policies. Especially when dealing with a topic as critical as the use of force, specifically deadly force. It is understood that it is the responsibility of the legislature (state and federal) to create laws. But with each state free to craft their own laws, it is unlikely that a consistent policy will be created. This points out the value of National Use of Force Policy as suggested by the IACP. While it is the responsibility of the various legislatures to create the laws, the courts have the ability to make rulings and decisions as to whether those laws are consistent with the overarching principles of the applicable state and U.S. Constitution. Since even state courts disagree among themselves about what is legal and appropriate, the federal courts may be the most appropriate entity to determine what criteria should exist within a national use of force policy that is applicable across the country. This is not outside the scope of the federal courts, especially the U.S. Supreme Court as they have already made various landmark decisions regarding policing and the use of force. Some of these include *Tennessee v. Garner*[5] and *Graham v. Conner*,[6] which deal with the use of deadly force and use of force, respectively. And these are directly applicable to local police agencies and officers.

Recommendation 7: The U.S. DOJ should conduct a variety of activities relative to policing and police agencies. This includes encouraging, assisting, educating, reviewing, and mandating police agencies to perform as expected. This would also include technical assistance, training, reviews regarding patterns or practices, other reviews and analyses, and consent decrees as might be warranted.

History has demonstrated that there has been a need for DOJ actions in some communities and police agencies. It is certainly reasonable to believe (with recent events verifying the ongoing need) that some police agencies need enhancement, encouragement, assistance, and even mandates to change their actions. The DOJ must utilize their complete resources to help or force agencies to correct behavior that is not legal, ethical, professional, fair, or impartial. DOJ actions must be more than just lawsuits, as lawsuits are generally reactive in nature. Proactive activities by DOJ (and other entities) enable changes to be made before damages can occur. Conducting independent reviews of police agencies is good as it provides information to agencies and communities. But in some cases, for various reasons, agencies and communities do not change on their own. In these cases, the DOJ must mandate these changes. This is generally done through consent decrees where the DOJ, the community, and the police agency consent or agree to make changes consistent with DOJ recommendations. These are supported by making the decree a binding legal document through the federal courts. The DOJ has the ability to actually force an agency to change and comply with the DOJ recommendations by going to federal court if the agency does not agree to make changes.

This power should not be used for political or frivolous reasons, but must be used where appropriate. Due to the cost of many of these agreements and the required changes, the federal government should help with some of the costs. A set of well-defined and comprehensive policies, procedures and guidelines must exist that set out how DOJ will perform its reviews and interactions with police agencies. This must include the standards and guidelines that will be used in identifying agencies for review; how the reviews will be conducted; opportunities for community and agency input; target time frames for the process; and releasing of the complete report to the agency and the community. There should also be procedures and time frames set out to implement any recommended or mandated changes, and how success will be measured. By having defined standards and procedures, reviews and actions will be guided by thought out guidelines. Politics and public pressure at the local and federal level should be removed from the process to ensure fairness and consistency.

DOJ activities should also be proactive to guide agencies and help them and communities avoid issues. This can be accomplished in many ways, including educational seminars, training, advisory notices, and technical assistance to police agencies individually and collectively. Agencies and communities should be encouraged to reach out to the DOJ and other entities for assistance in a proactive manner before problems develop or incidents occur.

Various federal statutes such as the Violent Crime Control and Law Enforcement Act of 1994,[7] Section 1983 Civil Action for Deprivation of Civil Right,[8] and others exist that give the Department of Justice the ability to examine police agencies that are accused of continually mistreating citizens. This does not mean that a single incident will automatically trigger a review of the agency. But if the incident is significant enough, or one in an ongoing pattern or practice of agency actions, then the DOJ can and should review the agency. Since most American policing is local, there is a need for consistency of treatment and actions regarding the basic core civil rights of citizens. The activity and interest of the DOJ in reviewing police agencies fluctuates from time to time depending on public pressure and political guidance from the president of the United States and the U.S. attorney general. Citizens are entitled to consistent treatment and protection of fundamental human rights regardless of state, county, or municipality. The DOJ is the only entity with the power to reach each police agency and review their actions. The DOJ and the federal government owe a duty to police agencies to review and assist them, while at the same time they also owe a duty to all citizens to protect everyone. This review power should not be frivolously or politically used, but it should be used to ensure the protection of all citizens.

Recommendation 8: The U.S. DOJ should create and administer a mandatory national database of police officers who have been terminated/dismissed for serious reasons or for those who have been decertified.

Due to the local nature of policing and the fact that officers are certified and decertified by each individual state using their own guidelines, there is no consistency regarding removal of officers from police service. While local agencies should still retain the rights and responsibilities to discipline officers, there must be some standard that creates some degree of consistency across the country. Officers who have been terminated, dismissed, or allowed to resign in lieu of termination should be documented in the national database. This assumes that such actions are for serious rule violations or criminal violations. Minor offenses should not be included in the database. It will be difficult to reach some complete consensus on what offenses should result in being listed in the database, but it should be possible to reach consensus on many violations, especially the most serious.

In 2000, the International Association of Directors of Law Enforcement Standards and Training (IADLEST) created the National De-Certification Index (NDI), which was designed to "act as a national registry of certification and license revocations relating to officer misconduct."[9] The DOJ has assisted in the creation of this resource by providing periodic funding through grants. This index receives data from forty-five states with five states not participating for various reasons. Since the index is voluntary, it is incomplete. The NDI should be administered by the DOJ and should be made mandatory for all agencies and state commissions.

Relying solely on the decertification process, and reporting only those officers who have been decertified doesn't recognize the differences that exist from state to state and allows for some officers to be further employed who were not decertified. By including those officers who were terminated, dismissed, or allowed to resign in lieu of termination, the database will include those officers who have not had their certifications revoked. But some of these officers have committed acts that should not allow them to retain their certification. This will improve policing, provide increased knowledge and information as agencies consider applicants, instill some consistency across the country, and provide greater safeguards for citizens.

Chapter 4

Core Foundational Beliefs

As highlighted previously, certain beliefs and philosophies should be the bedrock foundation of any police agency. These help guide the agency and its members in everything they do. Actions, activities, training, programs, policies, and procedures should all be built with guidance from these core beliefs. Some of these include:

- All citizens have worth and are entitled to be treated with dignity and respect.
- Police need the consent and support of the citizens being served.
- The police exist to serve and protect the citizens and community.
- Resolution of problems and issues that cause crime, fear of crime, and disorder should be the primary focus of police.
- Crime prevention should be the goal and priority.
- COP and POP are and should be philosophies, not programs.
- Personnel should strive to build trust with every contact, interaction, and action.
- The public has a right and responsibility to be knowledgeable of and involved in the actions of the agency.
- Procedural justice is mandatory and beneficial.
- Service should be delivered in a legal, ethical, professional, fair, and impartial manner.
- The sanctity of, and respect for, all life is paramount.
- Use of force should only be used when necessary, and then only to the extent minimally required to accomplish the lawful tasks.
- The community should be free from crime, disorder, and injustice.

These concepts and beliefs should serve as the constant, consistent, non-changing bedrock concepts that define why the agency exists and how it will perform its tasks. The Peelian Principles should be part of these beliefs as they provide great guidance regarding the role and responsibilities of the police agency and its personnel. To assist in documenting, memorializing, and defining these foundational beliefs, the agency should create documents that identify the mission, vision, and values of the agency.

Recommendation 9: All agencies should define, articulate, and publish the Mission, Vision, and Values of the agency.

All agencies must have written documentation as to why it exists (Mission), what it hopes to accomplish or its end result (Vision), and what concepts it holds as important to guide its actions and efforts (Values). The Mission, Vision, and Values (MVV) of an organization can and should provide guidance to the personnel, customers (in this case, every citizen), and every concerned entity as to why the agency exists, what it hopes to accomplish, and what it values. Part of the issue involving policing is that the broad mission of maintaining order has constantly expanded, or has been subjected to mission creep. Originally intended to keep the peace, prevent crime and disorder, and keep citizens safe, police agencies were assigned additional tasks such as dealing with homelessness, intoxication, and handling mentally ill persons who were not dangerous.

Mission, Vision and Values are the foundational items of any police agency, and all actions should be consistent with these foundational beliefs and philosophies. The MVV should provide long-term guidance, continuity, and support for the agency. These should be created by agency personnel, the profession, legal guidelines, and, most importantly, the community and citizens being served by the agency. These core items should change very little. Policy and procedures may and should change periodically. They are the manner in which the agency attains and complies with their MVV. The aspects that change are meant to indicate how the agency fulfills its MVV while remaining true to and consistent with its core beliefs. Every agency member, and all citizens should know why the police agency exists, what the ultimate goal is, and what values are important to the agency and the community. These are the foundational beliefs and philosophies of an agency, and all of its policies, procedures, actions, and activities should be consistent with them.

Recommendation 10: All agencies should adopt the Law Enforcement Code of Ethics.

A code of ethics identifies the values, standards, principles, and in many ways, the core foundational beliefs of a group. The Law Enforcement Code of

Ethics was adopted by the IACP in 1957 and has stood to guide law enforcement personnel ever since. It is imperative that all agency personnel, sworn and non-sworn, adhere to the code of ethics in all decisions they make. As a profession, law enforcement is critical to society and its citizens. Because of the role, responsibilities, and power vested in police agencies, there must be an overarching code that guides how police personnel will conduct themselves as they carry out their duties. The citizens depend on police personnel to function legally, ethically, professionally, fairly, and impartially. The code of ethics provides a foundation for the police actions and citizens to have confidence in the police.

Law Enforcement Code of Ethics,[1] as adopted by IACP is:

As a law enforcement officer, my fundamental duty is to serve the community: to safeguard lives and property; to protect the innocent against deception, the weak against oppression or intimidation and the peaceful against violence or disorder; and to respect the constitutional rights of all to liberty, equality, and justice.

I will keep my private life unsullied as an example to all and will behave in a manner that does not bring discredit to me or to my agency. I will maintain courageous calm in the face of danger, scorn or ridicule; develop self-restraint; and be constantly mindful of the welfare of others. Honest in thought and deed both in my personal and official life, I will be exemplary in obeying the law and the regulations of my department. Whatever I see or hear of a confidential nature or that is confided to me in my official capacity will be kept ever secret unless revelation is necessary in the performance of my duty.

I will never act officiously or permit personal feelings, prejudices, political beliefs, aspirations, animosities or friendships to influence my decisions. With no compromise for crime and with relentless prosecution of criminals, I will enforce the law courteously and appropriately without fear or favor, malice or ill will, never employing unnecessary force or violence and never accepting gratuities. I recognize the badge of my office as a symbol of public faith, and I accept it as a public trust to be held so long as I am true to the ethics of police service. I will never engage in acts of corruption or bribery, nor will I condone such acts by other police officers. I will cooperate with all legally authorized agencies and their representatives in the pursuit of justice.

I know I alone am responsible for my own standard of professional performance and will take every reasonable opportunity to enhance and improve my level of knowledge and competence.

I will constantly strive to achieve these objectives and ideals, dedicating myself before God to my chosen profession . . . law enforcement.

Police agencies should post the oath in various locations in all police facilities, and should develop operations, programs, and activities consistent with this code. It is also suggested that all police personnel review and recite the code annually so as to remind them of the values and expectations of the code of ethics.

Recommendation 11: Police services must be provided in an unbiased manner, and agencies must conduct relevant training.

All police services must be provided to all citizens in a legal, ethical, professional, fair, and impartial manner. Providing services in this manner builds trust, support, and legitimacy. People have to know and believe that they are being treated fairly and appropriately under the law. While the circumstances of any specific interaction or situation may change the outcome (warning or citation, etc.), the citizen should believe that the actions taken by the officer were guided by the law and the situation, not any bias, prejudice, or personal viewpoint the officer may have or utilize in making decisions.

Police officers are all human and have human traits. One of those traits is that all humans have inherent biases or preferences. There are positive and negative biases. People have positive biases for foods they prefer, sports teams they like, and places where they live. People have negative biases about different things, such as food, religions, ethnicities, and people that are different than they are. This kind of bias is referred to as implicit bias. It is not intentional, deliberate, or based on animosity or hatred. The person might not even recognize it is impacting them.

This is much different than explicit bias, which is considered intentional, known, and embraced by the person. It is often associated with animus or hatred. This type of bias is most easily characterized by Archie Bunker from the 1970s television sitcom *All in the Family*.[2] Archie was a middle-aged white male whose bias, as demonstrated by his bigotry for everyone different than him, was a main theme of the show. Even though it was eventually learned later in the show that his bigotry was not caused by malice (but rather the totality of his experiences and the era of his life), the outward display of his bigotry is considered the classic example of explicit bias. He knew he had these biases, openly displayed them, and did nothing to learn or change his behavior.

Every person has lived life to one degree or another, has experienced many situations, has heard many stories, and seen many things. All of these experiences reside in the human mind. At various times, these stories and experiences are brought forward in the mind and begin to have an impact on a person's views, opinions, and perceptions. These may present themselves as biases for or against a person, place, thing, or group based on various characteristics that are associated with that entity. How the entity, usually a person, is perceived can be impacted (positively or negatively) by the past experiences and information the person possesses about others. Oftentimes these perceptions are influenced by stereotypes about the person, group, place, or thing. In many cases, these stereotypes are often negative, especially if they are about people different than the viewer.

If left unchecked, these stereotypes (formed by stories, experiences, information, etc.) can impact how people perceive others or situations. If people are unaware of these perceptions, it might impact how one person treats or reacts to another. This can have harmful effects. The issue here is that as humans, everyone has implicit biases, good and bad. This does not mean that everyone, or people in general, are racist, sexist, and so forth. It merely, unfortunately, means they are human. There are several excellent resources that discuss implicit bias, including *Biased* by Jennifer Eberhardt,[3] *Blink* by Malcolm Gladwell,[4] and *Thinking Fast and Slow* by Daniel Kahneman.[5]

While it is important for all citizens to understand implicit bias, and to reduce and manage their own biases, it is critical that police officers do so. Police officers must provide the police services in an unbiased manner. Even though implicit bias exists to some degree in every person and every profession, because of the nature of policing, it is imperative that the police profession does everything it can to reduce the impacts of bias. Many agencies have implemented policies prohibiting bias-based policing, and the Commission on Accreditation for Law Enforcement Agencies (CALEA) has a standard (1.2.9)[6] that requires accredited agencies to have such a policy. Many states require training on implicit bias as part of their basic police academy curriculum or as part of their annual in-service training. Dr. Lorie Fridell's book *Producing Bias-Free Policing, A Science-Based Approach*[7] is an outstanding reference regarding implicit bias training for policing. This topic and its impact on policing is so important, that Bill Bratton (retired NYPD commissioner and LAPD police chief) dedicated a full chapter to "Implicit Bias" in his recent book *The Profession: A Memoir of Community, Race, and the Arc of Policing in America*.[8] In order to be successful, and provide unbiased policing to all citizens, officers and agencies must provide relevant training, appropriate supervision, and sound accountability mechanisms. This recommendation is consistent with many aspects of policing, including the previously mentioned Code of Ethics.

Recommendation 12: Legitimacy and procedural justice must be a foundation of all policing.

Legitimacy is the concept that citizens will support, trust, and have confidence in police agencies and individuals if the citizen perceives the agency and officer to be fair, legal, ethical, and professional in their actions. Legitimacy may ask the question, "Is the law, the agency, the officer worthy of compliance and respect?" If it is viewed that the law is proper, that it is being enforced fairly, that officers are treating the citizens reasonably and respectfully, then citizens are more likely to voluntarily comply with the law and more likely to comply with officer directions and actions. However, if citizens view the law as improper, or its enforcement is onerous, or unfairly applied, then resistance will exist to the law and those tasked with enforcing it. Legitimacy can be about what the law is as well as what police actions are used to gain compliance with the law. It is both substance and methodology.

Researcher and Professor Tom Tyler identified this concept in his 1990 book *Why People Obey the Law.*[9] His concepts have over the course of time become the foundation of the "legitimacy" concept especially when it comes to compliance with law, governmental mandates, and the police in general. Tyler advocates that the power of perceived legitimacy is stronger than the fear of punishment. He indicates that police agencies and government would be better off focusing on building the perception of legitimacy than on focusing on fear of punishment. More people voluntarily comply with laws, and police directions when they view the police, their actions, and their right to enforce the laws as legitimate or proper. If the police are trusted to enforce reasonable laws in a non-biased and fair manner, that is appropriate to the specific circumstances, then public support for and compliance with police directions and laws are increased. In those communities or areas where this perception of fair treatment during the enforcement activities is lacking, there will be increased levels of noncompliance and resistance.

Even though this concept was identified decades ago, it has only recently become a mainstream concept in policing. Police effectiveness has increased significantly in these decades but support for police and general compliance with laws has not increased to the same extent. This tends to indicate a disconnect between police effectiveness and societal support. Policing has traditionally looked at effectiveness as the primary measure of success. While it is important, the concept of legitimacy appears to indicate that a more important measure might be how the public perceives the police and their level of voluntary compliance with laws, as well as the levels of resistance to police efforts and activities.

Certainly, current events would indicate that there is a sizable deficiency in the levels of perceived legitimacy in various parts of American communities and society. This does not mean that overall support for the police is lacking, but it is certainly obvious that support for policing methods, activities, focus, and governmental regulation is lacking in parts of American communities. In recent times, more police agencies have been teaching and embracing the concept of legitimacy. It works very well with procedural justice, trust, confidence, and community-oriented policing concepts. By increasing training and utilization of these concepts, the police can be more successful. This could result in lower levels of resistance to police efforts, decreased uses of force, and less crime. This could also result in increased levels of support for the police, enhanced voluntary compliance with laws and directions, and an enhanced quality of life for everyone.

Procedural justice is closely related to and can help achieve legitimacy. But it is more focused on fair processes and how people perceive they are treated by the police, as opposed to the outcome of the encounter. The perception of fairness is critical to how people view the specific encounter and the police overall. People want to be treated fairly and to have their voices heard. It is generally agreed upon that there are four component parts to procedural justice. This version is used by Fair and Impartial Policing[10] (a leading training organization in implicit bias) and is derived from several studies by Tyler[11] and others.

1. Respect—Treating people with dignity.
2. Trustworthiness—Conveying worthy intentions, professional competence, and good character.
3. Voice—Allowing a person to share their point of view regarding the situation.
4. Neutrality—Making bias-free decisions.

If citizens are treated with dignity and respect by officers they view as trustworthy and legitimate; can actually voice their views about the situation they are in; and are treated fairly and impartially; they are more likely to accept the outcome of the interactions regardless of what those outcomes are. They are also more likely to perceive the interaction as appropriate for the circumstances and not as authoritarian or intrusive. Retired Philadelphia police commissioner Charles Ramsey highlighted the need and value of policing with dignity and respect in his TEDx presentation.[12]

As with any tool or technique, for it to be effective and useful it must be practical in the real world. These characteristics must be capable of being utilized in all police interactions given the nature of police-citizen interactions. And they can be, if the officers are properly trained, and the agency makes this a priority of how citizens will be treated, based on the agency's culture and expectations. All persons in all circumstances can and should be treated with respect and dignity. In different circumstances this might look differently. But officers can still perform all the tasks they need to accomplish, even use of force and arrests, in a manner that considers the dignity of the citizen, and is respectful to them. Officers can display trustworthiness through worthy, honorable intentions based on nonpersonal motives. By giving the citizen a reasonable opportunity to voice their concerns and opinions about the encounter enables the citizen to have some input on what is happening. This must be balanced with the circumstances, but even giving the citizen the opportunity to explain why they did what they did can substantially improve their perception of how they were treated. And if the citizen perceives that the actions of the officer were fair and were conducted without bias of any kind, then the citizen is more likely to accept the interaction and its outcome.

In essence, if the citizen is treated decently, consistent with the characteristics of procedural justice (how the citizen was treated), whether they were ticketed or arrested (the outcome), becomes less important. In addition to the tremendous benefits this can provide to officers, agencies, and communities, procedural justice training can reduce the use of force by police and can reduce citizen complaints about police.[13]

Recommendation 13: Arrest and charging activities should be used only when they are the best choice for everyone (including society) and when prudent and necessary.

The law enforcement function of policing is a tool that has applicability in many situations. But its necessity, prudence, and value is not always the best choice or option. There are hundreds of laws and regulations that exist. And yes, citizens are responsible for knowing the laws and for abiding by them. The saying, "Ignorance of the law is no excuse" is true. But with each state and, in some cases, localities having different versions of laws or completely different laws and regulations; it is common for citizens to not know or fully understand all applicable laws and their many nuances.

The issue of how a particular incident is handled involves fairness, appropriateness, reasonableness, severity, and value. The concepts of legitimacy and procedural justice are very applicable here. Without question all police actions must be fair to the citizen and society. But whether the incident is resolved by warning, citation, or arrest depends on many factors. Some factors are set out by law such as mandatory arrest for incidents of domestic violence in many states. But whether a citation is written or warning issued for a particular traffic violation is a matter of discretion exercisable by the agency and the individual officer. In some cases, the same is true for ordinance violations and minor crimes such as misdemeanors. While discretion can still exist for felony violations, the discretion is more limited due to the usual severity of the offense associated with a felony-level crime.

For example, a posted speed limit is not a suggestion. It is a binding traffic regulation based on the state's vehicle code, and compliance is expected. When the speed limit is 35 miles per hour (MPH), the lawful speed limit is 35 MPH. It is a violation to travel in excess of that posted speed, even if only 3 MPH faster. However, it is not reasonable, appropriate, or valuable to charge someone with speeding that is slightly over the limit. What is reasonable is subject to differing opinions and situations. In bad weather, road construction or when traffic obstructions exist, traveling at the posted speed limit may actually be too fast, unreasonable, and unsafe. In all but the most extreme circumstances, it would not be beneficial to write someone a citation for 3 MPH over the posted speed limit. It might not even be reasonable, appropriate, or valuable to stop someone at that level and warn them. While it is against the law, strict enforcement of all laws is not desired or practical. What the amount of violation that is acceptable also changes based on the environment and other factors. When speeding at a level of 10 MPH over the posted speed limit on an interstate highway may not be a concern, it might be in a residential area, and most certainly would be an issue in an active school zone. The enforcement actions of the agency and the officers must be viewed as reasonable and appropriate based on the severity of the violation under the specific circumstances.

The same is true for various criminal violations. Even though certain actions are against a state law, it might not be valuable to society to strictly enforce that law. For example, even though possession of a minor amount of marijuana has been illegal for years (this is and has been changing), making an arrest might not be the best action for the citizen or for society. A very small amount of marijuana might be destroyed on the street without charges being filed. Depending on the circumstances, this might be a proper use of discretion. If the arrest was made, it might be dismissed later and in such a situation the paperwork, charges, and processing the subject would have become a wasted effort on everyone's part. The same is true for other violations like underage possession or consumption of alcohol, operating a vehicle with an expired driver's license, or license plate. In some circumstances it might be better, more reasonable, and appropriate to give a warning than to engage in a formal charging process.

Any contact between police and citizens with a regulatory context that could result in an arrest or charge being made has the potential to escalate. People do not like to be told what to do. They don't want to be told they can't park here, or drive that way, or can't take that other person's property, or even that they cannot hit another person. While these are all good things and help to maintain order and protect everyone, people don't like it. And that is oftentimes what police are tasked with. So if very minor violations occur, it might not be worth it to society to have an enforcement contact occur.

However, that does not mean that enforcement actions should not occur overall. It is more about the benefit to be gained by taking enforcement action. And then, if a stop or contact is made, it might be better (reasonable, appropriate, valuable) for a warning to be issued, especially for the minor transgressions. For some violations like those that involve harm or potential harm to others, are excessive in the circumstances, or are repeat violations by the same person, it may be more appropriate, reasonable, and valuable for an arrest or charge to be made.

Another aspect of this concept involves arrests and how they are processed. For some offenses, a physical arrest is appropriate and reasonable. These would include offenses involving harm or threat of harm to persons, dangerous activities, or severe or repeat violations. For some minor violations, like possession of small amounts of drugs or nonorganized shoplifting, it might be more appropriate and reasonable to make the arrest but release the person on their signature and promise to appear in court later. Historically, this has been known as Release on (Own) Recognizance or ROR. In effect, the citizen agrees to handle the manner as prescribed by law (pay fine or appear in court) instead of being physically arrested and booked into a jail facility. There are many offenses for which physical custodial arrests are not necessary. It provides many benefits such as reducing the time officers are tied up on the specific call; reduces needed capacity in the jail facility; minimizes the impact on the citizen (bond, vehicle-towing expenses, time/emotional impacts etc.); and reduces the size and activities of the overall criminal justice system. Sometimes referred to as "cite and release," these types of programs have become more common. They should be considered by more agencies, courts, and communities.

The agency should establish policies and procedures that encourage and outline the use of diversion, warnings, and referral to other agencies. In many cases, an arrest or charge is simply not the best course of action. Public intoxication or publicly under the influence of illegal drugs (without any involvement of operating a motor vehicle) are more appropriately handled by a medical or health service provider than by a criminal charge and incarceration in the local jail. Yes, these are crimes as they violate various laws, but in many cases, the better course of action for everyone would be to ensure that the person is safe and healthy. Having procedures that allow for, and even in some cases require diversion and other alternatives to arrest is beneficial to society as a whole, and, in many cases, to the involved citizen. But this requires that alternative services exist.

Recommendation 14: Refresher training on all these concepts must occur on a regular basis.

People sometimes need to be reminded about various concepts. This includes doctors and the importance of bedside manner; retail store employees and being courteous to the customer; and police officers being perceived as legitimate, legal, ethical, professional, fair, and impartial in their actions. With the daily stresses of occupations and professions, sometimes the basics of service, demeanor, and respect get lost. In policing, with its exceptional stresses, the nature of its role, and the tasks that officers must perform in difficult situations, it is imperative that these foundational concepts and critical beliefs be reinforced through regular periodic training. This training should at times be stand-alone, but it also should be blended with and integrated into other topics in practical scenarios. The intent is to make these concepts part of the unconscious perceptions, thinking, and actions of officers. Better outcomes for everyone can be had by remembering and practicing these key concepts.

Recommendation 15: The agency should identify as a "police" or "police services" agency, not a "law enforcement" agency.

The primary mission of a police agency and its personnel, known by whatever name (police, sheriff, trooper, agent, investigator, etc.), is to provide services directed toward service and protection. Certainly "To Protect and Serve" is an appropriate motto for all such agencies. "Policing" represents the entire scope of tasks, responsibilities, and roles the agency and its personnel are expected to perform. This is a very broad concept of the reason a police agency exists. This is also the proper and more appropriate perception point for an agency.

"Law enforcement," however, is a part of the overall responsibilities of a police agency. It is a tool that is used in various situations. The primary role of a police agency is not, and should not be, to enforce the laws. It is an important part of an agency, but it is only one tool that the agency and its personnel have available to them and the community. Most of the tasks that police officers and agencies perform are more aligned with order mainte-nance, investigation and documentation of incidents, assistance, and provid-ing information. The majority of police personnel in a typical municipal type agency are found in the patrol group. This is the group of officers most people are familiar with and see. They are generally in full uniform and in marked police vehicles that are easily identifiable. The majority of their time is spent on routine, proactive, preventative patrol, and handling traffic crashes and traffic complaints, administrative matters, and report writing. Only a small percentage of their time is directly related to criminal matters, whether that be investigations, report writing, or actually arresting and processing an accused person. The time that an officer is actually engaged in law enforcement is a small portion of their daily shift.

How an agency and its personnel view itself is important. If the agency and the community view the agency's role as primarily "law enforcement," then the agency will focus its effort on enforcing various laws. If the agency views itself as a police service entity, then it will focus on providing a wide range of services to enhance the quality of life in the community. It is a matter of conceptualization and focus that impacts reality. Law enforcement is a neces-sary tool of policing, but should only be used to the extent that it is required to gain compliance with the laws and expectations of society. By focusing on police services, and working with society so that societal norms are main-tained voluntarily, law enforcement activities, especially as characterized by citations and arrests, can be reduced. It is widely known that an agency or society cannot arrest its way out of a problem. Focusing on police services will prove much more beneficial to society.

Recommendation 16: Agency culture must reinforce these core foundational beliefs.

The culture of an agency is a critical element of how an agency operates, treats people, and delivers services. It has as much to do with the history and long-term behavior of the agency as it does with current leadership. Culture, although not easily defined, is often easily observable. Agencies with a strong service culture, compliance with law, and adherence to principles of professional policing are recognized as those with fewer citizen complaints, better relationships with the community, less employee turnover, and overall better service. Those with a weak, ineffective, or poor service culture typically experience more citizen complaints, have more disciplinary issues, are feared and not supported by the community, and generally provide lower levels of service to the community.

The culture of an agency is critical as it guides how agency personnel view themselves and their role. It is truly a core foundational belief as it sets the tone for what is expected and what is accepted or tolerated by the agency. Agencies should create a culture of service, adherence to basic principles of American policing, working with the community and not functioning as an occupying force. Negative culture must be dealt with immediately as it cannot be allowed to gain support, either intentionally or negligently. Negative culture can grow and spread quickly within an agency, and usually starts in small workgroups. Constant vigilance is required. Positive culture must be constantly reinforced, demonstrated, and celebrated. All agency processes, especially those internal processes that deal with personnel issues must be focused on building and maintaining a positive culture. These include recruitment, hiring, training, discipline, supervision, and leadership. By setting appropriate expectations, and constantly monitoring agency and personnel performance and behavior, an agency can build and maintain a strong positive culture.

Chapter 5

Agency Actions

It is understood that virtually every recommendation made herein requires the agency to take some type of positive action. However, certain concepts are so fundamental to policing that they should be part of the core foundational beliefs and culture of the agency. These include things that the agency should do as a part of nature and very existence. The agency and its personnel should strive to be legal, ethical, professional, fair, and impartial in every activity, program, effort, responsibility, duty, and task in which they perform in. Every citizen should trust and feel comfortable around every police officer.

To do this, the agency and each and every one of its personnel must conduct themselves based on certain high standards. These standards exist in many ways, including organizational culture, training, supervision, and policy. The agency identifies the majority of its expectations through written directives and policy. Written directives and policy cannot cover every circumstance and situation. But if written thoughtfully, clearly, and comprehensively, directives, coupled with competent training, can give technical and foundational guidance that enables personnel to handle virtually any situation. Understanding foundational philosophies, guiding principles, applicable laws, and agency directives enables personnel to have a strong set of knowledge, skills, and abilities to competently serve the community.

Recommendation 17: Agencies should adopt and support the Policy Framework for Improved Community-Police Engagement as outlined by the IACP.

The International Association of Chiefs of Police is the largest and primary organization of police leaders around the world. It develops model policies, conducts training, discusses issues involving all of policing, and enhances the services provided by police agencies while increasing the professionalism of officers and agencies. For decades, it has stressed the criticality of partner-ships and strong positive relationships between police and the communities they serve. The Framework for Improved Community-Police Engagement[1] identifies seven key policy areas that the federal government through Congress should consider acting upon. These are:

1. Adoption of the National Consensus Policy on Use of Force
2. Mandatory Participation in the National Use of Force Database
3. Development of national standards for discipline and Termination of Officers
4. Development of a Police Officer Decertification Database
5. Enhance police leadership and culture
6. Implement improved recruitment, hiring, and promotional practices
7. Enhance ability of police agencies to implement effective discipline

Through this framework, the IACP, which consists of chiefs of all types and size agencies, acknowledges that federal involvement with policing issues can enhance the professionalism of policing. Some of the component parts have already been discussed. But this document recognizes the interconnectivity of various concepts and actions. Each of the items in the framework stands alone, and individually can enhance community safety. But collectively, these policies can help reengineer policing so that it is more effective, more professional, and more helpful to the communities being served by thousands of police agencies.

Recommendation 18: All agencies should embrace the concepts and implement the recommendations of the President's Task Force on 21st Century Policing.

In December 2014, President Barack Obama signed an Executive Order cre-ating the Task Force on 21st Century Policing.[2] This was in response to then recent events which demonstrated a continuing disconnect between police agencies and the communities they serve. The purpose of the task force was to "identify best practices and offer recommendations on how policing can promote effective crime reduction while building public trust." While polic-ing was focused on reducing crime, it had done so in ways that, in some cases, destroyed relationships with the citizens, causing a great deal of anger, mistrust, and reduction in perceived and actual legitimacy.

Due to the urgency of the issues and strength of feelings surrounding local policing, the task force was charged with acting quickly. Task force mem-bers, from various professions, conducted meetings around the country to listen to over a hundred citizens from numerous groups representing a diverse mix of views and experiences. Other groups and individuals submitted writ-ten comments and documents for the task force to consider.

In May 2015, a final report was issued which contained fifty-nine recommendations and ninety action items.[3] Each of these items provided opportunities for the enhancement of policing that enabled police to be more effective in their role while at the same time building trust, support, and partnerships with the citizens. The report identified six major topic areas they referred to as "pillars." These are:

- Building Trust and Legitimacy
- Policy and Oversight
- Technology and Social Media
- Community Policing and Crime Reduction
- Training and Education
- Officer Safety and Wellness

An additional section identified three recommendations regarding implementation of the various recommendations contained within the Task Force Report.[4] The task force also identified two overarching recommendations:

1. The president should support and provide funding for the creation of a National Crime and Justice Task Force to review and evaluate all components of the criminal justice system for the purpose of making recommendations to the country on comprehensive criminal justice reform.
2. The president should promote programs that take a comprehensive look at community-based initiatives that address the core issues of poverty, education, health, and safety.

This report provides a wealth of information that could and should have assisted communities, agencies, officers, and citizens in reengineering policing which might have helped make necessary and prudent changes, thereby avoiding some of the severity of the current issues being faced. A blueprint was laid out and many agencies did and still utilize the report to review their policies and operations. But the main support for the report, the federal level, stopped. This is why politics needs to be removed, and good, high quality, meaningful recommendations and decisions need to be allowed to develop and be implemented.

It should be noted that this was not the first federal commission convened to examine policing or the criminal justice system. In 1971, the National Advisory Commission on Criminal Justice Standards and Goals[5] was created. It produced six lengthy reports, including a nearly 700-page report on police. It created 107 standards with multiple items to improve the quality of policing. While many agencies implemented some of the recommendations, most of the recommendations, which are still applicable today, went unused.

For decades, policing has been reviewed, critiqued, and analyzed with hundreds of suggestions and recommendations formulated and advocated. If any significant number of these suggestions had been implemented across the policing profession, the current state of policing and quality of life might look completely different, and most likely for the better. It is certainly time to take actions based on the research, commissions, recommendations, and societal desire for change.

Recommendation 19: All police agencies should be accredited, preferably through the national/international accreditation body.

To enhance policing and improve the overall quality of life, there should be national standards and guidelines. Many of the suggestions herein and voiced (even demanded) publicly by citizens require some degree of consistency and basic minimum standards. This requires written policies to guide, control, and evaluate police performance. It also suggests that a set of consistent national standards should exist and apply to all police agencies and personnel. This is part of what has been recommended, and in some cases demanded by various studies, activists, and citizens.

Most professions are guided by a set of professionally agreed-upon standards which serve as the basic foundation for how they will perform the tasks and activities expected of them. Accreditation programs help to move entities towards compliance with universal expectations by creating standards and evaluating agency compliance with those standards. Most citizens would not attend a college or university that is not accredited, and they would not choose to be treated in a hospital that is not accredited. Accreditation programs exist for a variety of governmental services such as fire departments and even parks departments. So why would the citizens, the governmental parent, the agency, and its personnel not want, expect or even demand, that the police agencies that serve them also be accredited?

Based on the efforts of the four major executive associations in law enforcement (International Association of Chiefs of Police [IACP], Police Executive Research Forum [PERF], National Sheriff's Association [NSA], and the National Organization of Black Law Enforcement Executives [NOBLE]) and with assistance from federal grants, the Commission on Accreditation for Law Enforcement Agencies (CALEA) was created in 1979 as an accreditation entity.[6] The commission includes representatives from policing, courts, state, and local elected officials, governmental officials, academicians, and subject matter experts. Using a rigorous process, standards were developed with input from the professional and interested parties. These standards are regularly revised in number and content. The commission oversees the accreditation process which requires agencies in the program to comply with certain mandatory standards and at least 80 percent of "other than mandatory" standards that are applicable to the agency. The agency must continually comply with the applicable standards. Compliance verification occurs annually by a review of various standards documentation, and a periodic (currently every four years) physical review of the agency. Originally, approximately 944 standards existed that covered all aspects of police administration, management, and operations. Today, there are approximately 480 standards that include over 1,000 unique requirements.

Even though many of the standards apply to specific actions and situations, the standards are founded on and focus upon certain core foundational beliefs that should be part of policing. These include "procedural justice, ethical policing, community trust and engagement, transparency in service delivery, appropriate organizational culture, fairness in systems and processes, and consistency in what citizens should expect"[6] from police agencies. One key aspect of the accreditation process is public input. During each physical on-site assessment, the agency must provide at least three different opportunities for the public to provide input to the assessment team about the agency.

The main issue is that this program is completely voluntary. Only agencies that volunteer to go through this process become accredited. Approximately 1,200 agencies are accredited in the CALEA program.[7] And this includes communications agencies, university agencies, training academies, and foreign entities. Therefore, less than 7 percent of U.S. police agencies are accredited. Ironically, there are several foreign police agencies that are accredited or currently pursuing accreditation. It is a lot of work to become accredited initially as the agency must compile documentation showing that its policies and procedures comply with the expectations of the standards. In some cases, new policies and procedures are created while in many cases, there are several agency policies that require revisions. But once the initial accreditation is achieved, it can be easier to maintain the required "proofs" of compliance, if the agency strives to do so. But accreditation processes require effort.

For a variety of reasons, some states have created their own state-wide accreditation program. Most of the standards in these various state programs are very similar to CALEA standards. It is usually a little cheaper to be state accredited than CALEA accredited. Some agencies are accredited by both entities. The concern with state accreditation is the lack of consistency in standards and expectations around the country. The CALEA process is more comprehensive than state programs. While any accreditation is probably better than no accreditation, it is the lack of national consistency that has and is causing a lot of concern regarding policing.

Accreditation through CALEA offers many advantages to the agency, its personnel, and most importantly to the citizens. These include written policies that comply with national standards, periodic review of policies and procedures, and analysis of key concerns and activities to improve the information available to make decisions and to keep the public informed. Accreditation requires several time-based activities such as training, and review, analysis and reporting various statistics to the command staff and the public. As CALEA recently stated, accreditation is "perpetual action for public safety and criminal justice."[8] All agencies should be accredited at the national level to ensure consistency and compliance with nationally recognized standards. Even though there have been some efforts to mandate some type of accreditation program in various states, accreditation (preferably national) should be considered a mandatory cost of doing business. Additional support for this recommendation came when President Donald Trump signed Executive Order 13929 on June 16, 2020. This order came close to mandating accreditation by stating:

> The Attorney General shall, as appropriate and consistent with applicable law, allocate Department of Justice discretionary grant funding only to those State and local law enforcement agencies that have sought or are in the process of seeking appropriate credentials from a reputable independent credentialing body certified by the Attorney General.[9]

Although there are differences between "accreditation" and "credentialing," as defined in Executive Order 13929, CALEA has been designated as a certified independent credentialing entity. Meeting national standards can be beneficial to everyone.

Recommendation 20: Agency policies and procedures should be published online.

Citizens should have easy access to the vast majority of agency policies, procedures, and directives. They should be able to see, read, review, have knowledge of, and input into agency directives. Publishing them online allows citizens to have easy immediate access without having to contact the agency for these materials. Some people are intimidated by asking for items to review and, therefore, may refrain from doing so. By automating the directives, it also reduces the workload on agency personnel. Specific tactics would be excluded for officer and citizen safety, with this being affirmatively noticed. But the majority of directives and the fundamental concepts and guiding principles should be easily available.

Recommendation 21: Each police agency must prepare various reports regarding its activities, actions, outcomes, and conduct for internal use.

Agencies create a lot of information and data that can and should be used for various purposes. This data includes how resources such as personnel, vehicles, and funds are utilized, what programs and efforts are in place to accomplish the agency mission, and a tremendous amount of statistical data regarding every aspect of policing. While many agencies generate a variety of reports and analyses that review a lot of this data, some agencies do not. This is not effective leadership of the agency, nor appropriate management of agency operations. How can a chief make necessary and beneficial changes if they do not have information about what is happening? These various reports are a primary source of information that can and should be used as a management tool to ascertain efficiency, effectiveness, and the need for changes in policy, training, tactics, and equipment.

Reports and analyses should be regularly created and should cover a wide range of topics. This includes use of force, internal affairs cases and complaints, discipline, grievances, calls for service and other workload data, crime data, and other topics related to agency activities. These basic management tools are essential to the informed, intelligent, effective, and responsible operation of the agency. It is imperative that the agency creates, reviews, and utilizes these reports to enhance the services they deliver.

The agency must measure a lot of items. This includes agency efforts (output), but also agency results (outcomes). In some cases, the agency's ability to impact crimes (outcome) is limited, so it chooses to focus on its efforts (output). While this can be useful, it is the outcome, the results, the actual reduction of crime that is important to the public.

Other measurements that are important to the agency and community focus on statistics regarding all aspects of policing, such as arrests, citizen contacts, searches, traffic stops, complaints and many other items. The raw data must be collected accurately and completely. Partial information or inaccurate information is not only useless, it can lead to incorrect perceptions and wrong or counterproductive decisions. Therefore, appropriate data collection, analysis, and interpretation is essential if the data is to be used in a meaningful manner.

A topic of great concern for several years, decades even, centers around the real and perceived disproportionality of police actions. Much of the public believes that all police actions should be balanced and equal to the population in a community. For example, some believe that if the white population in town is 65 percent, then arrests, traffic stops, citations, and encounters with the police should involve whites 65 percent of the time. This is inaccurate. The residential population is not the proper comparison point for these actions. The proper comparison point is the percentage of people that are involved in the activity. If white males make up 85 percent of the population that commits bank fraud, stock insider trading, and insurance scams, but only represent 45 percent of the community population, the proper arrest percentage of white males for this set of crimes is closer to 85 percent. They make up 85 percent of the perpetrators of these crimes so they should make up very close to 85 percent of the arrests. It is the percentage of persons with certain characteristics that are involved in the crimes or activities that is important, relevant, and the comparison point, not the percentage of persons with those characteristics in the general community.

Part of the difficulty though is ascertaining what percentage of various groups is involved in various activities. For some activities, this can be more easily measured than it can for other activities. When it is difficult to measure the percentage of involvement, most people default to the resident population. This is primarily due to two reasons: first, it is easily available information, and second most people believe that crime is equally distributed and matches the population. Most researchers agree that the resident population is not the proper comparison point to use when looking at police activities. A DOJ/ Office of Community Oriented Policing Services document entitled "How to Correctly Collect and Analyze Racial Profiling Data: Your Reputation Depends on It!"[10] specifically states:

> This type of comparison-vehicle stop data against citywide census data-became the national trend. The 1990 Census and aggregate citywide demographics became the sole benchmark for many people and organizations. Racial profiling and discrimination accusations were launched against police agencies based on this comparison. Not only is this practice inaccurate-it is outright irresponsible, and actually contributes to negative perceptions in the community. Census data often fail to provide an effective data analysis benchmark or baseline. The census shows the percentage of citizens residing in a city; it does not provide the numbers or demographics of the actual drivers or traffic violators, which by most accounts yield the most effective baseline.

Dr. Lorie Fridell in her book *Producing Bias-Free Policing, A Science-Based Approach*[11] points out "the weakest benchmark is residential population as measured by the U.S. Census."

One of the biggest problems with using census data is that the resident population of a community does not represent the service population for the police agency. Others enter the jurisdiction for many reasons. This might include passing through on highways, visiting venues such as museums and commercial establishments, attending activities such as sporting events, conducting business at government facilities, and many other reasons. This changes the demographics of the service population, and is not reflected in the resident population.

Also the concept of disparity is greatly misunderstood. Disparity is simply a difference in numbers. It is the difference between what is expected and what actually occurs. *Merriam-Webster* defines disparity as "a noticeable and usually significant difference or dissimilarity."[12]

Just because there is a disparity in numbers does not mean bias or other inappropriate actions are occurring. Disparity is easy to identify, but the causes of the disparity are difficult. That being said, when a disparity does exist, it warrants an in-depth examination of all relevant issues. Disparity may indicate inequality which implies unfairness or injustice. That possibility warrants further examination. To ensure policing is fair, impartial, and balanced, the activities of police, the circumstances surrounding the actions, the activities of people generally and specifically, and the nature of the interactions must be examined.

Disparity must be examined with the intent of ascertaining why the disparity exists, what actions and conditions contribute to it, and what actions could be changed, stopped, or implemented to reduce the disparity. One of the most common causes of disparity is using a wrong comparison point, census data, for example. If a wrong outcome is expected, then the actual numbers will most likely be different from the expectation, thus resulting in a disparity. So selection of the proper comparison is critical to ascertaining if a disparity does in fact exist.

If a disparity is found to exist, a complete and accurate analysis must occur. It may be that bias, either individual, organizational, community, or other biases are impacting the actions and outcomes. It may be an unintended consequence of otherwise sound thinking and programs. There could and usually are many reasons why the disparity exists. In many policing issues, disparity is caused unintentionally, but is a foreseeable consequence.

A prime example involves how patrol personnel are deployed. Each community looks at its crime and calls for service to decide the number and size of individual patrol areas. In areas where the workload (calls for service and crime converted to hours) is smaller, the individual patrol areas will be larger. In areas where the workload is higher, the patrol areas will be smaller. This is to balance the workload and to allow for similar times in each patrol area for other approved and desired tasks to be accomplished. This means that in higher crime areas, the patrol areas will be smaller, and there will be more police officers in the community. More officers see more things and conduct more self-initiated activities like traffic stops. These actions result in more citizen contacts and correspondingly, more citations, searches, and arrests.

While the intent of providing appropriate levels of police service and presence to handle the workload is good, the unintended consequence is there are more interactions between the police and the citizens. This drives numbers up, and tends to increase confrontations. Not only does this cause a disparity but it harms police-community relationships. So an accurate understanding of disparity, comparison points, and data is critical to understanding what is happening, what are contributing factors, and what are viable options and actions to take to reduce the concerns. This will greatly assist in improving the real-world relationship between police and citizens.

Recommendation 22: All police agencies should publish various reports, statistics, and analyses regarding their actions for public information.

The actions, activities, efforts, and outcomes of police agencies and their personnel are of great interest to the public, even more so now after various incidents of concern. In addition to a strong interest, the public has an actual right to know what the police are doing and if they are efficient and effective. The previous recommendation called for agencies to create and utilize the information internally. The intent being to enhance performance through measurement, data, and current knowledge of issues and trends. This recommendation expects agencies to publish a large amount of the reports and data so that the information is easily available to the public. This improves transparency, knowledge, support, and interaction.

Chapter 6

Community-Oriented and Problem-Solving Policing

Understanding Peel's principles, policing should exist to prevent crime and solve the problems, factors, and situations that cause crime, the fear of crime, and disorder. While solving crime is important, it is much more important and beneficial to prevent crime. Every crime that occurs generates at least one victim and usually more. Most people understand that the primary victim is the one who directly suffered the harm. But others such as family members, friends, coworkers, and neighbors are indirect victims. They suffer too when a loved one or friend is directly victimized. It is virtually impossible to fully restore the peace of mind and feeling of safety in victims. So each crime should be viewed as much more than just a number or merely a statistic. It should be put into context that citizens have suffered physically, psychologically, directly, and indirectly.

The entire agency should be active in crime prevention and Community-Oriented and Problem-Oriented Policing. The largest pool of personnel, patrol, should be actively involved as they are the most visible and most present in the actual community. The concepts of preventive patrol, proactivity, and 40 percent noncommitted time are directly focused on prevention, community building, and problem-solving.

Recommendation 23: Crime prevention should be a primary concern, focus, and activity of all police agencies.

The values of crime prevention have long been recognized. In his first principle and his first core idea, Sir Robert Peel recognized the various values to police, citizens, and society of crime prevention. He understood the value of preventing crime instead of responding to it. These values and benefits are no less real today.

Each agency must have a core focus on preventing crime. It is much better for the citizens and the community overall. If crimes are prevented, there will be fewer victims which is certainly good for citizens, individually and collectively. It is good for society as there is less crime, less need for courts and prisons, and less risk of undesired consequences due to police-suspect confrontations.

But crime prevention is not solely the responsibility of the police alone. Citizens bear a responsibility to help prevent crime. In many communities, citizens leave their vehicles unlocked with valuables plainly in sight. Others see this and commit any number of crimes. Had the vehicle been locked and the valuables not in sight, it is likely that the crime would not have occurred. Now, it might have still occurred by force, but leaving valuables in plain sight with the vehicle locked or unlocked increases the chance that a crime will be committed. Communities and society in the larger context have a role and responsibility in preventing crime. Crime has many causes (poverty, lack of education, lack of jobs, lack of opportunities, lack of hope, etc.) that only society at large can resolve. By working on these larger issues, crime prevention can be more effective. Spending resources (time, funds, activities) on crime prevention can enhance the quality of life for everyone.

Crime prevention should not be a program or the responsibility of a single designated component within the agency. All police personnel should be focused on crime prevention. This serves the community and its citizens better than a focus on apprehension. Deterrence and prevention of crime has tremendous advantages, including the elimination of victims and their suffering; reduction of the costs and impacts of crime to the community; and reducing the number of people who commit crimes and, therefore, are processed by the police, courts, and corrections.

Having all personnel knowledgeable of crime prevention techniques enables all officers to help more citizens. A small component can only handle so many presentations, questions, and demonstrations. But if each officer were able to provide tips, information, and education about crime prevention, and actions that citizens could take, the amount of crime prevention activities would increase dramatically. Officers could and should provide prevention information when they respond to crimes; when they observe unsafe situations or conditions; when they are handling any call for service; and when they are interacting with citizens. A central crime prevention component could exist to coordinate larger events and house personnel who are additionally trained in topics such as "Crime Prevention Through Environmental Design" (CPTED), area-wide lighting techniques, commercial crime prevention, and so on. CPTED is defined as:

a multi-disciplinary approach of crime prevention that uses urban and architectural design and the management of built and natural environments CPTED strategies aim to reduce victimization, deter offender decisions that precede criminal acts, and build a sense of community among inhabitants so they can gain territorial control of areas, reduce crime, and minimize fear of crime.[1]

The values and benefits of a focus on crime prevention, to the community, to individuals, and to society overall are very real. In today's society, these benefits are more important and impactful than in Sir Robert Peel's time.

Recommendation 24: To assist with the order maintenance/public safety service aspect of policing, agencies should embrace Community-Oriented Policing and Problem-Oriented/Solving Policing. These concepts must be organization-wide philosophies and efforts.

Community-Oriented Policing (COP) has existed for decades in many formats in most agencies in one way or another. As originally conceived, COP is intended to have officers interact with citizens to identify concerns citizens have about crime, disorder, and other types of issues in the community. Then together, police and citizens look at the issues and concerns, identify the factors involved, and develop and implement potential solutions to the issues. The key is police and citizens working together for a mutually agreeable solution to the problems. Community interaction is key to COP.

Problem-Oriented/Solving Policing has also been around for some time. It is very similar to COP, but has as its focus solving problems in the community as they are identified hopefully by the police and community working together. POP has the police focus on things that are a problem in the community or neighborhoods, not necessarily those things that are technical law violations or things that the community is not particularly bothered about. It focuses on those things that are most pressing and important to the community.

Some projects that COP/POP have been involved with involve getting street lights replaced, adding stop signs, reducing vision problems caused by trees or signs, having potholes fixed, and other issues that have a safety component but might not be specifically police functions or tasks. However, COP/POP can and should examine the deeper issues that cause crime and problems. This might include a lack of parks and recreational activities; employment issues; or housing issues. Police wouldn't attempt to resolve these concerns on their own, but rather would assist and/or coordinate a larger governmental and/or societal response effort. Anything that improves the quality of life for the citizens is an appropriate topic for COP/POP. One of the big keys to both is the community and police working together. This is such an important concept that the U.S. Department of Justice created an office to assist police agencies and communities enhance its community oriented policing efforts. It is known as COPS—Community-Oriented Policing Services.

COP/POP should be the core foundational philosophies of all police agencies. These must be agency-wide philosophies and efforts if these concepts and practices are to be truly effective. The reason an agency exists is to serve the community, prevent crime, and resolve concerns before they become problems. These concepts are the essence of being proactive and participating with the community to enhance the overall quality of life. Every agency member must be focused on working with community members in identifying and resolving issues of community concern. These concepts and efforts cannot be the responsibility of a single officer, team, or component. COP/POP is not a program or only the concern of part of the agency. It must be embraced and practiced throughout the agency as a philosophy of how policing services are delivered in partnership with and for the benefit of the citizens and community. This goes beyond solely law enforcement issues and is truly focused on community safety. Plus, the community engagement aspect of these philosophies reaps numerous benefits.

Recommendation 25: Citizens and other entities must be involved in community safety and crime prevention/reduction.

Some factors that lead to disorder and crime are beyond the ability of the police to deal with. Not all issues that cause crime can be controlled by a police agency, no matter how skilled and competent they are. These include, among other things, unemployment; lack of quality education; lack of opportunities; insufficient community resources such as parks, transportation, or social services; poor housing conditions; poverty; insufficient positive role models; and substance abuse. How the police are trained, equipped, and tasked does not enable them to resolve these core issues that lead to crime and disorder. In fact, a police response may exacerbate these conditions, leading to more problems.

Citizens must play an active role in their own well-being, safety, and health. There are examples of individuals in any and all situations who have overcome severe adversity to "succeed" in society. But many people cannot, and no one should have the odds stacked against them. Governments and other entities must step up and assist with giving everyone a chance to be successful. This includes thinking differently about issues like education, housing, social services, employment, and those things that society as a group can improve.

Part II

ADMINISTRATION

What happens in the offices and conference rooms of headquarters and other police facilities has tremendous impacts on the service that is ultimately delivered to the citizens. Some of these actions and activities are part of the formal process of managing and leading any organization. These are things normally expected as part of the structure and tasks of any organization, including budgeting, personnel, training, supplies, and so on. Other types of actions and activities are less formal, sometimes unseen by outsiders and even agency personnel. But nevertheless, these items are critical to how an organization or agency operates. This includes leadership, decision-making, and key aspects such as the Mission, Vision, and Values of the agency. While part of the formal organization, these items have their own impacts on agency personnel and function. Leadership and decision-making are expected as part of the formal organization, but these often occur in numerous ways informally in the organization. And in many cases are more powerful than what is identified as part of the formal organization. This is true in any organization and is especially true, prevalent, and powerful in police agencies. This work is not intended to fully discuss all of these items in great depth. But rather, it is necessary to discuss some aspects in order to point out opportunities for enhancement that exist.

Chapter 7

Leadership

Leadership sets the tone for the environment in which the agency and its personnel operate. All actions and decisions must be consistent with the greater guidance provided by the Mission, Vision, and Values, and the core foundational beliefs and philosophies of the agency. Leadership is a heavily discussed and much studied topic. It has many aspects, component parts, and manifestations. Leadership involves getting a group of people to work together toward a common goal in an accepted manner. It is critically important in policing given the critical nature of the tasks, responsibilities, potential outcomes, and powers involved.

For police agencies, leadership includes innovation and moving the agency forward. It is the responsibility of the chief to move the agency past the status quo and into new activities that are focused on increased efficiencies and enhanced effectiveness. The chief must be a visionary who can see potential opportunities for improvements in service delivery, and then lead and direct the agency toward those new opportunities. Each chief should build upon the past of the agency and prior chiefs, while enhancing every aspect of the agency for today and tomorrow. Each chief should be the "best" chief the agency ever had, until the next chief takes over.

Chiefs must be advocates of building community relations and partnerships. They must take the initiative and create new opportunities for citizens and police personnel to interact for the benefit of everyone. COP/POP are excellent concepts to adopt in every aspect of policing. Community outreach, education, and partnerships are other activities that build effective relationships and produce better outcomes for the community.

Leadership must build a culture of service in the agency and among all personnel. An agency that has a culture of service, compassion, helping the community, crime prevention, de-escalation, and seeking out voluntary compliance with laws and societal expectations will have better relationships with the community, less use of force, fewer injuries to citizens and officers, and will have better outcomes including less crime and an overall higher quality of life for citizens.

Recommendation 26: The chief (agency CEO) should be experienced in policing, with a background in the art and science of policing. The chief should be educated in many ways, have at least a bachelor's degree and demonstrate extensive leadership qualities.

The position of chief of police is one of the most visible positions in municipal and local government. It is often one of the most important personnel decisions the manager or mayor will make as it has huge impacts on how policing is delivered and administered. Internally, the chief sets overall policy and can tremendously impact the culture, morale, focus, and behavior of the agency and its personnel. This can directly impact how policing is delivered to the community and impact the quality of life for all citizens.

The criticality of policing and the importance of the chief require that agency leaders have a working knowledge of policing theory and practice. This knowledge is essential if the leader is to make quality decisions about procedures, tactics, legal issues, and so on. They don't have to be an expert in all aspects, but they have to have the working knowledge of the profession in order to fulfill their role in the agency. The possession of practical experience in a real-world environment provides knowledge, skills, and abilities that cannot be as fully learned in any other method. Experience also buys a certain amount of legitimacy with the community, but especially with agency personnel. Electing or appointing people without any practical police experience is detrimental to the agency and the community.

In order to be effective as a police executive in today's society and times, the chief should have a knowledge level that is not only extensive in policing, but widespread in many other areas. Chiefs should possess a minimum of a bachelor's degree, with a graduate degree preferred. This is not to say that someone without a bachelor's degree cannot be an effective police chief. Rather it highlights that a bachelor's degree (and higher) can provide benefits to the chief, agency, community, and citizens. Also, the fact that someone has a bachelor's degree does not automatically make them a better chief, leader, or officer.

One of the primary benefits of having at least a bachelor's degree is that the holder has at least been exposed to people of different backgrounds and differing viewpoints. This diversity adds familiarity and understanding to the knowledge of individuals, and hopefully builds the skills to interact with different people in a positive manner. These are critical to being successful as a police officer and police executive. Another benefit of a bachelor's degree is that the person should have learned to write in an enhanced manner, articulate and advocate views in a professional manner, and learned to research materials and analyze options. Each of these skills will prove invaluable to a police chief as they have to make decisions about policies and procedures.

The chief should also have successfully attended advanced police training and attained advanced certification. This includes training such as the FBI National Academy, Southern Police Institute Administrative Officers Course or the Northwestern University School of Police Staff and Command. These courses are ten- to fifteen-week intensive courses designed to elevate an executive's skills, knowledge, and abilities through academic study combined with real-world experiences. Other courses that can provide excellent educational value for a police executive include PERF's Senior Management Institute for Police (SMIP) and Harvard's Senior Executives in State and Local Government. These programs are shorter but expose the participant to different ways of thinking, considering different points of view, and making decisions while building relationships.

The chief should possess the highest level of state certification possible. This reflects ongoing and advanced training and learning specifically in the police field. Many states have advanced levels of certification that require extensive ongoing, continuing training to earn the advanced certifications. These demonstrate continued learning which is important for a chief. All of this education and training serves to create an individual who is well-rounded, open to new ideas and information, and hopefully supports lifelong learning and skill enhancement.

Having many years of policing experience does not in itself qualify someone to lead a police agency. They might be an excellent investigator but may not be able to lead the agency and make those critical decisions that are necessary. The chief must have qualities such as team building, active listening, a servant leadership mentality, conflict resolution, building morale and esprit de corps, innovation, change management, and decision-making. They must be capable and skilled in interacting with different groups and people including, elected officials, community groups, special interest groups, and representatives of other agencies and departments.

Recommendation 27: The chief and staff should actively participate in professional organizations.

Learning is a lifelong activity. Just because someone has become chief (CEO) or any high-ranking official does not mean they know everything and have nothing else to learn. Policing is a profession that is constantly changing, with new situations being encountered; changes to laws, court decisions, and policies constantly occurring; and new or changing expectations and demands being made of the police. It is imperative that police leaders, especially chiefs, continue to build knowledge, learn, and stay informed of trends and opportunities for enhancement. All of this has the goal of enhancing the organization and the service being delivered to the citizens. This is accomplished by participating in professional organizations, attending training of various types, and staying informed via reading, research, and conversation. Examples of these organizations include the International Association of Chiefs of Police, National Sheriffs Association, Police Executive Research Forum, National Organization of Black Law Enforcement Executives, state chiefs and/or sheriff's associations, and local groups. This continuous learning can have tremendous benefits for the agency and the community, and oftentimes translates directly to enhanced services.

Recommendation 28: The chief should be an active, visible, and accessible member of the community.

It is imperative and hugely beneficial for the chief to be actively involved in the community. The chief must be active within and viewed as part of the community, not apart from it. This translates into being a positive role model for other agency personnel. It sets the tone as to what is expected of other police leaders and police personnel. It also builds familiarity with the community and helps to build trust, confidence, and transparency. A police chief can have significant impacts on the community. Being out and about, interacting with citizens in groups and individually gives a sense of comfort. In most communities, people want to know who the chief is, and they want to hear from and talk with them. The chief should be involved in various community groups, activities, events, and discussions. The chief should make an effort to meet and interact with various community leaders on a regular basis. Besides building a working relationship, it can help when incidents occur, can assist with recruiting, and can enhance the levels of trust and legitimacy within the community.

As the public face, leader, and primary representative of the agency, the chief needs to be visible in and around the community. The chief needs to be seen around various areas and neighborhoods of the community, and needs to be engaged with the community and interact with the citizens. People want to perceive and believe that the chief cares about the citizens, their concerns, and the environment in which they live. And being seen out and about in the community helps the perception and reality of knowledge and caring. The chief is the leader of the organization and being out in the community serves as a role model for other staff members and personnel, while giving citizens some comfort. It also provides opportunities for the chief to see what is happening in the community so they can gain a current understanding of the conditions, talk knowledgeably about the issues, and make better decisions as to how best to respond to citizen concerns.

The chief must also be accessible to the citizens. In most communities, the citizens want to occasionally talk with the chief. It might be to voice concerns, ask questions, offer compliments, or even just say hello. But people want to see the police chief much more than any other city department head in most cases. The chief should make efforts and set time aside to go out into the community to actively listen to what the citizens have to say. Some methods that can be used to accomplish this contact and interaction include programs and efforts such as "Chat with the Chief," "Coffee with a Cop," and monthly press conferences. These activities enable the community to have opportunities to see and talk with the chief away from the police facility. It makes it easier, and sometimes more comfortable for citizens. Being active and visible in the community makes it easier for citizens to interact with the chief in less formal settings which can facilitate conversations and awareness. These outreach activities allow for more positive interaction between the chief and the citizens, and generally in a more relaxed and productive environment. This builds positive contacts and impression, helps with legitimacy and transparency, and facilitates dialogue, support, and better service delivery.

Recommendation 29: The chief must be a reasonable advocate, and the primary spokesperson for the agency and its personnel, especially in times of crisis.

When there are concerns about police actions, the chief needs to be visible. At times the chief needs to be a strong advocate for the agency, especially when the agency and its personnel did the right thing or performed in an appropriate or even admirable manner. But they also need to be outspoken, to the extent allowed by law, when the agency or one of its personnel failed to live up to expectations. It is in these critical times that the public wants to hear directly from the police chief.

While many agencies have a designated spokesperson, a public information officer (PIO), there are times when the chief must be visible and heard. These are generally very critical situations and incidents such as when an officer or citizen has been severely injured or when some unusual event has or is about to occur. People tend to view comments by spokespersons like PIOs with a degree of suspicion as they perceive it is their job to give limited information with the intent of calming things down. The same comments from the chief are generally viewed more favorably. Plus, the chief is the CEO and leader of the agency. They are the ones who are ultimately responsible for the agency, its actions, policies, and its personnel. Having the chief talk about significant events or critical incidents lends more credibility to the agency and comments, offers more comfort to the community, and shows that the chief is informed, engaged, and responsible.

Recommendation 30: The chief must hold themselves, the agency, and its personnel accountable.

Because of the great power that police officers have, and the tremendous and difficult responsibilities they bear, a higher standard of behavior is expected and is appropriate. The chief must be a role model for the agency and the community. Integrity and compliance with all rules, laws, and standards is mandatory. But with all the expectations placed on police personnel, and the fact that they must make significant decisions in crisis situations, in split seconds, the reality is there will be mistakes, sometimes intentional acts, and in some cases, just better decisions could have been made. The chief must hold the officers to a higher standard than to that which citizens are held.

In some cases, officers get involved in an issue when off duty. If it reflects negatively on the agency, or impacts the ability (perceived or real) of the individual officer to legally, ethically, professionally, fairly or impartially perform their duties, then the chief must take action. To the extent allowed by law, the chief must be open and transparent about such issues. The chief has a responsibility to inform the public about the applicable directives and laws when an officer is involved in an investigation. The community needs to know what to expect so they can have informed reactions. The public has to know that any transgressions will be dealt with appropriately and that they can trust the chief, the agency, and the officers, to do the right things.

Recommendation 31: A variety of police-community boards and committees should exist to increase and enhance communication, trust, participation, and transparency. One such board should be a "Chief's Advisory Board" or a similar type of structure to share information and receive feedback. Agency personnel must actively participate in these boards.

These types of entities are designed to provide an opportunity for the chief to meet with a group of citizens to discuss issues related to policing. The group should meet directly with the chief on a regular basis (quarterly or at least semi-annually), to discuss issues, concerns, trends, major policy changes, and so on. In some cases, the group may discuss critical incidents such as an officer-involved shooting, police response to crimes in a specific area, or police response to disturbances. These groups should have diverse participation to represent the full community. There might be more than one group, with each consisting of a different population to discuss issues that may be relevant to them. Examples would include business leaders, religious leaders, Hispanic concerns, black issues, the LGBTQ community, or neighborhood watch leaders. The goal is to get information directly to and from the chief, while understanding that different groups may deal with different issues and concerns. This two-way, high-level communication builds support, transparency, information flow, and enhances the overall level of service delivered to the citizens and various communities.

These advisory boards, commissions, task forces, and partnerships can increase police-citizen interactions away from the law enforcement aspect of policing. The boards would focus on various topics such as recruiting, crime trends, use of force, equipment, and policy development. They could be boards looking at community-wide issues or just focusing on specific neighborhoods and areas of the larger community. The agency and the community benefit greatly when more interaction exists and more public input is received. These activities work to increase information flow; build trust, transparency, and confidence; and enhance overall relationships. The possibilities are almost endless as are the benefits that could be derived by increasing citizen participation and input regarding the operations of the agency.

The more that citizens can interact with police personnel in nonenforcement situations, the better the understanding of and relationship between police and citizens will be. Officers, sergeants, support personnel, as well as command staff should participate in these activities. This builds citizens' familiarity, trust, and comfort with more officers. At the same time, it benefits officers as it allows them to hear from and interact with citizens about issues, while providing agency personnel a chance to develop by their participation in agency decision-making. While it is important for the chief to be involved, they should not be the sole agency participant or representative. This increased positive interaction also helps to reduce any negative stereotypes that may exist among and about citizens and officers.

Recommendation 32: Citizen participation must be encouraged, solicited, and accepted.

Policing should not be done to people, it should be done with people. The police cannot be effective as an occupying force. There must be an active and ongoing partnership between the police and the citizens they serve. As Peel outlined nearly 200 years ago, policing requires the consent and cooperation of the citizenry. If the public as a whole decided not to voluntarily comply with a specific law, or even all of them, the police and government would be physically incapable of forcing compliance. Citizen participation is not only a beneficial aspect of policing; it is an essential requirement. Benefits to be derived by increased citizen participation include enhanced trust, transparency, legitimacy, cooperation, support, and better information and decision-making due to more diverse viewpoints and opinions. It is not good enough to have a few opportunities made available when people inquire. The agency must actively announce and recruit for citizen participation. And the participants must have diverse backgrounds, experiences, and perceptions. It does not have real benefit and can be counterproductive if all citizen participation is limited (intentionally or unintentionally) to people with similar views and backgrounds.

Recommendation 33: The agency must have training and directives in place that discuss, encourage, and properly regulate discretion.

As previously mentioned, there are times when strict enforcement of various laws may not be desirous. In some cases, strict enforcement or making a charge or an arrest may actually be counterproductive to the interests of the community, the involved citizen, or the officer and the agency. Enforcing the law through arrest and/or incarceration may actually negatively impact community safety or the mission of the agency. Strict enforcement may be viewed as excessive, unnecessary, or vindictive. This could lead to negative perceptions, loss of support, and even increased overall resistance to the agency, the officer, or laws in general. Examples of these include very minor transgressions where enforcement may not have the desired end result or value that education and a warning might have.

The agency should train personnel to balance the need for strict enforcement with reasonableness. After all, the end result should be voluntary compliance with laws and societal expectations. Traffic law enforcement is the most common contact point between police and citizens. In many cases, a warning can be much more productive than a citation or ticket. If a ticket is issued or an arrest made, animosity toward the agency and laws in general might increase. It is likely that future voluntary compliance will be reduced. However, if the officer uses discretion and educates the person and issues a warning, there is a greater chance that the citizen will have more respect for the officer, agency, and law, and therefore the chance of future voluntary compliance is higher. Since so many people are killed and injured in traffic crashes each year, having a large focus on traffic safety is certainly appropriate. And enforcement is part of traffic safety. But so is education. If an officer writes a citation to everyone they stop, or writes no citations whatsoever, there are some concerns. Giving everyone a citation or no one a citation is not a balanced method of encouraging compliance with traffic laws. Some people should be ticketed and some do not need the citation to learn to obey traffic regulations. In most cases, if the person has a "clean" driving record and has not committed an egregious violation, it may be more productive to issue a warning. This may build support for the agency, show understanding by the officer, and allow the citizen to change their behavior. If their behavior doesn't change, then most likely they will be stopped again and at that subsequent traffic stop, a citation would be more than appropriate and warranted.

By allowing and encouraging the reasonable use of discretion, the agency is demonstrating that it is more concerned with community safety than the number of tickets or arrests. It also shows compassion for the citizens as it recognizes that occasionally everyone speeds a little bit, or commits other very minor violations. Now, should the violation be egregious, then other more severe actions would be warranted. The agency must train its personnel when discretion is warranted and useful so that each individual officer does not make an arbitrary decision. If left unchecked, the decisions may become arbitrary or based on biases, favoritism, or other inappropriate factors. The agency should encourage discretion where the benefit to the community is greater than the benefits derived from full strict enforcement.

Other examples of when discretion would be preferred involve many situations that could be more social, health-related or assistance-related. These include public intoxication without other criminal activity; panhandling in a nonaggressive, non-traffic interfering method; homelessness in general; or mental health-related issues. In these cases, it would be much better for the involved citizen and society if other diversionary options existed and were utilized. Absent other criminal charges, it would be best to divert these persons to resources better equipped to handle them and their issues. Issuing citations, transporting them to jail, or otherwise entering them into the criminal justice system serves little value other than removing them from the specific location at the moment. It really has no long-term benefit and does nothing to help resolve the situation. But in order for this to happen, agencies need to encourage officers to use their discretion, consider diversion, and utilize available resources as appropriate and existing.

Another significant issue here is that in most communities, sufficient social and community resources do not exist to help those in need. Officers can only divert persons to services that exist. Part of the problem that has led society and American policing to the current situation is that there is a tremendous lack of resources. Because of this lack of resources, the police, jails, and the criminal justice system became the default service provider. Society needs to step up and provide better options for many of these issues instead of requiring the police to handle these situations and individuals.

Recommendation 34: Education should be a primary focus of the agency, with community outreach and interaction being stressed.

Educating people about safety precautions, risks, trends, scams, and other threats to community safety and order provides greater benefit than arrests, tickets, or charges. Educational programs can inform people of the risks, and possibly help them make better, more informed decisions. It is also imperative that police use various methods, techniques, and technologies to educate the citizens. The efforts must consider where the people are. It cannot be just one method, but rather must be different methodologies. This would include outdoor education, programs at schools, work environments, on roadsides, websites, and most definitely social media. For education to be effective, it must reach the citizens, and therefore multiple methodologies must be used.

A prime example here is seatbelt usage. By educating the public about the benefits of seatbelt usage, and the dangers of not wearing them, people can make a more informed decision about wearing them. While they need to realize it is the law, they may decide they don't like the law or they may opt to take their chances about being observed, stopped, and cited for the violation. But hopefully, through education, people will realize that they are at a risk for greater injury if they don't wear seatbelts and make a good informed decision to wear them. Police depend on the majority of people to voluntarily comply with laws, regulations, and safety directives. Police alone cannot enforce full compliance with laws and the courts could not handle strict enforcement of all laws. Therefore, education is a much better and productive method to gain compliance.

Positive interaction between police and citizens has numerous benefits. These include but are not limited to:

- Less fear and suspicion between police and citizens
- Reduced uses of force, and reduced injury to officers and citizens
- Reduced biases based on race, sex, profession, economics, and so on
- Increased knowledge of issues impacting a community
- Increased support for the police
- Increased quality of life for everyone

Multiple activities and methods should be used, as no one method is universally effective. Some activities that exist include:

- Park-Walk-and-Talk, Officers Out of Cars
- Requiring police personnel to engage in proactive positive contacts between police and citizens
- Chat with the Chief, Coffee with a Cop, Shop with a Cop, Fish with a Cop
- Trust Talks, other meetings where police and citizens sit together and talk about issues, concerns, and perceptions to reduce misinformation, produce better understanding, and build positive relationships

There are hundreds of different programs and activities that can be used to bring police and citizens together. Anything that works for particular neighborhoods and communities should be supported and utilized. It might be different activities in different areas, but if it works to bring police and citizens together peacefully, then it should be supported. This support includes financial support from the agency and governmental parent, and private businesses; materials support, such as educational and supportive materials and equipment; and time for agency personnel to plan and participate in these events. Some activities may be large and planned in advance, while other activities may be a spur of the moment opportunities for an individual officer to just talk with a citizen for a minute or two. These activities can reap tremendous benefits for everyone.

Recommendation 35: Utilize police and community resources (funds, assets, people) to enhance public safety and the general improvement of the overall quality of life. This specifically includes using a sizeable percentage of asset forfeiture funds for outreach, community, crime prevention, and educational efforts.

Significant aspects of police resources (budget, personnel time and efforts, facilities, etc.) should be directed toward improving the general overall public safety in non-law enforcement manners. This includes the use of funds for community outreach, crime prevention, Police Athletic League (PAL), and other community-based events. In some cases, laws or regulations will need to be changed to allow agency funds to be expended on items related to these efforts and events such as food and giveaways like backpacks, bicycle helmets, child car seats, and so on.

Events and activities discussed here are larger scales than those previously discussed, and therefore require more planning time, personnel resources, and actual funding. In many communities, there are private businesses and corporations that help support these events. But the governmental parent (city, town) must also support the efforts. These events help on so many levels to create positive interactions, build trust, and show that policing is more than law enforcement.

It is understood that there are strong opinions about asset forfeiture programs and how they are operated. The reality is the program allows agencies to seize assets used in crime or derived as the fruits or benefits of crime. These funds can then be used by the agency to acquire equipment, provide training, or support crime prevention programs. It basically takes crime-based funds and turns them into funding to help support public safety. This not only removes the monetary or financial benefits of crime, but it allows communities to utilize those funds for the benefit of the community without the community having to use taxpayer funds for the items and activities.

By using a substantial amount of the assets for outreach, community, crime prevention, and educational activities, there is more direct benefit to the community. Agencies should expend at least 33 percent of asset forfeiture funds within these specified topics. This would assist in probably one of the most important aspects of policing which includes those core philosophies of crime prevention, service, and education. It would allow additional funds to be spent on areas that typically have low levels of funding, and would have direct tangible benefits in many ways. It would also reduce some of the concerns the public has about these programs and how the funds are spent.

Chapter 8

Personnel

Policing is all about people (police personnel) supplying services directly to other people (citizens). This makes the selection of high-quality personnel critical. In fact, one of the most important decisions a chief of an agency can make is whom to hire. Since each officer will probably operate alone, at all hours of the day, and in any conceivable situation, it is imperative that only high-quality personnel be hired, employed, and retained by the agency. These individuals will make decisions regarding whom to contact, whom to stop, whom to arrest, and how much force to use. They will make decisions that involve the use of discretion, whether to charge anyone, and if so will it be a physical arrest or release on signature. Each contact they have will have an impact on how the individual officer, the agency, and the profession is viewed. Each individual interaction will either hurt relationships and perceptions or it will build trust, support, and confidence. Therefore, it is imperative that high-quality personnel are hired to provide these critical services to the citizens. To accomplish this, a reliable selection process must exist that is comprehensive, consistent, and fair. Detailed procedures must guide the process so only the best persons are selected, and that all citizens perceive and believe the process to be fair and inclusive.

RECRUITING

Recruiting involves those efforts focused on identifying and attracting qualified and desirable candidates to the agency. This involves advertising the agency and the profession so people are interested in the profession and specific agency. Since there is considerable competition between agencies, any particular agency must be proactive to attract potential candidates. Police agencies not only compete among themselves for candidates, but they also compete with other public careers and with the private sector. Everyone is looking for good, high-quality candidates with common sense and good backgrounds who can interact with different people and make good decisions under pressure. The competition for people with these qualifications is high.

Current issues and opinions about policing also impact the potential candidate pool. With a lot of negative perception, and the conversations and efforts involving defunding the police, the pool of high-quality candidates is much smaller than in prior years. In many cases, families do not want loved ones or close friends to enter the policing profession. This reduces the potential candidate pool and increases the competition for quality candidates. Recruiting is an essential activity that helps to ensure the agency and the community it serves have enough high-quality candidates to fill available positions. An excellent resource that talks about various issues associated with recruitment is a COPS/IACP project entitled "Law Enforcement Recruitment Toolkit."[1]

Recommendation 36: The agency must be proactive in recruiting. It must have an active recruiting plan with defined goals and objectives, and it must be reviewed and adjusted at least annually.

Since policing is a person-centric service delivery operation, the personnel selected to be police officers and police support personnel are critically important to the agency and community. It is these personnel that deliver the actual services to the citizens and community. It is imperative that the agency be proactive in recruiting high-quality people to deliver these critical services.

If the agency is to be successful in hiring quality personnel, they must plan for it. The recruiting plan is the guidebook that advises an agency regarding how they will attract a diverse workforce to provide services to the citizens. The plan looks at where an agency is, where it wants to be, and outlines policy, procedures, and actions to take to reach its goals. The goals and objectives should be specific, defined, and reachable. The purpose of the plan is to ensure the agency has qualified personnel of diverse backgrounds, skills, and experiences. An Equal Employment Opportunity Plan and Statement are not sufficient on their own, but have a supporting relationship to the recruiting plan.

A comprehensive recruitment plan should identify specific, obtainable goals that focus on recruiting high-quality people with diverse characteristics. It should identify venues, entities, and groups which the agency can focus attention on to increase the exposure of the agency, and let those entities know the agency is looking for good people. It should identify key stakeholders in the community that can assist in recruiting, people that have good connections throughout the community. It should identify training for recruiters and identify personnel to function as recruiters that would represent the agency well, and are capable of positively talking about the profession and the agency.

The mechanism of the plan is to be proactive. It is not good enough to simply advertise locally and expect or hope that a diverse, quality applicant pool will respond. Certainly some very desirable candidates will apply on their own as they want to be with the specific agency. But in order to attract a sufficient number of quality applicants, the agency must basically advertise its openings and then go to various events, venues, and locations to develop and solicit interest. The agency should make heavy use of social media and other technologies to have a wider reach to potential candidates.

The agency must actively recruit where desired candidates live, work, and relax. The agency must build relationships with community leaders and other entities to assist in identifying quality candidates. This includes religious leaders, ethnic groups, schools, military, colleges (especially historically minority universities), and college programs. And these relationships must be built before it is time to ask for recruiting (or other) assistance.

The agency should work with the parental government's (city, town, county, state) Personnel or Human Resources group as they have certain expertise which can assist the agency. The agency must be an active and proactive participant in its recruiting efforts and activities. It cannot turn all activities and responsibilities for recruiting and selection over to another entity. The agency must proactively recruit qualified personnel. The recruiting plan helps to build a pipeline of potential applicants and candidates.

While the agency has the primary responsibility for recruiting, it is not solely the responsibility of the agency. The governmental parent (city council, county commission, etc.) and the community also have a role and responsibility in recruiting high-quality personnel to the agency. All groups and entities must help identify, recommend, and support high-quality citizens to pursue careers in the policing profession. Members of the community know more people than agency personnel. And they know the quality of their friends and family better than agency personnel. Citizens, community leaders, and community groups should be supporting the police agency, encouraging others to apply, and recommending good candidates to the agency. This participation also helps to build enhanced relationships between the community and the police agency. Community partnerships and assistance, and proactive efforts by the agency should be part of the aforementioned recruiting plan.

The recruitment plan must be reviewed and adjusted annually. Without periodic review and analysis of the plan, it is meaningless. The review should look at the goals and objectives, the actions of the agency, and the results gained. It should identify what activities were fruitful and resulted in quality applicants and candidates, and which actions did not provide positive results.

Depending on the number of personnel being hired throughout the year, the agency should consider semiannual or even quarterly reviews. These would supply a timelier status and update of how successful the agency is being in meeting its goals and objectives. The review should examine the timing and reasons that candidates leave the hiring process. This informs the agency regarding any disconnects between who is being recruited and who is successfully hired and completes the basic training. With high volume needs and activities, waiting a full year to review the plan may cause the agency to expend resources and efforts on nonproductive activities while missing other opportunities that might be more fruitful. It should show the agency is actively reaching out to diverse populations in an effort to hire people who can police the diverse communities of America.

Recommendation 37: The plan should include the goal of having the agency workforce mirror the community it serves.

The agency workforce, sworn and support, individually and collectively should mirror the demographics of the community being served by the agency. Having a workforce that mirrors the community has many benefits. The IACP effectively outlines the numerous benefits in a 2007 statement stating,

> having a department that reflects the community it serves help to build community trust and confidence, offers operational advantages, improves understanding and responsiveness, and reduces perceptions of bias.[2]

Additionally, having a diverse workforce provides opportunities for people to see and interact with people like them in the agency. This is very powerful in several ways including recruiting efforts, building trust and confidence, and making it easier for people with various characteristics to have a little more comfort in talking with people with shared or common characteristics.

But building and maintaining an agency that is diverse and mirrors the community is not easy. There are numerous reasons this might not be the case in any police agency at any given time. Some factors are beyond the agency's control, but the agency must be proactive and aggressive in recruiting diversity. Mirroring the demographics of the community is a higher standard than the legal standard of approximating the available workforce. But this is the appropriate standard because the agency provides services to the entire community, not just the available workforce. It is incumbent on the agency to let everyone know that they are welcome in the agency if they meet the legal and professional standards. While the agency may have difficulty meeting this goal, it is the appropriate goal as it gives the agency a high level to strive toward, and can help build a better and more legitimate police agency.

Recommendation 38: Agencies should identify desirable characteristics for its personnel. This should include some mix of education, knowledge, service, and life experience. Police agencies should adjust their recruiting messages to reflect the type of people desired, and the type of tasks and activities they will perform.

The agency should develop an inventory of characteristics that it desires for its personnel to have. This can greatly assist and guide the entire personnel process. These characteristics must include all types of demographic characteristics as discussed previously. But other characteristics that can enhance the quality of police personnel must be considered. These include education; experience interacting with persons of diverse and different backgrounds; the ability to remain calm; the ability to communicate with others; and high moral character. Each of these characteristics will be essential in competently fulfilling the role of a police officer.

In addition to the general benefits of education, it provides exposure to new information and different viewpoints. In most educational settings, the environment enables, and in many cases, requires students to interact with others. This builds skills in many areas such as tolerance of others viewpoints, learning other viewpoints, being able to discuss differences of opinions, and building human interaction skills. It can also teach one how to listen to others and be patient as others explain their views and opinions. All of which will enhance the ability of the person to serve as a police officer.

Having experiences with people of diverse backgrounds, views, and characteristics exposes one to different views, opinions, ways of life, and perceptions. There are many different ethnicities, religions, preferences, beliefs, and numerous characteristics in the world. If a prospective officer can demonstrate that they have successfully interacted with people "different than they are," it will help them serve as a police officer wherein they must interact with all the different types of people in their community. This is beneficial in reducing implicit bias and building skills of acceptance, interaction, and understanding, which will result in better service delivery.

It is also imperative that police personnel remain calm in various situations, especially when dealing with crisis situations or persons in crisis. Police are expected to respond to a situation and establish order, calmness, and resolution. If the officer cannot remain calm, then the situation can deteriorate further and the service delivered will be less than desired. Calmness in the officer can go a long way to reducing stress and anxiety in others which is good for everyone.

Having good or high moral character is critical to policing. Police personnel must be depended on to exercise their role in an honest, legal, ethical, professional, fair, and impartial manner. There can be no question regarding the integrity of an officer, and agency, or the profession. The integrity, truthfulness, and judgment of the officer must be beyond reproach. In many cases, it might be the word of the officer that decides if a citizen will be arrested, charged, jailed, and possibly even found guilty. Also citizens must have confidence that the police will treat them with dignity, respect, fairness, and legality in every interaction. After all, in many circumstances, police officers have access to people's homes, personal information, and yield a tremendous amount of state power. It is critical that each police employee have good and high moral character.

A variety of knowledge, service, and life experience can add competence to a police officer. This becomes the true value of diversity. Personnel with different backgrounds and experiences increase the views, opinions, and perceptions of the agency as a whole. The agency should require some amount of specific attributes to ensure that the applicant is well rounded and capable of interacting with different people in different situations. These attributes should include at least two years of college, with four being preferred. The Tulsa, Oklahoma, Police Department requires a bachelor's degree for decades and they believe it enhances the quality of its personnel without negatively impacting recruiting. Some of the values of and recommendations for additional and higher education beyond high school have been enumerated herein. In addition, several studies and commissions point out the value of higher education. These include a PERF study entitled "The State of Police Education: Policy Direction for the 21st Century,"[3] and the National Advisory Commission on Criminal Justice Standards and Goals "Report on Police"[4] to name just a few. Higher education has also been shown to be related to fewer serious disciplinary actions.[5]

Another attribute that agencies should value is military experience. There are many advantages to military service that directly relate to policing. Serving in the military exposes people to other viewpoints, opinions, and demographics. Military personnel must learn to live with, get along with, and interact with people of different backgrounds and characteristics. This is especially helpful as a police officer, since the officer will be required to positively interact with people of various characteristics and background. This is a critical skill for police officers. The military also provides excellent training, some of which can translate to policing. This would include weapons skills, defensive tactics, understanding rules of engagement/laws, and various types of supervisory and leadership training. Military experience also indicates that the person can function in a structured, rule-laden environment, which is very similar to the paramilitary structure of most police agencies. In some cases, military experience can provide examples of calm action in stressful situations which police officers will be required to demonstrate. As long as the military experience is positive and the person leaves in good standing (honorable discharge), military experience and service should be a desired attribute and be favorably received.

The agency should look for life experience in its applicants. Generally, life experience is gained by living and can be associated with chronological age. But this is not automatically true as some young people have experienced a lot of situations in life, while chronologically older persons may not have been exposed to as wide a variety of life experiences. Since police officers will be dealing with all types of people in all types of situations, the more life experience an officer has, the more likely they are to be compassionate, understanding, calm, and logical in their perceptions and actions. Plus, a variety of positive life experiences, with people of different characteristics can indicate that the person is more capable of successfully dealing with different people.

The agency can consider these attributes in many ways. It can have "either/or" preferences surrounding these attributes. It could require some amount of college or military experience with demonstrable positive life experiences or it could have a mix of them. For example, it could require (or prefer) a bachelor's degree, or military experience, or demonstrable positive life experiences. Or it could mix and match them such as two years' college and life experiences, or military service. By seeking these attributes, the agency is indicating that it is looking for an applicant with some additional life experiences beyond just high school. By default, this would also increase the minimum age to at least twenty-one. The goal should be to identify those candidates who have life experiences that will enable them to competently perform the difficult tasks, responsibilities, and roles of a police officer.

Currently, too many police agencies have recruiting videos and materials that highlight Special Weapons and Tactics teams (SWAT), action, tactics, arrests, and weapons. While all of this is part of policing, and unfortunately part of the necessary tasks asked of police officers, it does not represent the vast majority of tasks that officers will perform. Most officers use very little force, and the vast number of officers in America never fire their firearms at a person during their entire career. The recruiting message, materials, advertisements, and efforts should be directed at the kind of person that is most desired by police agencies and the citizens. If the recruiting message is all about action and force, then that is the kind of person that will be drawn to the agency. However, if the desire is to hire people with diverse backgrounds who can think, possess a service mentality, have excellent skills of communication, patience, and self-control, then the recruiting message should focus on persons with those attributes. This is not to say that police will not have to make arrests or possibly use force to accomplish the lawful tasks of the position, because unfortunately they probably will at some point. But it is about what is the primary type of person the recruiting message is reaching out to.

The recruiting message must match the characteristics and attributes of the desired applicants.

HIRING STANDARDS

Every organization has a set of hiring guidelines or standards that identify the type of person the organization desires to hire. The hiring standards are generally the foundation for who gets hired and who does not. These usually include a mix of skills, knowledge, and abilities (SKA) that generally focus on technical skills, competencies, and educational levels. They also include minimum requirements or qualifications that have been deemed necessary by some entity. Depending on the organization and type of occupation, there may be a certifying body that establishes these minimum hiring requirements. Most professions (policing, law, medicine) have these entities but some other occupations (teaching, various trades) also have an entity that oversees licensing or certification.

Policing has its own set of hiring standards based on the tasks, responsibilities, and role of police personnel. Some of these standards are set by state commissions that govern various aspects of being a certified police officer in each specific state. Standards set by a state commission are considered as minimum standards. Agencies must comply with the state-mandated minimum standards but are generally allowed to add or enhance these minimums with their own standards. Police standards place a heavy focus on the character of candidates and officers. These character attributes include "good moral character," lack of prior criminal charges, honesty, integrity, and lack of prior drug use (to varying degrees). The concern is that the job requires police personnel to be of good moral character since they will be entering people's homes, will be dealing with criminals, will be required to act appropriately in difficult situations, and will be required to testify truthfully. Much of this is verified by a mandatory comprehensive background investigation.

Other types of police standards involve educational proficiency of varying levels, successful completion of a comprehensive medical examination, passing a psychological examination, and maintaining some degree of physical fitness. All of these are directly related to the tasks of competently serving as a police officer. Under the current structure, each state sets out the minimum requirements to be a police officer in the respective state. While there is general agreement and consistency with many of the standards, each state can set its own standards. Most states require a person to be at least twenty-one years of age, but many have a lower minimum age with several only requiring the officer be eighteen years old. Recently this has begun to change as more scrutiny has been placed on policing. There are many reasons that support a higher minimum age. These include more years of life generally means more life experience, more interaction with other people, and a more fully developed mind, mentally and emotionally.

Every state requires a minimum of a high school diploma, or a GED (general educational development test). In late 2020, California announced it was considering requiring either a college degree or being at least twenty-five years of age.[6] Some states require a mix of college education and/or experience. Some agencies (in the past or currently) have additional educational requirements of either sixty semester hours or more up to a bachelor's degree as minimum requirements. A few states (Florida and North Carolina) require candidates to attain a 10th grade reading comprehension level before entering the basic police academy. Research has shown that persons with a reading comprehension level below 10th grade have a significant likelihood of failing either the academy or the field training program.[7] Some agencies also place a value on military service and may substitute all or part of any educational or experience requirement for military service.

Police hiring standards have existed for many decades and have changed over time. As the tasks, responsibilities, and role of police change, and as the expectations of society regarding policing change, it is imperative that police hiring standards be reviewed to ensure they match the needs and expectations of the agency and society.

Recommendation 39: Agencies must ensure that their hiring standards are lawful, relevant, and appropriate.

Every business, employer, and profession has hiring standards to help them hire qualified personnel. Due to the nature of policing, it is critical to hire personnel who can perform the required tasks legally, ethically, professionally, fairly, and impartially. Leonard and More point out "The caliber of police service is almost completely determined by personnel policy, and very largely at the intake by recruiting standards."[8] This reinforces the criticality of proper personnel selection, which is guided by hiring standards. Many standards are set out by state law and are required by a state certification body. These standards are mandatory for all hires and applicable to all agencies with sworn personnel. Some standards are set by the individual agency and enhance the state-mandated requirements. State standards cannot be waived by the agency, but agency standards can be changed.

Many current hiring standards make good sense such as no felony convictions or crimes involving ethics or moral turpitude. But some standards should be reviewed and considered for adjustment or elimination. Examples would include a conviction for underage drinking or operating a jet ski without a current registration. Some actions that occurred as a juvenile or many years ago should not be an automatic bar to police employment. The use of illegal drugs has been a common disqualifier for a lot of applicants. For years agencies have been reviewing, and in some cases changing the standards regarding illegal drugs, especially marijuana. This is to reflect the actual reality of current society. It might not be appropriate to eliminate a twenty-four-year-old college graduate or military veteran for smoking marijuana five times five years ago. But it also may not be appropriate to hire someone who "blazed up" on the way to the interview. Finding a good balance is necessary to protect society while not ruling out otherwise good candidates for minor drug use in the past.

Care must also be taken to understand and review the impact of various hiring standards. If a particular standard tends to rule out more of one group than another, then the standard is suspect and must be evaluated. The standard should give everyone, regardless of characteristics like race, sex, or ethnicity, the same opportunity to pass and succeed. Regardless of whether state mandated or agency guidelines, the standards should be reviewed periodically to ensure they are legal, relevant to the job and tasks, and that they are appropriate for the police service and society.

Recommendation 40: Agencies should not restrict their hiring to only already certified officers.

There are basically two types of people agencies can hire as police officers: those who have a police certification and those who do not. Additionally, those with certifications are of two types: those who have the certification only and those with certification and actual experience as a police officer. While all applicant types can be excellent additions to a police agency, each has certain benefits and disadvantages.

To earn a police certification, the person has to have successfully completed an approved basic police academy and passed a state-mandated certification examination. Attending the basic academy is generally accomplished in two ways. First, and historically most common, is the recruit is hired by a police agency and then sent to the academy to be trained. This has been the primary method for decades. It enables the agency to select who they want and then send them to the academy as an employee. This benefits the agency in that they can have more control over the recruit and they have a fully certified officer ready to work once they successfully pass the academy and certification examination. For the recruit, it is a benefit in that they are earning a paycheck while attending the academy, and they know that if they pass, then they will have a job waiting for them. This is good for both the agency and the individual.

Another way to attend the academy is for the person to apply to and pay for the academy themselves. This has the benefit of having the person complete the academy without financial risk to the agency and at the same time enables people to earn the certification and then apply with the certification in hand. The negatives to this are that many potentially good officers cannot afford to pay for and attend the academy on their own. They may have to work to live while supporting a family. Then to attend the academy in addition to regular life is extremely difficult. Recently, many agencies have done this more frequently as it is a cost savings to them. Another concern with this model is that some entities that run certified police academies allow persons into the program that cannot be certified under state certification rules. This is unfair to the student in that they spend time and money completing training and then can never be certified. It is also a disservice to the other potential applicants and society in that limited seats are now taken up by persons who cannot become police officers.

Additionally, many agencies will now only hire officers who already possess the certification. One large issue with this is that people without a certification in hand are basically shut out of the opportunity to be a police officer. For the agency and the community, this has a huge negative impact. First, the pool of already certified police officers is not very diverse. The majority of police officers in the United States are white males. Females make up roughly 12 percent of all sworn officers, while 71.5 percent of all officers are white, 11.4 percent are black, 12.5 percent Hispanic, and 4.7 percent are either other or unknown.[9] Since the existing pool of certified and experienced officers is not very diverse, if an agency hires only already certified and experienced officers, the odds are they will not enhance the demographics of their agency. And except for those few new officers entering the profession as officers move around or retire, the profession itself will not increase its overall diversity. Second, the profession does not bring in younger people that might have different ideas about society and policing. This could possibly reduce the amount of innovation and reflection of current societal views.

Another issue with only hiring certified and experienced officers is that some officers change agencies to get away from something. This might be a lack of opportunity, a "bad fit" with the agency or community, or disciplinary issues. On the other hand, many officers that change agencies are good officers who are making changes for positive reasons such as family reasons and better opportunities. The issue is that, when hiring already experienced officers, the agency must include a review of the officer/applicant's personnel file. They must examine how the officer performed at their current or previous agency. In some cases, the new agency will have to deal with prior training and procedures that might not be consistent with the new agency's expectations. An already experienced officer may have "baggage" that needs to be dealt with.

Hiring a noncertified person and/or non-experienced officer has many advantages. First, it gives the agency more hiring options as it does not automatically eliminate noncertified applicants. And the reality is that there are many thousands of applicants without a certification that would make excellent police officers. It also broadens the pool of diversity in the agency and the profession which has benefits of its own. Sending an applicant to the academy as an employee, whose job is to successfully complete the academy and pass the certification exam, enables the recruit to fully focus on the academy, and on developing the necessary, SKA expected of them. They may still have a family and all the responsibilities associated therein, but they do not have to worry about a different job while attending the academy.

Depending on the size of the agency and needs of the agency and the community, there may be times where it is "better" to hire a certified or certified/experienced officer. If there is a genuine, articulable reason for doing so, then it should be done. But if the only reason that noncertified personnel are being excluded is to save money, then the agency should immediately rethink its overall needs in light of having a professional diverse workforce. In most cases, agencies should be hiring noncertified people and training them, as the primary method of hiring officers. It can be supplemented with hiring certified and/or experienced officers, but this should not be the primary method of hiring.

BACKGROUND PROCESS

Recommendation 41: A comprehensive background process must be utilized.

Due to the tasks demanded of police officers, and the responsibility and power they possess, it is imperative that only highly qualified personnel be hired. The background process is designed to look deeply into the past of the candidate, to determine if there are any actions or factors that indicate the person would not be a good police officer. Since society cannot know what a person will do in the future, or how they will react to a particular situation in the future, the best criteria and indicator is to look at past actions.

Most states mandate a certain minimum background process, with some states mandating very good processes. As with hiring standards, some agencies supplement the state mandates with additional components to ensure they hire quality personnel. The process should be clearly set out in detailed written directives with all information documented. At the very least, a comprehensive background process should include:

• A comprehensive personnel history, completed by the applicant, that details all past residences, schools attended, driving and criminal records, immediate family, debts, and so on

- This personnel history must be reviewed and utilized by the background investigator to verify all applicant-supplied information and gain additional information about the applicant
- A criminal history and driver's license check must be performed
- Interviews of family, friends, and coworkers
- Review of social media accounts

All of these are intended to give the agency as accurate and complete a picture of the candidate as possible. Each aspect is designed to ascertain if the applicant has a violent past, has excessive driving violations, demonstrates biased attitudes in life or on social media, or has anything in their past that might indicate they may not be able to perform the expected tasks in the manner desired by the agency or deserved by the citizens. While it is hard to define good moral character, that is exactly what the process tries to do.

Recommendation 42: If the applicant is or has been a police officer, the agency must expand its background process to review personnel files from current or prior agencies and any relevant databases. To this end, all police agencies should be legally required to provide full assistance to other agencies, specifically regarding the provision of all personnel, performance, and complaint records.

Since past behavior is the best predictor of future behavior, examining the personnel files of certified police officers can provide a wealth of information about the candidate's real-world policing behavior. The files that must be reviewed include the personnel file of the officer/candidate in every agency they currently or previously worked. This would provide information about evaluations, commendations, complaints, training, discipline, and so on. Internal affairs in all prior agencies must be checked to understand the nature and outcome of complaints. The National De-Certification Index (NDI) must be checked to see if there have been actions regarding the officer/candidate's certification due to serious misconduct. The certification commissions of all states that the officer/candidate was certified must be examined to see if there were any issues within the state. To facilitate these checks, the officer/candidate should complete an authorization form to release all records from prior agencies. This will reduce issues of other agencies not providing personnel records. If the officer declines to sign such authorizations, the officer should be dropped from further consideration for a police position. These actions will help reduce the movement of problem officers from one agency to another.

Since every agency will hire new personnel, and sometimes that will include already certified, experienced police officers, each hiring agency will need access to the files of another agency. They should, therefore, cooperate and assist other agencies when the various personnel files of current or past agency personnel are requested as part of a hiring background process. It is mutually beneficial for agencies to share information, and is certainly good for communities and society. Some agencies (and their governmental parents) are reluctant to provide such information for fear of being sued by the officer-now-applicant to another agency. In some cases, the full files are not released while in other cases no information is provided, even with a signed form authorizing release of all information. Also, all agencies should cooperate as part of their obligation to society in general. If necessary, laws should be amended to allow and even require release of this information to other police agencies.

OTHER HIRING PROCESS COMPONENTS

Recommendation 43: A comprehensive battery of examinations should be utilized in the hiring process. This would specifically include a written test, an initial Physical Abilities Test (PAT), at least one board/ panel interview, a medical examination, and a psychological examination. Standards should be set and all applicants should be required to successfully pass each and every aspect of the process.

Policing requires a substantial amount of basic education skills including reading comprehension, problem-solving, writing, and some degree of mathematics. An entry-level written test helps to determine if the applicant has the basic educational levels to be successful as a police officer. The test should measure reading level skills, as some studies indicate that low reading levels lead to more failures in the academy and more attrition during the first two years of service. Because of this, the mandated reading level should be at the least a 10th-grade reading level, but a 12th grade level is greatly preferred. Those states with a minimum threshold have generally used a 10th-grade reading level as that equates to the reading level of a high school diploma. As previously mentioned, research indicates that persons with a reading comprehension level of below 10th grade are more likely to fail in the basic academy.[10] Minimum passing scores for math and writing skills are generally set at 70 percent. Writing skills are essential since officers will be composing various written reports to document their investigations. These must be accurate and comprehensive to be useful in court.

The written test is also beneficial due to the amount of basic educational skills that will be used in the police academy. The academy is heavily focused on increasing basic knowledge of the law and police processes. Plus, throughout the career of an officer, they will be required to read and understand laws and procedures that change periodically. The test also helps identify those that most likely will not be able to pass the academics portion of the academy and allows available background, hiring, and instructional resources to be focused on those most likely to pass. Care must be exercised to ensure that the written test is valid, reliable, and fair.

Successful completion of an initial PAT should be required. Policing is a profession that requires physical exertion and stamina in various situations and conditions. Certainly, the position requires the ability to protect oneself, protect others, and make arrests even when there is resistance and force used by the citizen. But also, the position requires running, climbing, and substantial time in all weather conditions performing tasks such as traffic direction, investigation, and evidence gathering. Physical stamina and the physical capabilities to perform the required functions are essential to protect citizens and officers.

The entry-level test should measure the physical tasks of the position as closely as possible. Most states have a validated Physical Abilities Test (PAT) that reflects the demands of policing and it is usually used as one of the required tests that must be passed to graduate from the police academy. The entry-level test should mirror that test but require a lower passing level in the application process. For applicants, the initial test should require the applicant to demonstrate capabilities of approximately 65–75 percent of the academy end passing level. This indicates that the applicant should be able to reach successful performance levels during the academy training. Some agencies require the applicant to pass the full PAT, this is problematic. First, the applicant will have the entire length of the basic recruit academy to build the necessary skills to pass the full PAT. In most academies, there is a fitness aspect that includes training, general fitness development, and actual passing the full PAT as a requirement to successful completion of the academy. The academy training curriculum is designed to take citizens from a reasonable point to a fully trained police officer. It is not practical nor necessary to expect an applicant to pass the full PAT prior to going to the academy. Second, requiring the applicant to pass the full PAT as part of the application process, causes otherwise good candidates to fail the application process and never make it into the academy and hence, becoming a police officer. This eliminates people unnecessarily when they can reach the intended levels by participating in the academy. Third, it might expose the agency to lawsuits if the application PAT requirement results in disparate impact to certain groups. The application-based PAT must be valid, reliable, fair, and job-related.

There should be at least one interview board component. To this end, each agency should implement a standardized oral board interview component as part of the hiring process. This requires the applicant to demonstrate the ability to answer basic questions, and should focus on ethical issues and reasoning skills. Very technical questions such as what law is broken in this scenario should be avoided as an applicant wouldn't reasonably be expected to have detailed technical knowledge before they are fully trained. The board interview should examine the ability of the applicant to be calm, think, and communicate with other people. The board members should include someone in the position being sought (officer), a supervisor, and a citizen. Others such as a representative from city Human Resources/Personnel can participate as desired. The board should also be diverse to reflect the agency's support of diversity, to make the applicant more comfortable, and to reflect the diversity of the citizens that will be served by the applicant. The board must be consistent in member makeup and questions asked. By having a citizen on the board, it offers a citizen's perspective on the process and the candidate, while giving another opportunity for citizens to participate with the agency.

A comprehensive medical examination must be administered and passed. Most state certification processes require a full medical examination prior to hiring. Some agencies require a more comprehensive examination for various reasons such as insurance, pension, or general preference. This examination is near the end of the process and is geared toward the final hiring decision. It is not the physical examination that some agencies require just to participate in the initial physical abilities test. This medical examination is intended to ensure the applicant is medically and physically capable of safely performing all of the tasks expected of them. The agency should identify the licensed medical doctor to perform the examination using criteria that is appropriate for the position in question. The doctor should be familiar with the demands of being a police officer, including the various tasks and responsibilities required of the position. They should also be required to document in writing whether the candidate can or cannot perform the tasks of the position. It should be a very comprehensive examination and paid for by the agency. This examination must also be job-related and use established tests, testing methods, and criteria.

Because of the tasks, functions, and responsibilities of police officers, each candidate should be subjected to and pass a psychological examination. The examination is intended to ascertain if the candidate has the mentality and personality to perform in the high stress, rapidly changing environment of a police officer. This includes a battery of written tests which is reviewed by a qualified and licensed professional. The professional should conduct an interview with the candidate after reviewing the written test results. A standardized interview should be used that is supplemented with questions derived from the candidate's written and oral responses. The examination should specifically look at how the candidate interacts with and responds to people, especially people who are different from him. Looking for examples of dealing with diverse persons can give an indication of how well the candidate can interact with others and how aware of and in control of their implicit biases the candidate is. Remembering that police officers must interact with a wide diversity of people in various situations, it is critical to determine if the candidate can do this. A comprehensive report should be completed and provided to the agency to assist in its hiring decision.

Recommendation 44: The decision to hire or not hire should be made by the agency.

In compliance with detailed procedures, the agency should make the final hiring decision. This is due to the fact that the agency is the entity that will be held responsible for the decisions and the ultimate acts of its personnel. Policy should clearly define the hiring process and what factors will be considered and with what weight if appropriate. The chief or their designee (an individual or a board) should make the final hiring decision. Many communities have a public safety or police commission that makes such decisions. Some use a very strict civil service process wherein the chief or agency has no or very little say whatsoever in who is hired. These types of processes have several problems and deficiencies including hiring people who test well on a written test but may not have the personality for the job. Some communities use only written tests and a point-based rank-ordering system that requires selection of the top score. The heavy or sole reliance on a single test has previously caused a lack of diversity in some agencies. This is not to say that people of diverse backgrounds cannot test as well, but historically, there have been issues with how some tests were constructed. In some cases, who moves on in the selection process or who is offered a job may be decided by tenths of a point. And very few tests are so well constructed as to be capable of determining by tenths of a point, which candidate will succeed in the process or more importantly which candidate will be the better police officer. The reality is there is much more to being a police officer than scoring high on a single written test.

The chief and the agency can be held accountable for their hiring decisions and they should be. They should be required to document why a particular person was hired or not hired. The hiring decision should be based on the whole person. The hiring process should answer the question: Does this applicant possess the necessary requirements to be a police officer, and do they bring other desired qualities or benefits to the position, the agency, and the community.

Recommendation 45: Residency should not be an application, hiring, or employment requirement.

Some agencies and communities require that police officers (and possibly other employees) reside in the community either before they apply, before they are hired, or shortly after being hired. This is done by some towns, cities, and counties. Residency should not be a requirement for police personnel for a variety of reasons. First, it unnecessarily limits the applicant, candidate, and employee pool. Second, it can have negative impacts on diversity. Third, it may cause the agency to have unfilled openings, especially if the community is a wealthier one, where many residents already have careers or where potential applicants are looking at other careers. Fourth, the cost of living in the community may be higher than an entry-level police officer can afford.

Community knowledge is a good thing, but sometimes growing up in and living in the community can cause reluctance or hardships for the officers and their families. Community knowledge can and should be gained once employed. By hiring people from outside the community, there is the opportunity for diversity in backgrounds, thoughts, experiences, and viewpoints to add positive benefits to the agency and community. The one individual where there can be a requirement to reside in the community is the chief. This makes it easier for the chief to be seen in the community, to better understand the community, and to be part of the community. The chief should not be required to reside in the community until they have been hired, and then they should be allowed a reasonable time (no longer than six months in most cases) to move into the community.

Recommendation 46: The agency should review its overall hiring process and decisions on an annual basis.

An annual review and analysis should occur and be documented in a written report. The hiring process is so critical to an agency and the community that review and analysis is crucial. The report should identify numbers and demographics of applicants, who progressed to and through each step, who failed at each step, and who were eventually hired. This is not person-specific but is individual specific so as to understand if there is any bias or adverse impact to any particular group of people. By examining attrition at each step of the process, the agency may be able to identify problems that unnecessarily and possibly inappropriately eliminate applicants and candidates. It may also identify opportunities for enhancement of the process itself or its components. The report should be reviewed in conjunction with the recruitment plan and then the entire process examined as a whole. These reports should be published for review and consideration by governing bodies, the Personnel or Human Resources component of the governmental parent (city, county, state), and the public.

Chapter 9

Training

Training police personnel is a critical function. It is time-consuming, difficult, and expensive. But failure to properly train agency personnel is much more expensive and results in injuries, death, lawsuits, protests, riots, loss of trust, and many types of damage to officers, communities, and citizens. All states except Hawaii currently prescribe some amount of basic training to be certified as a police officer. This training differs in hours and topics, with anywhere from 340 hours to 1,150 hours of basic training required, depending on the state. The overall average length of basic recruit academy training in the United States is 840 hours or 21 weeks.[1] States also require different topics and amounts of periodic training in order to maintain certification. Individual agencies can, and many do, require additional training topics and hours for either new officers or annual in-service training. Some individual agencies require substantially more training than the state-mandated minimum. This training varies greatly from agency to agency, state to state.

Since all citizens have a right to expect certain basic levels of service, and certain basic competency levels by their personnel, some standardization is appropriate and necessary. This standardization has generally been accomplished by state boards or commissions that set minimum mandatory levels of training. These minimum standards include training topics and the number of hours for each topic. But as identified above, there is a wide difference in the amount of state-mandated minimum hours. These state-mandated minimums quickly become the state standard as most agencies require only that minimum amount mandated by the state. Training is expensive financially and in lost available manpower. So too many agencies complete just the minimum amount of formal training that is required by applicable state standards.

Just as the federal courts have issued rulings impacting all policing, it is appropriate for some federally mandated minimums to exist. This would provide some degree of consistency in topics and hours to which citizens are entitled. This is a controversial topic as it impacts state's rights. But some minimum guidelines should be established which would be good for officers and citizens.

BASIC TRAINING

Recommendation 47: The federal government should mandate certain topics and hours of training for all basic police academies.

As demonstrated, there is a wide difference in basic academy programs. Some states require very little training (three months or less) while other states require more. Only three states require over six months of basic training. Understanding there are some differences in state laws and local practices, states do have a legitimate reason for teaching different topics. But these differences should be conducted as additional hours, beyond a universal core of mandated topics.

Some of the topics that should be mandated consistently throughout the entire United States include sanctity or reverence of life, use of force, deadly force, proper defense and arrest tactics, constitutional protections, duty to act and intervene, ethics, implicit bias training, de-escalation, communication techniques, human interpersonal skills, first aid, procedural justice, legitimacy, and others. The concepts and items identified in the National Consensus Policy on Use of Force, the 21st Century Policing Report, items within the IACP Framework for Community-Police Engagement, and agreed-upon standards of accreditation should also be taught. Doing so would enhance the consistency of training and possibly the service levels for all citizens.

The number of hours should be a mandated minimum so there is reasonable belief that each and every officer received comprehensive and competent training in all topics. The training should focus on the practical demonstration of learned skills, knowledge, and abilities. Training should be scenario-based, realistic, and integrated. This means that scenarios should be used that incorporate a variety of skills and knowledge instead of just teaching one topic in isolation of other skills or techniques. While having a set number of hours for each topic does not guarantee the quality of the instruction or the level of learning, it is a common measure to help ensure some probability that the material is being taught comprehensively and that appropriate learning is occurring. With many topics, demonstrating mastery of the concepts and expected competencies may be a better measure of learning. However, since some testing does not measure all competencies, the hours-of-instruction method has been the default measure of quality teaching. In reality, there should be some mix of the two measurement methods (course hours and competency demonstration) to ensure full mastery of the pertinent skills, knowledge, and abilities.

Recommendation 48: The basic police recruit academy should be at least six months long, if not longer.

As previously mentioned, current state-mandated basic recruit training ranges from 340 to 1,150 hours. With the average length being 840 hours or about 5 months, expanding the basic academy by at least another 160 hours (or one month) should not be that onerous on anyone. And the reality is that every hour of quality training that an officer receives can enhance the officers' skills, build better interactions, result in better outcomes, and enhance the quality of life for everyone. This is a tremendously short training period when one considers the skills, knowledge, and abilities that need to trained and mastered, and the tremendous impacts that police officers have on individuals and society. Police personnel are required to possess detailed knowledge of laws and apply that knowledge very quickly in confusing and frequently chaotic situations. They are expected to be experts in human relations and must be able to positively and beneficially interact with persons of all characteristics, including people who are different than they are. And when interacting with citizens who are in various levels of crisis, they must be capable of de-escalating situations. If necessary, they must be able to use force to overcome resistance in a manner that is the minimum required to resolve the situation. They must learn technical skills such as defensive and arrest/control tactics, enhanced driving skills, firearms and weapons proficiency, and first aid. They must learn how to investigate crimes and traffic crashes, and how to interview witnesses, victims, and suspects. But it is the interpersonal skills areas, such as de-escalation, dealing with mental health issues, stress reduction and wellness for officers and other such skills that need to be enhanced. It is these skills that officers use most often and they represent only a small portion of academy training.

In most cases, the skills, knowledge, and abilities that are taught in the recruit academy are new skills, or at the very least are an enhancement to the level of skills the recruits possess. The recruits must also demonstrate a mastery of everything they have been taught in the academy. It takes time to learn and master everything that is expected of a police recruit. In many agencies, the new officer, who just graduated from the police academy will be required to begin functioning as a full police officer as soon as they complete the academy. Therefore, it is critical they leave the academy as well trained as possible.

While most academies provide excellent training, it is difficult to believe that 340 hours is enough to properly equip a new officer to face the issues they will be asked to deal with on the street. Even the average (which means that some academies are longer and some are shorter) academy length of 810 hours causes the question to be asked: "Is this enough training for someone to perform the complex tasks, responsibilities, and role of a police officer in America?" Additional quality training that is integrated with various topics and concepts, and requires practical demonstration of the mastery of skills and knowledge provides enhanced opportunities for new officers to be successful on the street. This additional training provides additional opportunities to learn and master skills. It better prepares the recruits to function as police officers. Police officers have tremendous responsibilities and power in our society. Because of what society expects of police officers, the initial training should be at least six months and really should be closer to a full year. The federal government should mandate certain topics and minimums for all police recruit academies. But each state should supplement these minimum federal requirements with additional hours to teach topics deemed necessary by the states. These could be additional topics and/or hours, but would be customized to each state's needs and concerns.

Recommendation 49: Funding and opportunities for candidates to attend basic police academies should be provided.

Historically, and as previously discussed, most new recruits were hired by a police agency and then sent to police academies for basic training. These academies were operated by the hiring agency, the state training commission, and/or a technical/community college. But in almost all cases, the recruit was paid to attend and participate, with that serving as their employment. This had the benefit of providing training to those who might not be able to afford it on their own, gave the hiring agency more interaction with their recruits, and kept the recruit focused on the training instead of another job.

Over the course of recent years, many agencies have moved away from operating their own academies. This was primarily due to two reasons. The first was due to costs. Operating an academy consumes resources such as budgets, administrative and instructional personnel, facility operating costs, and paying the recruits a salary while attending the academy. These costs could be shifted elsewhere if the agency did not operate the academy. Second, community colleges sought control of the academies in order to offer and control the programs in exchange for funding, student count, and other issues related to community college operations. This doesn't mean that all community college programs are bad; many are very good. But they must still conduct the state-mandated curriculum.

But one of the problems with these programs is that students must pay for the training themselves. This makes it difficult for some candidates as they must pay tuition, attend classes, work to pay living expenses, and possibly raise a family. These are big issues that can impact who applies and completes academy training, and in effect who is hired. Another concern regarding community college programs is they sometimes accept students into the program who cannot or will not be hired as officers. They may not meet the state-mandated requirements to be a police officer, or if they do, something in their background may cause most agencies to not hire them. These expectations and situations are unfair to the student, and they waste academy seats.

If the trend is to have community colleges provide the training, then there should be some mechanism to help the students, the agencies, and the communities. Some positive actions might include: prescreening all students to ensure they fully meet the requirements to be a police officer; being sponsored into the academy by an agency that has already completed the background process so that the student will have a job when they complete the training; having a funding stream or entity that pays the tuition for the student, such as the government or college funding based on hours and so on; and having the funding available for the student to be a paid employee of the agency. Each of these options would enhance the ability of policing to hire diverse, qualified, and well-trained candidates.

Recommendation 50: The basic academy curriculum should be controlled by the certification body.

Notwithstanding the prior discussion about federal involvement in basic academies, each state certification body should set the curriculum for basic police training within their state. They should be required to comply with any federal mandates (including minimum length and topics) regarding such training. But the state should set the curriculum, resources used, instructor certifications, minimum passing standards, and general academy operating guidelines. While this exists in most states, as mentioned the minimum training standards and curriculums vary widely from state to state. The curriculum should not be controlled by the community colleges as their focus may be different than the state certification body. The community colleges should be involved in curriculum discussions and revisions, but adjustments should not be based on costs or profits.

The state curriculum should be continuously reviewed. Most states do this now. But there is great reluctance to increase the number of hours due to additional costs in dollars and costs in personnel. The curriculums should include many of the topics already discussed with expanded hours for some. Most curriculums focus on technical skill development and proficiency, with a much smaller number of hours focused on interpersonal skills. But once again, it is the interpersonal skills areas, such as de-escalation, dealing with mental health issues, stress reduction and wellness for officers and other such skills that need to be enhanced.

Recommendation 51: The passing grade should be raised to 80 percent in all topic areas.

While some agencies and academies use an 80 percent passing threshold, most still use 70 percent. This passing threshold generally applies to technical skills (firearms, driving, etc.) as well as basic knowledge items such as law and other informational topics. Some academies use a pass-fail threshold for certain topics such as driving, the practical aspect of first aid, and defensive or arrest/control tactics. For the practical applications of some of these skills, a pass-fail option may be appropriate as it would be difficult to quantify an 80 percent competency level in some skills. But it should require a high level of mastery to pass. Due to the impact and severity of the decisions police officers make, an 80 percent passing threshold is more reasonable. It would be more difficult, and could result in more academy attrition, but an expanded academy length would provide more time for training and subsequent mastery of knowledge and skills. All of this would result in better trained and more highly qualified and skilled officers, which is desired and beneficial to everyone.

Recommendation 52: Academies should provide more tutoring and assistance to students.

Since academy students have already passed significant background investigations and hiring examinations, reasonable assistance to students is appropriate. There is a lot of material to learn in an academy in a short period of time. With a higher passing threshold (80 percent), the academy should provide assistance to students, such as tutors, study sessions, and study guides. More classroom hours, as previously recommended would increase the time to discuss and learn the material. The academy should not be a process focused on weeding out students. Academies with high attrition rates should be carefully reviewed to determine why the failure rates are high. An examination of the primary reasons for failure in basic academies reveals that additional training and tutoring would probably be beneficial. The primary reasons for failure are voluntary withdrawal (34.9 percent), academic failure (22.5 percent), physical standards (13.1 percent), injury/illness (9.6 percent), firearms performance (5.7 percent), discipline (5.1 percent), sponsoring agency withdrawal (2.5 percent), driving performance (1.6 percent), and all other reasons 5.0 percent.[2] The three competency-based categories (academic, firearms, and driving) account for 29.8 percent of all failures in a basic recruit academy.[3]

This indicates that expanded instructional time (even with a higher passing mark), and increased instructional assistance could reduce attrition in the academic, firearms, and driving topics. It might also assist in reducing voluntary withdrawals. This is not meant to suggest that everyone should pass by any means possible. High standards need to be set (such as 80 percent), and students should honestly and fairly meet those expected standards. But if fair, proper, ethical, and reasonable assistance can assist them in reaching that high standard, then that should be seriously considered. But most certainly if a student cannot pass the material, with reasonable assistance that is appropriate, then they should not move forward. The impacts and costs to society of having a poorly trained officer are too high.

Recommendation 53: Dishonesty, untruthfulness, or cheating of any kind in a training course should be grounds for immediate dismissal.

While this should be obvious, some academies have more lenient policies and penalties. When a police academy student cheats, there are several issues that must be addressed. First, it is against the ethics of policing to cheat. This is a moral issue that begs the question, "If they cheat on an academic test, what else will they cheat on or be dishonest about?" Dishonesty cannot be tolerated in policing and officers must act ethically at all times. As previously mentioned, it is imperative that police officers are truthful and honest in their actions, reports, and statements. Their statements are relied upon in reports, investigations, and in court. Because of the impact of an officer's statements or testimony, there can be no doubt about the accuracy and truthfulness of the officer.

Second, they cannot cheat on the examination and then be expected or depended upon to have learned the material to a sufficient degree to reliably perform their tasks in a legal manner. In a real-life situation, the officer will often be required to make quick or even immediate decisions that can impact a person's life, liberty, or safety. They may not have someone else present to rely on or to cheat off of. While the officer is not expected to know every law that exists, and in many cases can either read the law, a procedure, or ask for guidance, in some situations they cannot. They must know the main points, common aspects, and key principles of the laws. These are what are generally tested upon in an academy setting. So if the student needs to cheat on these items in an academy test, they most likely have not sufficiently mastered the knowledge to apply it in a real-world situation. Society simply cannot afford to have officers that cheated on exams to gain their certification. This recommendation applies to annual refresher and all police training courses.

Recommendation 54: Fitness standards should be relevant to the job, with training being reasonable.

Policing requires officers to have a certain level of physical fitness. This is necessary to perform various functions such as spending hours outside in the weather, standing and directing traffic or securing an area, and unfortunately having to overcome the resistance and force used by citizens. Fitness training should be focused on building stamina and overall fitness, not just bulking up. Certainly, strength training is a component of good overall fitness training, but it should not be the primary focus. Also arrest and defensive tactics training should focus on accomplishing the tasks in a manner that uses minimal force and involves the least amount of risk to officers and citizens. Use of a valid, reliable, and job task-relevant test, such as a validated PAT is recommended as it directly relates to the tasks required of an officer.

Fitness, defensive tactics, and response to resistance training should not be brutal or result in unreasonable injuries. Some academies fail or hurt too many students because of the exercise standards, requirements, or training methods related to the fitness and tactics areas. The national average of reasons for failures, as previously mentioned, indicated that physical standards accounts for 13.1 percent of failures and injuries/illness accounts for 9.6 percent of failures.[4] It is unknown what part of the 9.6 percent injury/illness number is due to academy-based injuries and what is not related to academy training. But an examination of the physical standards and injury issues is warranted due to these failure percentages. If the applicant entered the academy having passed a reasonable physical abilities test, then they should be capable of passing the academy-based physical training and standards. The training should develop and enhance the skills of the recruits in a demanding but balanced manner. These training topics should also include verbalization and de-escalation as component parts.

Recommendation 55: An annual review and analysis of academy training should be completed.

An annual review of academy training should be completed that focuses on performance data. Some of the data that should be reviewed includes test scores, passing rates for individual topics and the overall academy, and the passing rate for the state certification examination. By examining this data, the academy staff and other interested parties can understand if the training is effective and if any instructor, section, or topic causes a high attrition rate. If students continuously score lower in certain topics, then that indicates that the training needs to be reviewed to ascertain why the training isn't sufficient to produce successful learning. The training should be of such a quality that students should pass the tests if they apply themselves in a reasonable manner.

By examining the passing rate of the state certification examination, the agency and/or training center can further determine if the training materials, instructors, and methods are sufficient to enable a student to pass the examination. If there is a significant percentage of students who pass the academy but fail the certification examination, then there is a disconnect between the academy program and what the state deems as essential knowledge to be certified. The review of academy and state certification performance should include an analysis of passing rates based on group characteristics. There should be very little disparity among different groups regarding passing the academy and state certification. Any level of disparity should be examined to determine the causes and to ascertain methods to eliminate the disparity. Training methods, instructors, materials, tests, and/or testing methods may need to be adjusted to produce better results.

Recommendation 56: Academy training should be integrated, scenario based, and include additional training in human interaction skills.

In many academies, each topic is taught as a stand-alone topic. This results in a silo type of mentality regarding teaching and learning. Certainly, each topic should have time and effort directed toward learning that topic and its intricacies. But real-world application of the knowledge and skills does not happen one topic at a time. In real-life situations, numerous topics are present and required. For example, a traffic stop involves vehicle operation, radio usage, camera activation (if not automatic), officer safety awareness and skills, communication skills, and an understanding of the law and the rights of citizens.

Integrated scenario-based training places the student in a scenario where they must utilize all of the skills they have learned. They learn that a traffic stop is much more than just enforcement of traffic laws, and they learn how they present and conduct themselves can often times impact the flow, environment, and outcome of the traffic stop. Another example involves use of force training that should not just focus on technical skills. Certainly, the student must learn and master the technical skills, but they must also understand to use those skills in the context of the law and the situation encountered. Use of force training should include applicable laws, rulings, guidelines, de-escalation, verbalization, safe positioning, and ethics. Certainly, the technical skills of arrest and control procedures, defensive tactics, firearms, driving, and other technical skill topics are critical. But they should not be taught in a vacuum. Training in an integrated, scenario-based manner also allows the various topics to be reviewed, reinforced, and observed multiple times in various circumstances. Many academies and state commissions have started moving toward this type of training in recent years.

Historically, police academies have focused quite heavily on teaching the technical skills of the job, and only lightly on how to interact with and respond to people. This was due to the view that most people had learned how to communicate with others and did not need that much training in these areas. It was (and to a large extent, still is) believed that the limited academy time was better spent on teaching students technical skills like defensive tactics, arrest control, firearms, evasive driving, first aid, and understanding the law. Therefore, the number of hours spent on human interaction skills generally represented less than 20 percent of the academy curriculum. In fact, the most recent survey of police training academies indicates that less than 5 percent of training hours is spent on communications and professionalism.[5]

In recent years, there has been a push and necessity for officers to have enhanced interpersonal and communication skills. Some academies have increased the number of hours and topics regarding these skills. Since an officer must be able to effectively communicate and interact with citizens, increased training in these skills must occur. Academies can no longer assume that students can effectively communicate with others, especially in the role of a police officer. Being in the role of a police officer changes the dynamics of the interaction and requires a different and expanded skill set. Academy training must be increased in the areas of verbalization, positioning, appearance, de-escalation, patience, legitimacy, and procedural justice. It must specifically include training regarding interactions with persons who are in crisis and/or have mental health challenges. An increased ability to use these skills can reduce the need to use other more technical skills such as arrest techniques and response to resistance. In some circumstances, enhanced de-escalation skills can reduce the need for using force, including deadly force. In reality, virtually every call, self-initiated activity, or police interaction requires some degree and level of human interaction skills. It is imperative that these skills be taught, enhanced, and evaluated during police academy training. The more officers can gain compliance and successfully complete their tasks by using interpersonal skills, the safer officers and citizens are.

Recommendation 57: State certification should require successful completion of a state certification examination. No person should be allowed to function as a police officer unless they have passed an approved basic academy and a state certification examination or process.

Completion of a basic police academy, even using the state-mandated curriculum and procedures should not automatically grant officer certification to an academy graduate. Before a person is certified to perform as a police officer, they should be required to take and pass a state-mandated certification examination. Most states currently do this, but it must be made mandatory for all states permanently. Some states do not require passage of a state-wide certification examination.

By requiring passage of a state certification exam, citizens can have more comfort that each new officer possesses the basic required knowledge to perform as a police officer regardless of which academy program they graduated from. This process is to ensure that quality training is delivered by each academy, and that each new officer has acquired basic knowledge. It helps to build consistency at the state level.

Due to the tasks, responsibilities, and roles of a police officer, and due to the impacts of the actions of a police officer, all persons should be trained and certified before being allowed to function as a police officer. While this seems to be very common sensical, and actually being a "no-brainer," it is unfortunately legal in various states for persons to function as police officers without training or certification. Several states allow persons to function as police officers for various periods of time, ranging from three months to indefinitely before attending training.[6] This is simply unacceptable.

Some states allow already trained officers, who have been certified in other states, to transfer their certification. They must demonstrate various levels of experience; show that the training they have received is consistent with the current state's training and requirements; and in most cases, must complete a short transfer course involving law and/or "high liability" areas, and/or pass a "challenge" or "comparative compliance" examination. This is very standard and is consistent with professional expectations. This is also very different from functioning as a police officer without any training.

Recommendation 58: All agencies should have a Field Training and Evaluation Program.

Upon completion of academy training, and successful passage of the state certification examination, new officers should participate in a Field Training and Evaluation Program (FTEP). The purpose of these programs is to supplement academy training with agency-specific training such as an awareness of agency procedures, policies, and practices. They are also designed to actually observe the new officer in the real-world performance of various police tasks such as traffic stops, arrests, investigations, driving skills, knowledge of the community, and interacting with citizens. It is a real-world learning environment that focuses on the practical application of the knowledge, skills, and abilities required of a police officer. While many agencies have these programs, there are many versions of them. Only five states require any type of FTEP, and these programs range in length from 40 hours to 960 hours.[7] Some agencies require a week or two of familiarization with the agency and community, while others require a three-month or longer program that is very comprehensive. The better programs, and the type that should be required, are the longer programs that have detailed procedures, trained mentors, and require extensive documentation.

The FTEP should include Field Training Officers (FTO) that are trained in how to train and evaluate new officers and in how they document additional training and skills performance. The program should include reviews of key agency policies such as use of force, ethics, emergency response, camera utilization, and investigative skills. The FTO should observe the new officer/trainee actually performing various tasks to ascertain if the officer can perform them legally, ethically, professionally, fairly, impartially, and in compliance with agency directives. The trainee should be tested on a regular basis regarding policies and procedures. All testing, training, and performance should be documented on a daily basis, with the performance of the trainee being reviewed so they understand any deficiencies.

Most programs are divided into several phases, most usually four phases. The first phase is an orientation wherein the new officer rides with an FTO, begins learning key agency policies, the areas of the community, and other basic information. In the second phase, the new officer is assigned to a different FTO and begins performing various tasks such as driving, handling the radio, learning directions and travel routes, and beginning to conduct investigations. In the third phase, the new officer rides with yet a different FTO and handles more of the workload. They start to multitask such as driving and handling the radio simultaneously, and they conduct more of the investigations and more significant aspects of investigations. The last part of the program should be structured so that the new officer handles all the calls for service, driving, and proactive patrol, with the FTO there just to observe and verify that the new officer is capable of functioning alone. At the end of the program, the trainee should be capable of performing as a single officer unit. By changing FTOs throughout the training, the new officer is exposed to different personnel with different methods of fulfilling the role. This also ensures that the new officer is evaluated by more than one FTO which provides benefits of different perspectives and opinions, different knowledge levels, and helps to ensure fair treatment to the new officer and the agency.

These programs expand the academy training and allow for observation of the new officers as they perform various tasks in real situations. But they do so under the guidance of trained experienced officers for the duration of the program. This assists in officer development while protecting the agency and community during this expanded on-the-job-training program. There should be some degree of consistency in these programs to ensure that citizens are served by officers that have as much training and experience as possible.

IN-SERVICE TRAINING

In order to keep the skills, knowledge, and abilities of police personnel viable and current, agency personnel must receive annual in-service or refresher training. It is simply insufficient to provide recruit training at the start of a police career, and then not provide regular, annual refresher training. The skills that officers learn and need are perishable. The skills must be refreshed and officers should be required to demonstrate mastery or proficiency in the skills on a regular basis. Some of the knowledge that officers learn and need is also perishable due to regular changes in criminal, civil, and procedural laws as well as changes in best practices. It is unreasonable to believe that regular training to refresh skills, knowledge, and abilities, and to demonstrate periodic skill proficiency should not occur or be required.

Most states mandate some amount of annual refresher training, but it currently varies from zero to over forty hours annually. The average is twenty-one hours, and two states do not require any annual training.[8] Some states require a certain amount of hours every two or three years instead of annually. Of the states that mandate some amount of in-service refresher training, most identify the specific topics that must be covered. Many of these provide the complete training curriculum including lesson plan, learning objectives, tests, and any pertinent videos. Some states provide the refresher training through a learning portal of some type that is delivered in an online format. Some states mandate a certain number of hours and allow the agencies to pick some or all of the training topics from among a mandated list. There are various options of this mix and match option. As with basic recruit training, many agencies require more in-service training than is mandated as a minimum by state law, regulations, or commissions. The annual training should cover certain basic topics every year, and then provide refresher training or skill enhancement training in various topics every two to three years. Certain topics should be reviewed every year and various proficiencies should be tested and demonstrated annually. These generally are those that could be considered critical or high liability skills and knowledge. Once again, training is expensive and time-consuming. But failure to train, and failure to train properly can be devastating in so many ways. The periodic refresher training should be structured on an annual basis for key topics, with some topics structured over a two- or three-year period. The importance of training does not end when an officer is sworn into a police position. But based on the tasks expected, the powers involved, and the possible impacts and consequences, this training is essential.

Recommendation 59: In-service training should be integrated and include legal, ethics, and professional aspects in each topic.

Integrated training brings together various topics that should be considered with different skills, knowledge, and abilities to handle situations in a more comprehensive manner. In the real world, no incident stands alone requiring only one skill set or type of knowledge. Each call that an officer responds to involves numerous skills, knowledge, and abilities. All will require the ability to interact with citizens. Other calls may require additional abilities such as the ability to interview people, apply a current understanding of the law, utilize technical skills such as defensive tactics or arrest/control tactics, or the need to provide first aid. And virtually all will require the ability to document what happened and what actions the officer took. Therefore, training should encompass and include various topics to resolve the incidents that will be encountered. Core topics such as legal issues, ethics, de-escalation, officer fitness and wellness, and professional behavior should be part of all training. Legal updates as a stand-alone topic and integrated with other topics should be part of the mandatory annual training and testing.

Recommendation 60: The agency should create a multi-year refresher training program. Certain topics should require annual refresher training. This includes legal reviews and updates, the use of force and all related policies, fitness and wellness, de-escalation, and human interaction/interpersonal skills, and professionalism. Other topics should be on a multi-year schedule.

Some topics are so important that officers should have annual refresher training regarding these topics. In some cases, there are changes within the topics such as changes to laws. It is imperative that officers stay current and competent in knowledge and skills. Since officers enforce the laws they must be knowledgeable regarding the most current laws. Every year, state legislatures change, delete, and add laws. Some changes are major while other changes might be subtle wording changes. But the officer must be aware of these changes so they can properly act consistent with current laws. Also, each year various court decisions impact how laws are interpreted and might even find some laws unconstitutional. These court decisions have real impact on how the police can act. It is, therefore, critical that agencies provide officers with the most current legal updates. To do this, the agency may need to issue new directives at any time and provide immediate training regarding the changes. But, at the very least, the agency should provide annual refresher training regarding legal changes and updates.

Due to the issues surrounding a police officer's use of force or response to resistance, all agency personnel should be required to attend annual refresher training that reviews every aspect of the use of force. This specifically includes applicable laws including any recent changes due to legislative or court actions, as well as a complete review of the agency's use of force policies. This training should include any information provided by the agency's legal counsel, local prosecuting attorney, state attorney general, and any information or training provided by the applicable state certification commission or body.

The training should include when force can be used, what level of force can be used, and what weapons are authorized by law and agency policy. It should occur with and as part of actual firearms or other force-related refresher training or proficiency demonstration. While it should be an integrated part of these trainings, it should occur at the start of or prior to other related training. This is to refresh and enhance the understanding of force usage, and acts as the foundation of all force-related training. This enables the subsequent training and proficiency demonstrations to occur in the context of and in compliance with, the most recent and current training.

Due to the physical demands on officers, their fitness should be evaluated annually. This would be part of a mandatory fitness and wellness program discussed later. The fitness test should be validated for the activities performed by officers and should be a version of the state-mandated PAT used for applicants and academy graduation. If reasonable and allowed by law, the standards should consider the age of the officer. Some agencies have excellent programs, but unfortunately most have no programs. Being physically capable of performing the tasks of the job, including overcoming resistance to arrests, might reduce the use of increased levels of force, including deadly force. It will also keep officers healthier and reduce injuries, worker's compensation claims, insurance costs, and many lines of duty pension payouts related to injuries or stress.

The officers should also be educated regarding the need for overall wellness, both physical and mental. Stress is a serious issue in policing and contributes to heart attacks, strokes, poor habits regarding eating, substance abuse, and can lead to poor or improper job performance. A fit police workforce is a benefit to the officers, the citizens, and the community as a whole.

De-escalation refresher training should be required annually. De-escalation is a skill that can be used in many of the tasks officers are involved in on a daily and constant basis. Since most people are not happy about the situation that leads to contact with officers (vehicle crashes, victimization, traffic stop, or being arrested), de-escalation techniques and skills can be used in virtually every contact between police and citizens. De-escalation is also important in dealing with persons with mental health issues, persons who are in crisis, or citizens who are involved in disputes. Annual training should involve role-playing exercises, a review of existing and new techniques, and new studies or other information about the topic. De-escalation should be a topic of its own, but should also be integrated into other training such as traffic stops, persons in crisis, and persons who are resisting lawful orders. Success stories from the agency and policing in general should be shared.

Since interpersonal skills are used in every police-citizen interaction, they should be refreshed and reviewed annually. For this purpose, interpersonal skills include communication, verbalization, empathy, courtesy, and treating people with respect. Professionalism skills here are defined broadly and include ethics, implicit bias training, procedural justice, and legitimacy. These skills and factors are crucial to police being accepted, supported, and trusted by the citizens. Treating people with respect, dignity, and courtesy can go a long way to gaining support and compliance.

In many cases, citizens want to be heard and want an opportunity to explain their actions and/or the situation. Some studies indicate that allowing a citizen to reasonably voice their view, opinion, or reason for their actions can have a larger positive impact on outcome and citizen perception than if the person does not get a ticket. Unfortunately, some officers get into the habit of being very short with citizens including not listening to them or offering an opportunity for the citizen to explain themselves.

Sometimes this is referred to as the Sergeant Friday response. In the old TV show *Dragnet*, Sergeant Friday would often tell people, "Just the facts ma'am." This left the impression that he didn't care about perceptions, feelings, or emotions, and that all he wanted was the facts so he could move on to the rest of the investigation or to another call. This doesn't just apply to citizens who might be on the receiving end of law enforcement actions. Even citizens who have been victimized or involved in a traffic crash want the attention of the officer for at least a few minutes. Also this might be the only contact the citizen has ever had with police, and their situation most likely will be very important to them. Officers should take the time to hear the citizen out. Most citizens hate to be brushed off when they are dealing with police, especially if they are victimized and/or trying to report something to the police. Officers should be capable of, and take the time to, positively interact with all citizens regardless of background, demographics, or situation. Granted, citizens play a large role in how encounters evolve, but the officer has the primary responsibility to de-escalate, positively interact with citizens, and to try make all encounters as pleasant as possible.

Some topics and training are not necessary or applicable to annual training. This includes first aid, hazardous materials, civil disorder training, and other topics that are less critical or do not require training on an annual basis. These topics should be regularly scheduled in the multi-year training cycle so requisite skills and certifications are maintained. If new material such as changes in law or procedures occurs, the training topic should be moved up in the cycle to ensure officers are utilizing the most current information and procedures. The use of a multi-year training cycle allows the agency to better plan its annual refresher training, and to be more efficient in the use of its overall training time.

Recommendation 61: Officers should be required to qualify with all weapons and firearms, at least annually, and at a skill level of 80 percent.

After the refresher training regarding the applicable laws and policies regarding the use of force (deadly or otherwise), then training and proficiency demonstration should focus on the technical skills related to force usage. This training should include recent and new information and studies regarding the use of force such as relevant academic and professional studies. Officers should be aware of what general studies and actual incident reviews have learned about human emotions, reaction times, and effectiveness. By understanding and analyzing real-life incidents, agencies and personnel can be better prepared to deal with potential and actual use of force situations.

The use of force or response to resistance is a critical and high liability activity. While necessary and reasonable in the vast majority of incidents, it has resulted in public concerns, numerous injuries, lawsuits, protests, and riots. By requiring all officers to re-qualify or demonstrate proficiency with each weapon or firearm at least annually, the agency can ensure that appropriate skill levels are maintained. The training should include all weapons for which the particular officer is authorized to carry and use. This includes baton, pepper spray, conducted energy/electrical weapon (CEW) (Taser), pepperball, and other less-than-lethal weapons authorized by the agency. It also includes all firearms whether handguns, shotguns, or rifles.

Due to the serious nature of using any force weapon or firearm, it is imperative that the officer has significant proficiency in the use of these items. The training should include general refresher training on the use of the weapon, demonstrated proficiency in its use, a review of applicable laws, and a review of the agency use of force policy. All of this training should be based on a recently approved lesson plan, by instructors certified to teach the weapon, and documented regarding attendance, performance, and what was taught. A written test covering the basics of each weapon and the agency use of force policy should be part of all relevant training. A score of 80 percent should be required to pass. This training and testing should be performed at least annually.

For firearms, the training should be conducted at least annually and should include general handling and safety methods, relevant laws as are updated, agency policy, a written test, and a demonstration of proficiency. It should also include a focus on de-escalation including the use of cover and distance. Many states require some type of periodic firearms re-qualification, but the training should be much more than just re-qualification. The proficiency demonstration should include day and night proficiency and all testing, including proficiency, should require 80 percent to pass. Procedures should

exist for those who fail to pass the proficiency testing including a prohibition from carrying the weapon or firearm until additional remedial training
and subsequent demonstration of proficiency can occur. These practices will
require additional materials associated with the training and demonstration of
proficiency, as well as personnel time such as instructor time and time away
from primary assignment for students. But based on the issues surrounding
use of weapons and firearms, this training and its related costs are prudent,
reasonable, and necessary to protect officers and citizens.

**Recommendation 62: Officers should train on state-of-the-art decision-
making simulators.**

In addition to refresher training regarding new laws, and actual demonstration
of proficiency in the use of weapons, including firearms, all sworn personnel
should receive training using decision-making simulators. These sophisti-
cated learning systems present various scenarios with multiple options to the
officer, and require them to use a variety of skills to respond to and successfully resolve the scenarios. Using realistic video scenarios or vignettes, the
officer is immersed in the scenario. The officer is required to use a variety
of skills (cover, verbalization, de-escalation, and possibly various weapons)
to respond, control, and resolve the incident presented in the scenario. Each
scenario has multiple options, paths, or outcomes that can be controlled by
the instructor and can be dependent on how the officer acts and reacts. This
allows the officers to realize that in some situations, their actions such as verbalization and de-escalation may allow them to avoid using various weapons.

These training simulators provide realistic scenarios with many being common situations officers may face on the street. They are capable of increasing officer stress and can measure various aspects such as when a weapon is
drawn, used, and the accuracy of the officer. Different systems have different
characteristics and options, but most allow the officer to select from various force and weapons options including voice, baton, CEW, OC (oleoresin
capsicum)/pepper spray, and various firearms. Depending on the options
selected, the size of the physical training environment, and the number of
personnel that can train simultaneously, prices can range from approximately
$25,000 to well over $100,000. They are relatively expensive but the training
they offer is outstanding and has many advantages.

The training is much more than accuracy with firearms. Many of the
scenarios can be resolved without using a firearm or other weapon. The
scenarios are customizable and responsive to the actions and directions of
the student-officer. It can enhance verbalization, de-escalation, and officer
safety skills. It also has been shown to reduce implicit bias due to forcing the
officer to observe and respond to threats, not demographics such as race, sex,
ethnicity, or other characteristics.[9] The scenarios also provide the opportunity

for feedback and additional training that can provide officers with multiple options instead of or in addition to force. Most systems also document reactions and accuracy which allows for additional training opportunities. While these simulators are not a substitute for actual qualification with weapons and firearms, they provide substantially more learning opportunities than just the technical skills of aiming and discharging a firearm. These simulators encourage and generally require an integration of various skills, knowledge, and abilities such as verbalization, de-escalation, officer safety (positioning and cover), and decision-making regarding what weapon to use if any. The benefits of these training tools far exceed their cost.

Recommendation 63: The agency must have a written remedial training policy.

It is critical that personnel be provided remedial training when their performance does not measure up to agency expectations. This deficiency may be a failure to meet expected performance levels in a classroom/learning/training situation or may be a failure to meet performance expectations in the actual performance of duties. In either case, remedial training should be required. Remedial training is designed and intended to rebuild the skill set of the person so they can meet minimum performance expectations. It is not just getting someone to pass a test, but rather is intended to build the actual skills, knowledge, and abilities of the person. After all, the overall intent is to ensure the person can competently perform the tasks and duties of their position.

The policy should be integrated with the disciplinary system and should require some degree of remedial training in most disciplinary situations. If someone is disciplined for an action or deficiency, remedial training should be included to build the skill set of the person so future deficiencies do not occur. The remedial policy should require the person to participate in training designed to correct the deficiency and meet at least the minimum level of acceptable performance. Remedial training should be appropriate to the topic and deficiency and should be documented. Remedial training can improve individual performance and can protect the officer, the citizen, the agency, and the community.

Recommendation 64: All in-service refresher training should be based on written lesson plans and delivered by qualified personnel. All training must be fully documented.

Lesson plans are necessary for each training course as they provide the operational plan for the course. Lesson plans should be reviewed annually before training is conducted to ensure the material is current and accurate. The lesson plan should include the instructors name, last revision date and by whom, who reviewed and approved this version of the lesson plan for training, materials required and used, tests and answers, resources used in building the lesson plan, and the learning objectives of the training. The lesson plan provides guidance for how the training will be conducted and helps to ensure consistency of the training. It also provides documentation of the training.

State standards should exist regarding instructors for certain topics and may require special certifications for instructors to teach certain topics. These topics are usually considered high liability and include firearms, weapons, defensive tactics and/or arrest techniques, driving, and first aid. All state certification requirements regarding training and instructors must be adhered to. Periodic recertification of the instructors in these identified topics should occur to ensure they are knowledgeable of the most current information and techniques.

Each agency training course should be documented in a file that contains at least the following information: comprehensive lesson plan, tests and scores, attendees, instructor, and the dates, times, and length of training. It is imperative to ensure that all training is fully documented so it can be verified that each person successfully completed all mandatory training. Documentation is also necessary to show what was trained in case there is a concern about training method or content. This information is necessary to have for litigation purposes and to assist in ensuring current information and best practices are being taught. The individual files of each officer should also be updated after each training course to reflect the training they have completed.

PROMOTIONAL TRAINING

As personnel are promoted, they will assume new responsibilities. It is critical that personnel receive appropriate training in these new tasks and responsibilities, and that they develop new skills, knowledge, and abilities. It is also beneficial to everyone that an understanding of and competency regarding these new roles and responsibilities exist prior to assuming the new position. Promotions usually involve moving from one level to another, with most involving additional responsibilities as a supervisor. Each upward promotion indicates that the newly promoted supervisor is responsible for supervising more people and/or making more critical decisions, with these decisions having a wider impact on more people. Supervisors in many police agencies have increased abilities to approve officer actions such as arrests, warrants (search and arrest), and approve other actions by agency personnel. In some cases, they will be involved in performance evaluation, complaint investigation, and/or discipline. It is imperative that supervisors are capable of providing competent and accurate guidance, and making appropriate decisions from the moment they assume the new role. Promotional training is a critical aspect of personnel management and ensuring that police personnel function legally, ethically, professionally, fairly, and impartially.

Recommendation 65: Personnel should receive training relative to their new position and role within six months of being promoted. Immediately upon assignment, they should be provided a mentor to guide them as they start to function in their new position.

Since personnel assume the tasks and responsibilities of their new position on a given day, it is reasonable to expect that they are capable of exercising those responsibilities in a competent manner when they begin acting in the new role. Other personnel depend on this newly promoted person to be able to make the decisions commensurate with the position when they assume the position. Being inadequately trained to make decisions, or perform the tasks expected of the position is a disservice to other personnel, the agency, and the citizens. Appropriate training in new tasks, procedures, and responsibilities is necessary to ensure the proper operation of the component, and to ensure the citizens are served legally, ethically, and professionally.

Optimally, this training should occur before the person actually starts performing the new job. Some agencies provide training either before the new position actually begun or the newly promoted person is sent to training as the first task, and occurs before the new supervisor actually begins serving in the new position. Some agencies have excellent promotional training programs that include classroom training, scenario-based training, practical field experience, and mentoring. For many agencies, providing this training immediately prior to or upon assuming the role isn't practical. This is generally due to agency size and the need for the newly promoted person to immediately assume the position. In these cases, the agency should at the very least provide some type of role familiarization, mentoring, and on the-job training. The newly promoted person should then be provided additional training as soon as possible, but it should occur no later than six months after the promotion is effective.

A mentor, who is skilled in the aspects of the relevant position, should be appointed for the newly promoted person. This mentor should be someone who has served in the specific position and can be available for training and discussion sessions as well as when the newly promoted person has questions. The mentor can act as a resource, guide, and trainer as the promoted person learns the roles, tasks, and responsibilities of their new position. This should include relevant procedures, processes, forms, tasks, and possibly training in new concepts. Just as a new officer goes through a field training program, a new supervisor should be guided as they learn different and critical tasks.

POSITION/ASSIGNMENT TRAINING

Police agencies have a lot of specialization. This is intended to build specific skills so incumbents can perform at the highest levels. Just as newly promoted personnel must have time to learn the aspects of their new position, so too must personnel who are transferred, assigned, or promoted into new assignments. Personnel must be trained in the roles, tasks, and responsibilities of any new positions. This is essential for them to function competently while serving the citizens.

Recommendation 66: Various positions may require additional or specific training. Therefore personnel assigned to new positions should be trained on specific items or aspects. Depending on the tasks, responsibilities, activities, or skill sets, this training would be required prior to assumption of the new tasks, or within six months of being assigned.

This type of training generally focuses on the development of skills related to the new position. Personnel assigned to a new position should be provided training and education relative to the new position being assumed before they are allowed to practice those skills unassisted. In some cases, this training may be focused on procedures and directives, while in other cases it may involve learning new technical skills and abilities. Upon assignment, the person should be familiarized with the new position and what it entails. As soon as practical, but no later than six months after being assigned, the officer should be given sufficient training to allow them to function independently in the position.

One example of this type of position would be assignment to a traffic crash investigative unit. The newly assigned person would possess the minimum abilities to investigate routine traffic crashes. Then either prior to assignment or upon assignment, the person would be sent to various advanced crash investigation courses. This provides additional training and the new team member would begin to utilize the new skills as part of an investigative team. As they develop and refine their skills under guidance and direction from other team members, they would begin to handle more of the tasks until they can perform additional tasks on their own. This type of mentoring, field training, or on-the-job training helps build skills with minimal risk of error. This does not preclude additional training, mentoring, or partnering as is prudent. But certainly, no individual should be allowed to perform tasks for which they have not been fully and properly trained.

While personnel may be assigned to a new position, in certain positions they should not be allowed to perform various tasks until they have been trained. Persons can be assigned to the component, and can perform routine tasks for which they have been properly trained. A prime example of this would include assignment as a motorcycle operator. It is impractical and dangerous to everyone to allow an untrained person to start functioning as a motorcycle operator before they have been trained to safely operate a motorcycle. Even someone that has ridden motorcycles previously should be required to demonstrate their proficiency before being allowed to operate a police motorcycle in the public.

Another example is assignment to a Bomb Team. Personnel newly assigned to a Bomb Team rarely have the training to function as an Explosive Ordnance Disposal (EOD) technician prior to assignment to the team. They should be allowed to observe and perform certain support-type tasks but should not be allowed to actively perform typical EOD functions. As soon as possible, they should be sent to an appropriate training course to learn the fundamentals of EOD operations. Upon return, they should begin to perform additional tasks under the direction and guidance of a training officer or the entire team. As the skills are developed and minor tasks and additional training is conducted, the person should be allowed to handle more difficult and specialized tasks, until they can perform all reasonable tasks. Other examples include SWAT, K-9, aircraft pilots, and Hostage Negotiators. The risks and criticality of these positions are so high that training must be accomplished prior to assuming the tasks of the position.

Specialized assignments and teams exist because they are expected to perform enhanced tasks using specialized skills, knowledge, and abilities. These are talents that exist beyond those possessed by the average officer with only a basic recruit academy level of training. As mentioned, agencies have a variety of specialized assignments and teams so they can develop enhanced and specialized skills to be able to perform various tasks and investigations that require additional skills. It may be a latent investigative unit and additional training might consist of enhanced interview or interrogation skills. It could be assignment to a drug or narcotics unit whose purpose is to conduct in-depth investigations relative to drug offenses and drug trafficking where an increased knowledge of drugs is needed, or the ability to operate in an undercover assignment. Or it might be some of the various components previously mentioned.

Regardless of the type of assignment or component, additional training is needed and beneficial. This training provides enhanced skills, knowledge, and abilities that enable the incumbent to competently and safely perform the relevant tasks. It also helps to ensure that actions by the individuals and the overall team are conducted legally, ethically, professionally, fairly, and impartially. The agency should proactively and in advance identify what training is required, desirable, and beneficial for personnel to possess. The training should be identified including specific courses that may be relevant. Any mentoring, in-house training, and on-the-job training that would be beneficial should be identified. And new personnel should be provided the appropriate training with such training being fully documented.

Chapter 10

Discipline

Due to the powers that police have and the responsibilities they are tasked with, it is imperative that policies, procedures, and guidelines exist to regulate officer behavior. It is critical that police personnel (especially those with sworn powers) act and perform in a manner that is consistent with legal, ethical, and professional expectations. This includes the Law Enforcement Code of Ethics as previously discussed. Processes need to be in place to ensure proper conduct, and to prescribe how violations and complaints will be handled. Commonly referred to as disciplinary processes, these must be comprehensive, timely, fair, and consistent.

The purpose of discipline is to ensure that behaviors and actions are consistent with expectations. If there is a deficiency in officer actions, the disciplinary process should be focused on correcting behavior to ensure future behavior is in compliance with expectations. Punitive actions or punishment are not and should not be the purpose of a disciplinary system. The system should include a variety of methods to correct behavior including counseling, written letters and/or reprimands, training, suspension, demotion, and termination. Which action is best depends on many factors, such as officer history, and the type, circumstances, and severity of transgression. The process should utilize progressive discipline, with discipline becoming stronger or more severe for repeat violations of a similar nature or severe transgressions of a singular nature.

Discipline's primary focus is to change individual behavior, but it has an impact on others. Discipline involves more than just the subject officer. Other personnel and sometimes the public are watching what the agency does. This includes whether the agency sustains any charges or rule violations and the type and severity of any disciplinary action taken. While in many agencies, disciplinary action is confidential as part of a personnel record, information still gets out about what action was taken. In other agencies, the information is public record so others definitely know what action was taken. Disciplinary action can serve notice to agency personnel and the community that if violations occur they will (or will not) take action. It impacts the level of rule compliance within the agency and can positively or negatively impact agency culture over time.

Most disciplinary processes are documented in agency directives, governmental policies such as personnel rules, civil service rules and regulations, and/or collective bargaining agreements. Each of these specify how accusations or concerns of rule violations, misconduct, or citizen complaints will be handled. Most processes today are very detailed including time frames, forms, findings, and penalties. All are based on creating a process to ensure that agency personnel abide by and comply with the various rules, regulations, standards of conduct, policies, procedures, directives, and oaths associated with the position.

Several myths exist surrounding police disciplinary processes. One myth believes that officers do not report or file complaints about other officers. This is generally false. The majority of police complaints are internal complaints. In other words, these complaints originate from within the agency and generally focus on either behavior or rules compliance. The second myth is that the agency and/or the chief have total say over the discipline process or even the final decision. This is also false. All disciplinary actions must take place within the context of the disciplinary process. How the investigation is handled and that it must occur within certain time frames impact the process. What decisions can be rendered based on the findings are also controlled by applicable procedures. In many cases, even what types (letters, reprimands, suspensions, demotions, termination, etc.) of discipline and the severity of discipline are controlled by established procedures. In some environments, the chief can only make a recommendation while in other environments, the chief can make the decision. In some cases, the decision is made by a city manager, city personnel department, public safety board, or by civil service board. And, in most cases, the decision is subject to review and appeal to or by one or more other administrative, quasi-judicial, or judicial bodies. These final decisions may vary greatly from what the chief desires.

Many agencies have implemented different types of disciplinary processes, with different focuses and varying degrees of success. Some agencies have and continue to use a matrix type process which identifies a range of discipline for various offenses and situations. Other agencies, such as the Los Angeles Police Department (LAPD) have implemented mediation programs (Alternative Complaint Resolution–ACR) wherein the citizen complainant and the involved officer meet to discuss the incident.[1] This is usually reserved for minor complaints and is voluntary for both the citizen and the officer. The Los Angeles County Sheriff's Department (LASD) implemented a program focused on education, training, and learning. The Education Based Discipline (EBD) program focuses on behavioral change through education instead of punishment.[2] Other types of processes that either replace or supplement traditional disciplinary processes include peer review and civilian review boards.

Recommendation 67: A set of written directives must exist to guide and detail general behavior and an overall code of conduct for all agency personnel. It must specifically require all personnel abide by applicable directives, laws, regulations, and expectations.

There must be a comprehensive set of written documents that detail policies, procedures, standards of conduct and generally how personnel will perform their tasks and conduct themselves. Some of the expectations are generally documented in general directives, standard operational procedures (SOPs), rules and regulations, and codes of conduct. General directives and SOPs usually focus on procedural aspects of how personnel are expected to perform the various tasks assigned to them. Some will be more detailed than others, but they must be sufficiently clear to identify what level of service is expected and what actions are not allowed. It is necessary to identify and document what officers can do, what they cannot do, and how they are to conduct themselves, especially while performing the tasks of the position. Written directives serve to document the agency's expectations of its personnel as it is the obligation and responsibility of the agency to identify all such guidelines and requirements. Granted, no directive can cover every possibility, eventuality, or situation, but the directive should provide sufficient guidance so there is general understanding of what is legal, ethical, and professional. Conversely, the concept of discretion should be fully discussed and officers granted the ability to use said discretion within certain parameters.

Documents known as rules and regulations or codes of conduct generally focus on the personal actions of agency personnel. Most agencies have numerous documents that outline how agency personnel should perform and behave. These directives cover such activities as courtesy, behavior, service, appearance, demeanor, fitness for duty, off-duty behavior, untruthfulness, and numerous other aspects associated with possessing police powers. These rules and regulations require behavior that is above that expected of citizens and is directly related to the powers and position of a police officer. In many cases, these rules guide how an officer behaves and how they perform their duties overall as opposed to the specific procedures that guide how a specific task will be completed. While most agencies have these, all agencies should have these in written form. These types of behavioral rules directly relate to the characteristics of agency personnel, and focus on fairness, honesty, integrity, courtesy, and many other characteristics that transcend and impact every action of the officer.

It should be specifically stated that personnel are expected to comply with the directives, rules, regulations, policies, procedures, laws, and the oaths of their office. While it should not be necessary, and sounds strange to have a directive which requires all personnel to comply with all directives, it is nonetheless prudent and necessary to have such a directive. All directives must be appropriately worded to ensure everyone understands what is required and what is recommended. Using words such as "shall" or "must" are more definitive and require compliance. Other words such as "may" and even "should," tend to allow for options depending on the situation and circumstances. While it is appropriate for some directives to allow for options or discretion, many directives are mandatory and need to be written as such. This specific admonition and requirement clearly identifies that compliance with expectations is mandatory.

Recommendation 68: A written directive must exist that details the disciplinary process.

Most agencies have these, with many being found in civil service rules and/or collective bargaining agreements/union contracts. These written descriptions of the disciplinary process should be comprehensive as they are basically the rules or procedures of how the disciplinary process will function. It is imperative that the procedures be fully documented and described so everyone has fair and full notice of how the process will operate. The directives must outline all aspects including time frames, procedures, employee rights, and management rights. It is imperative that management and supervisors fully understand the procedures as any errors or mistakes, such as missed time frames, can result in a loss of ability to take action regarding an officer's actions. The directives should be focused on determining the facts of any situation so appropriate decisions can be made. Decisions should take into account the nature of the specific incident, past behavior of personnel involved, and what is fair and balanced for all involved, including the subject officer, the complainant, the agency, and the community.

Recommendation 69: The disciplinary process should be completed in a timely manner.

In order for discipline to be productive, fair, and beneficial, the process must be completed in a reasonable time frame. There is little benefit to the agency, employee, or community if discipline for an action occurs a long time after the action. Since the intent of the disciplinary system is to correct past behavior and positively influence future behavior, it is imperative that these adjustments be made as soon as practical. It should be noted that the time frame discussed herein is different than the time frame to conduct the actual investigation. Here, the focus is upon taking action and actually issuing any appropriate discipline after a comprehensive investigation has occurred. These factors (length of investigation time and quickness to issue discipline) are linked, but they are different.

The time frame for issuing or conducting discipline should be as short as is necessary to ensure that the investigation is complete and to consider what the appropriate level or method of discipline is. In some cases, this may be hours for very minor transgressions wherein the officer understands the transgression, and there is no history of concerns. In other situations, that include a more serious transgression or repeated transgressions, a small number of weeks may be required to ascertain the appropriate level of action to be taken. Other factors that must be considered include what actions have been taken for other violations of this nature with similarly situated officers. In other words, the discipline must have some consistency to it.

Recommendation 70: Discipline must be appropriate when matched to the rule violation. It must be consistent but fair to the agency and the individual considering the circumstances.

The level of discipline administered must be such that it demonstrates that the officer's actions were not consistent with expectations, and should be sufficient to prevent future occurrences. Insignificant discipline is meaningless as it does nothing to shape future behavior. But it might be counterproductive in that it may give the impression of nit-picking or heavy-handedness, and eventually breeds contempt for rules. However, excessive discipline is unreasonable as it is perceived as unbalanced compared to the violation. In many cases, excessive discipline destroys morale, and frequently it is overturned by reviewing authorities if appealed. Having disciplinary decisions reversed or overturned is harmful to management and the entire process. Discipline must be balanced and in order to be truly effective, must be viewed as fair by the totality of personnel.

A concern that is sometimes overlooked is how the disciplinary action will be perceived by the community. Citizens must also perceive the discipline as appropriate considering the violation. If the community believes the discipline is too little for the violation, they may perceive that the officers can get away with anything and the agency will not hold them accountable. This could easily result in a lack of faith and trust in the agency and could result in citizens believing there is no reason to report perceived misconduct. Many feel that this is commonplace, and believe that this encourages officers to break the rules as they know they will not be punished. However, various reviews have indicated that citizen review boards that can look at discipline, generally either support or reduce the agency issued or contemplated discipline. Regardless, it is incumbent upon the agency to educate the community about the disciplinary process and applicable rules and guidelines.

Discipline must be consistent yet fair. Given similar circumstances, and considering officer histories, like discipline should be administered for similar transgressions. This does not mean that all discipline has to be exactly the same for each violation. The circumstances of the transgression and the officer's history must also be taken into consideration.

For example, there can be a policy that states a second at-fault traffic crash will result in a one-day suspension. If Officer Jones and Officer Smith each have their second at-fault vehicle crash on the same day, giving each the same discipline of a one-day suspension would be consistent, but might not be fair and appropriate. If Officer Jones has been an officer for six months while Officer Smith is a twenty-year officer, the discipline, even though identical, is not the same and would not be considered fair, balanced, or consistent. The reality is that the officers are not in similar circumstances. Care must be exercised in issuing discipline in this manner, as the agency must avoid any appearance of favoritism.

Recommendation 71: The disciplinary system must be based on progressive actions and have training as a key component.

As mentioned, the purpose of a disciplinary system is to ensure that behavior is consistent with expectations. With that understanding and philosophy, changing behavior to meet expectations should be the focus of the actions taken, so as to meet the desired end result of rule and expectation compliance. Also, from a practical consideration, if the officer is not terminated from employment, the agency must try to ensure future performance and behavior matches expectations. Since the officer remains with the agency, mere punishment is not sufficient. Retraining must be used to document that the officer was in fact shown the proper methods so that any future transgressions are not a training issue.

Some transgressions can actually be a training issue. If the officer was never trained, or poorly trained, or has not performed the task in a lengthy period of time, they might not legitimately know or recall how to perform the task as expected. In these cases, training is the best response and should eliminate future transgressions. However, if the officer was properly trained, and has been performing the task, sudden and/or recurring transgressions are generally not a training issue but rather are a disciplinary issue.

Training is one of the best methods to ensure that the officer is aware of desired performance expectations. Virtually all disciplines should involve some aspect of training. This might range from a review of the pertinent procedures up to and including attending a remedial training session with proficiency testing. What is best once again depends on the circumstances, but all disciplines should at least include a review of desired expectations.

Progressive discipline should be the foundation of the process. Understanding that education and ensuring compliance with expectations is the goal of the disciplinary process, the least severe punitive actions that would succeed in changing behavior should be used. Disciplinary actions should become more severe as the number and/or severity of transgressions increases. The minimum action necessary that would reasonably ensure future compliance should be used. This has benefits including reasonableness of penalty compared to violation, not overreacting by being too severe, and encouraging the employee to learn and go forward. Punishment that is too severe runs the risk of alienating the employee so they no longer wish to function as a member of the team, but nonetheless still remain in the agency. Discipline that is perceived as too severe or as unfair is often resisted and, in many cases, is appealed. While appeals can be beneficial, they can delay a final decision, cost time and money, and can in some cases be overturned. If transgressions continue or a single transgression is so severe, then progressively more severe discipline is warranted. Many of these concept-based recommendations interrelate and work together.

Recommendation 72: A directive should identify the probable range of disciplinary and corrective actions available for various violations. It should also identify those actions, violations, or transgressions that would generally result in termination.

By providing a list of potential disciplinary actions for various transgressions, everyone is made aware of what can happen for various violations. Many agencies have disciplinary matrices that outline different penalties for transgressions that are sometimes grouped into violation classes. Most agencies, however, do not have a written document matching transgressions to possible penalties. The reason is that some agencies believe that such a document would limit their ability to act and that it restricts their freedom and management rights. It is also more difficult to construct as it requires the agency to think more about the disciplinary process in advance, plan accordingly, and gather input from the community and agency personnel regarding a range of potential actions.

The reality is that if done correctly, such disciplinary matrices can provide good information to agency personnel and the community about normal ranges of actions to be taken. This advance notice assists with fairness and consistency concerns generally. In his article "Police Employee Disciplinary Matrix: An Emerging Concept," Jon Shane states, "the purpose of a disciplinary matrix is to leave the police department with a predictable, progressive, and uniform guide for dispensing discipline that accounts for the seriousness of the infraction, the prior disciplinary history of the officer involved, and the aggravating and mitigating circumstances."[3]

The matrix should also provide a range of disciplinary actions to account for seriousness of the violations, officer history, frequency of violations, as well as mitigating and aggravating circumstances. It should also indicate that repeat violations of the same or similar type of rules would be considered. This avoids an officer from having four counseling sessions for four different rule violations in a short period of time. A disciplinary matrix can also be perceived as fairer by the employees since they know what the range and likely disciplines will be. There is also less variation in the issued discipline between different cases, which causes less resistance to the entire disciplinary process. These documents and processes, if done correctly, can benefit the officer, the agency, and the community.

Realizing the purpose of a disciplinary process is to correct and change behavior, and that progressive actions should be taken when feasible, sometimes behaviors or violations are so egregious that only severe disciplinary action is appropriate. For some violations, no amount of training or punitive action would suffice to change behavior or ensure that subsequent behavior or decisions do not reoccur. In some cases, the violation is so damaging that the agency has lost trust and confidence in the officer and their ability to act as expected. In these cases, the officer can no longer perform as a police officer. The disciplinary process should identify those violations that would generally result in termination.

Being a police officer requires that personnel can be depended upon to act legally, ethically, professionally, fairly, and impartially in all matters. Since officers act alone in most situations, their judgment, decision-making, knowledge, and actions must be as expected and within commonly accepted parameters. The chief, the community, and other agency personnel must be able to depend on the officer to do the right thing, especially when no one else is looking. Citizen freedoms and liberties are at stake. So is the reputation of the agency, community trust in the profession and the agency, and the ability of the agency to function with community support.

Violations that involve honesty, integrity, adherence to laws, and the ability of the officer or agency to competently perform the duties of the position are very severe. They threaten the core concepts of legitimacy, trust, support, procedural justice, and violate the oath of office. Examples of such severe violations include untruthfulness or false statements, planting or tampering with evidence, excessive force with serious injury, theft, assisting criminals improperly, accepting bribes or payoffs, and being charged with certain crimes.

Once an officer has been found to have committed any of these offenses, they have lost the ability to competently perform as an officer because they cannot be trusted. In many cases, it is the officer's word against that of a citizen regarding if a crime was committed and that could impact the citizen's liberties. The agency, the courts, and the community must be able to rely on what the officer states or writes in a report. If there is any question of truthfulness, legality, or ethical behavior, then the officer becomes worthless to the agency.

Certain court decisions (Brady,[4] Giglio,[5] and subsequent cases) have held that if an officer has been found to have been untruthful in any matter, then that raises questions about their character and their ability to testify truthfully. Accordingly, such information must be provided to the prosecutor who must provide the information to the defense attorney. This results in many prosecutors determining that they cannot trust the testimony of such an officer, and therefore they will not use them as a witness in any cases. If an officer cannot testify in court, then the agency cannot let them be involved in the investigation of any criminal cases.

In situations like this, and based on a comprehensive investigation that results in a finding of guilt, the officer should be terminated from employment. Other steps regarding certification and notice should also be taken, but it is imperative that the officer be removed from the agency and profession.

Recommendation 73: Officers should have a predisciplinary hearing/ meeting prior to the implementation of any significant discipline.

Prior to making a final decision regarding the imposition of significant discipline, the officer should have the opportunity to speak to a command-level person, preferably the one that will either make the decision or make a final recommendation to the chief. This provides the involved officer an opportunity to explain their actions, offer mitigating circumstances, and offer any other pertinent information they want to voice or have considered. For purposes herein, significant discipline includes demotion, suspension, or termination. The command officer or chief should consider this information, and if warranted conduct additional investigation, prior to making a final decision. The officer should also be able to have someone with them to help articulate the desired information. This process helps to ensure that the officer has the opportunity to present any information they believe relevant prior to the final decision being made. For any discipline, but especially significant discipline, it is best to ensure that all information is heard before final decision and imposition of any decision.

Recommendation 74: A review of the public nature of disciplinary records should be conducted.

This review should include what disciplinary records are public, what are protected as personnel records (or other classifications), and what records can be released to the public. Different states have different guidelines, with some states granting the municipality the discretion to decide what is public and what is not. In some states, the entire disciplinary record of an officer is public, while in other states only very limited information is public. These various laws, rules, and guidelines create a hodgepodge of situations which are difficult for agencies and communities to navigate.

There should be some degree of uniformity and consistency to ensure that the rights of officers are protected while at the same time protecting the interests of the citizens. The officers have a reasonable expectation that any small transgression does not hold them up to public ridicule or make it more difficult for them to accomplish their lawful duties. The citizens have a reasonable expectation of knowing that their public servants are competent and comply with the rules and regulations pertaining to how police personnel perform their duties. There should be a careful review of applicable laws and guidelines, with input from officer groups, management, government, and the community, and then informed changes should be made as appropriate and beneficial.

Recommendation 75: A disciplinary notice should be sent to the state certification body regarding all discipline.

Currently most state certification bodies are not made aware of the vast amount of disciplinary actions taken by agencies. This is partially due to the fact that the vast majority of actions are minor such as counseling, training, or written documentation of some type. And in most situations there is no need for further action as the discipline administered has served its purpose to transform behavior. But, in many cases, even severe discipline such as suspension or demotion, and in some cases termination, are not reported to the state certification body. This is predominantly due to the fact the state certification body only acts on a certification if they are made aware of a serious issue or if the officer is terminated from an agency. In some cases, the certification body does not act on the officer's certification unless they apply for a job elsewhere within the jurisdiction of the certification body. Partially, this is due to workload and staffing. Most certification bodies are lightly staffed. So the decision is made that certifications are only reviewed if needed, such as if the officer applies to another agency in the jurisdiction. If the officer is terminated but never applies for another position in the jurisdiction, then why waste the time acting on the certification? The problem is this does not help the profession, other agencies, or the citizens at large.

Such notice to the certification body would include a summary of the incident, what kind of investigation was conducted, the agency finding, and what actions were taken by the agency. This notice would enable the certification body to be aware of and capture all discipline generally, but also specifically on all personnel who are certified by the body. If desired, the certification body could request the entire incident investigation and disciplinary documents for further review and action as deemed appropriate. This would enable the certification body to more closely monitor certified personnel, take action when or if an agency failed to do so, track misbehaving personnel across agencies, and provide general data and information about violations for statistical and training purposes.

While this would add significant workload to the certification bodies, it is a reasonable and necessary step to ensure the public and profession are protected. It would reduce some of the issues that the profession is facing, and it is a reasonable cost of doing business. It would also provide some consistency at least at a state level. Agencies would also face additional workload but it would be relatively minor and basically consist of sending various forms and paperwork to the certification body. Some agencies might balk at this process arguing that it takes away some of the agency's ability to handle its own personnel issues. But the reality is the agency could still take the actions it deems appropriate as long as it is reasonable. The bottom line is there is little reasonable argument for not doing this while there are numerous benefits supporting this change.

Recommendation 76: Annual disciplinary summaries should be published.

Each agency should be required to review and analyze its disciplinary process and activity on an annual basis. It should also be required to publish the results of the analysis so the public understands the issues surrounding the discipline process and the steps the agency took to correct and enhance behavior. The analysis should be a numerical analysis of all disciplinary actions taken. It should include what actions were taken for what violations and the numbers of each violation type and disciplinary action. It would not list individual officers or cases, but rather look at the process and agency as a whole to determine patterns. These patterns would include work component, time of day, week of day, and so on. The report should also include what actions were taken based on the violations and patterns revealed. This might include changes in training, equipment, policy, procedures, or other actions. Reports of these types are helpful to the community and the agency in guiding decisions regarding how to continually improve agency and officer performance and service. It can also serve as an excellent tool to educate the public about the disciplinary process.

Chapter 11

Complaints and Investigations

Every business or profession must have some way for customers, clients, or interested parties to voice complaints and concerns about the services, products, and personnel of the business. Many utilize a "customer service" component that includes a phone number or email contact point. Very few offer the ability to actually go in and make a formal complaint. Policing has had one of the most comprehensive complaint functions of any business or profession for decades. Complaints can be filed for virtually any reason and can be filed in person, via email, telephone call, and even through regular U.S. Mail. Policing also offers one of the most comprehensive processes for handling and investigating complaints.

It is critically important that complaints, questions, or concerns about the service provided or the demeanor and actions of police personnel be fully investigated. This is to ensure that agency and officer actions are legal, ethical, professional, fair, and impartial. It is also beneficial in that it ensures that agency policies, procedures, equipment, and training are appropriate. While this reasoning is actually applicable to any business or profession, it is especially pertinent in policing. Due to the powers, responsibilities, and possible outcomes of police action, reviewing all aspects of police service is appropriate on so many levels.

It is no secret, that most officers dislike complaints and the resulting investigations. This is true for virtually all people in any business or profession. People do not want to be complained about, especially as it deals with their employment. But for officers, the stigma and enduring record of a complaint investigation adds to the stress of going through a complaint investigation process. But, in reality, it is often the only manner in which the facts can be ascertained and the officer either found to have committed a violation or, on the other hand, be found to have performed as expected. Many complaints about police conduct are false, having been filed by a citizen as a way to get back at the officer, discourage them from performing their lawful duties, or in an attempt to force them to drop criminal charges against the citizen. In most agencies, the filing or not filing of a complaint has no (and should not have any) bearing on the criminal charges filed against the complainant. Many other complaints against officers are based on a lack of knowledge of what the officer can or cannot do.

But some complaints are true and these must be encouraged and fully investigated. The problem is that it is impossible to ascertain which complaints are true and which are false until the complaint is investigated. Therefore, all complaints need to be appropriately investigated. Depending on the size of the agency, and severity of the complaint, investigations may be performed by an immediate supervisor, other designated manager, or individuals assigned to an entire component. Oftentimes these components have names such as Internal Affairs (IA), or Professional Standards. Regardless of title, they exist to provide skilled investigators so that competent investigations can be performed regarding crucial issues of trust and compliance with agency expectations.

Recommendation 77: Written directives should detail a comprehensive process and procedures for handling complaints.

Most agencies have detailed directives that outline the steps and procedures to be followed in complaint investigations. They may specify that certain types of complaints can be and should be handled by the immediate supervisor while other types of complaints are to be handled by a designated component. Many processes are also set out by civil service rules, personnel directives, and/or collective bargaining agreements. The process should be publicly available so that citizens understand how the process works, and so that officers are fully aware of the process.

The directive should include a definition of the possible findings or outcomes of the complaint investigations. Standard findings include:

- Sustained—There was sufficient evidence to prove all or part of the accusations regarding misconduct were true.
- Not Sustained—There was insufficient evidence to prove or disprove the accusations.
- Unfounded—The act complained of did not occur.
- Exonerated—The act complained of did occur but was legal, justified, and proper.
- Misconduct Not Based on Original Complaint—A rule violation occurred but was not the original complaint.

While there may be minor wording differences, and in some cases an additional finding category, these are the most prevalent and cover the gamut of likely outcomes. Citizens should be advised of the outcome of the investigation, including the definition of the finding so that the complainant is fully aware of the outcome.

Recommendation 78: All complaints should be investigated, even anonymous complaints.

Because of the power, role, and impacts associated with policing, all complaints should be fully investigated. Most police agencies investigate all complaints even those that are anonymous. Some agencies do not investigate anonymous complaints, but they should, at least to some degree. And there can be different levels or extents of investigations. For some complaints, it may be sufficient for the supervisor to interview the complainant and officer (separately), to ascertain the facts, circumstances, and issues. For other complaints, it may be necessary to have formal statements made on tape with specific investigators, and then have additional investigation take place. The magnitude and depth of the investigation should be consistent with the nature of the complaint, and sufficient to determine the facts of the situation and to determine if the officer's actions were appropriate.

Victims might be reluctant to provide their identity. But they may provide enough information to enable an investigation to occur and either prove or disprove the complaint. Just because the complaint is anonymous doesn't mean it is false or should be discounted automatically.

Recommendation 79: The agency should utilize proactive accountability measures.

Virtually every complaint and/or internal investigation is reactive. The complaint is made or the investigation launched after an action has occurred. The investigation begins as a reaction to a citizen or internal complaint. While this is often necessary, it can only verify that an improper action did or did not occur. This means any harm (real or perceived) has already occurred. If the investigation determines that the action was improper and sustains the complaint, then the improper action already occurred. Depending on the extent of the violation, the officer may have already soiled the uniform, tarnished the badge, and damaged the credibility and reputation of the agency. Any harm or damage to the citizen has already occurred. Reactive investigations are necessary as they can verify or disprove the complaint and action. They can even prevent future transgressions if the agency utilizes the investigation to enhance training or supervision.

Since most investigations are reactive in nature, the agency and the community cannot make the internal investigations function the cornerstone or foundation of its "good policing" efforts. The agency must be proactive in its efforts to ensure that policing is delivered in a legal, ethical, profession, fair, and impartial manner. Training and supervision play a heavy role in this effort. Proper training can build the skills, knowledge, and abilities of agency personnel. It equips them with the skills to perform the tasks and role of the position in the manner expected. Supervision provides additional proactive efforts in that it can ensure compliance with performance expectations. It can reinforce positive actions and performance and can interrupt negative performance or actions.

The agency should utilize a variety of proactive efforts specifically in its internal investigations function. This can take several forms and can serve to verify that agency personnel are performing as expected. Various examples of proactive efforts in internal investigations can include periodic examination of bank records of agency personnel involved in vice investigations. This would include narcotics, prostitution, gambling, and organized crimes investigations. Due to the amount of money involved in many of these activities, it is possible that agency personnel might become directly or indirectly involved in these activities. This participation may involve looking the other way, providing information, providing protection, robbing criminals, extortion of participants, or running an independent crime group. Unfortunately, there are too many examples of police personnel who have succumbed to the temptation of vast amounts of money involved in these activities. By checking bank accounts, the agency might get advance notice of improper officer income and be able to take action before the activities progress. Obviously, this would not identify every case of wrongdoing as the money may not make it to the known bank accounts. But it is a proactive effort that the officers would be aware of and cues them that the agency does proactive investigations.

Another method of proactive investigation may involve various types of "integrity checks." These are various situations which might be created to ensure that agency personnel are acting appropriately. It might involve situations wherein various amounts of cash are turned in to the agency and then ensuring that all of it is handled according to agency procedures. The agency can check to see if the full amount made it into evidence and thereby verify that agency personnel are acting as expected.

Other methods can also be used, and are in fact limited to the creativity of the agency. One of the most useful proactive methods involves viewing of body and car camera video. This can show how an officer acts and conducts themselves on a daily basis in routine and critical situations. Each method used must be carefully built and monitored so it can be successfully used to verify integrity and proper conduct while being sufficient to use if the officer acted improperly. The agency should ensure that agency personnel are aware of the general proactive nature of its efforts, that it will be conducting various proactive investigations, and that the investigations will be reasonable.

The agency may also need to announce the concept as part of a collective bargaining agreement. The agency should make every effort to ensure that the program is viewed as a proactive accountability mechanism and not as a way to entrap or trick good officers. How the concept and program is set up can be critical to its success. But the agency should utilize a variety of proactive mechanisms and efforts to ensure policing is occurring in the manner desired.

Recommendation 80: The agency must have trained investigators available to handle serious complaints.

As mentioned, immediate supervisors can handle certain complaints. These should be identified by policy, and the supervisors should have some degree of training to handle complaints. But these types of complaints should be limited to complaints such as courtesy, unfair treatment, and other specified complaints. Complaints of a more serious nature, more complicated, or time-consuming should be handled by trained investigators. Depending on the size of the agency, this might be a designated position or person in the agency, or it might be an entire organizational component.

Personnel should be experienced investigators trained in interview techniques, general investigations, and then additionally trained in conducting internal affairs investigations. They should be extremely knowledgeable regarding general police procedures and specifically about agency policies. The investigators must have an understanding of any applicable civil service rules and any collective bargaining procedures relating to complaints and internal investigations. It is critical that investigators are aware of Garrity[1] provisions and other court decisions and rules impacting internal administrative investigations. (Garrity basically indicates that officers involved in administrative or disciplinary investigations can be required to answer questions related to the administrative investigation. But it also preserves the officer's right against self-incrimination in a criminal case by prohibiting any Garrity-based comments from being used in a criminal case. This enables the police agency to fully investigate a situation or complaint.) The investigators should be able to put complainants at ease to elicit all the facts and issues surrounding a complaint while building trust that the complaint is being fully investigated. They must also be capable of questioning officers regarding their actions and must operate from a position of knowing procedures while understanding the environment in which officers function.

The investigators must understand that their role is not to protect or condemn officers. But rather they are fact finders, who are seeking to understand what happened and possibly why it happened. They should also understand that their role is critical to the officers, the agency, the citizen, and the community. Everyone is depending on the investigator to ascertain the full circumstances of the incident and gain the facts so appropriate decisions can be made.

Competent investigators conducting thorough, unbiased investigations are key to agency performance, community trust, and the protection of everyone.

Recommendation 81: The complainant should be kept informed of the status of the complaint, including when the investigation is complete, and as to the outcome as allowed by law. Applicable laws should allow the complainant to be advised of the outcome of the complaint and investigation.

The complainant has a right to know that the complaint is being investigated, how it is being investigated, and who is handling the complaint. They should be informed of a probable time frame and kept apprised of the status if it takes longer than originally anticipated. The complainant also has a right to know if the complaint was valid and if the officer's actions were improper. Since states have different laws about personnel investigations, the complainant should be informed of the outcome as allowed by law.

In some circumstances, the public becomes aware of incidents that result in internal investigations. This may be due to the incident occurring in a crowd, or the incident having been recorded by a citizen and then disseminated in some manner, usually social media. In these situations, the public is either aware of the complaint, or might even advocate for an investigation. When this happens, the agency must also make statements to the public regarding the status of the investigation, and depending on applicable state law, they should be made aware of the outcome of the investigation. This greatly enhances the transparency of the agency and can build support for the agency, if the action taken is viewed as appropriate by the community.

While the complainant most definitely should be informed of all information available under applicable laws, in some cases that simply is not enough. Since some states do not allow the final determination or the discipline taken to be released, the complainant may be left with not understanding if the officer's actions were appropriate or not. This is simply unacceptable. Laws should be changed to allow the complainant to be fully informed of the outcome of their complaint. At the very least, the complainant should be informed if the complaint was sustained or if the officer was found to have acted appropriately. It is more important for the complainant to understand if the actions were appropriate or not than to know what corrective actions or discipline was issued.

Recommendation 82: Knowingly false complaints should result in appropriate charges.

If a citizen makes a complaint against an agency or its personnel, that the citizen knows is false, then the citizen should be charged with an appropriate crime. Since filing complaints against police personnel can result in an expenditure of time and resources, and such complaints can have a negative impact on the officer, the agency, and the community, knowingly false complaints must be discouraged and dealt with. A few agencies have such a policy, but in fact they are rarely used.

Some advocate that such policies could have a chilling effect on citizens who want to make complaints against police. They argue that the potential of criminal charges might cause someone with a legitimate complaint to either be reluctant or to not file the complaint at all. The reality is that these types of policies are only used when the complainant makes a knowingly false complaint. It does not apply to complaints that were not sustained or were filed because the complainant did not know what the police could or could not do. It simply does not apply to complaints filed with good reason and honest intentions.

But unfortunately, there are a number of complaints that are filed against police officers and agencies that the complainant knows to be false. These include complaints filed in hopes of getting the officer or agency to drop criminal charges, to get police to reduce pressure in an area, or complaints designed to attack an officer. Some people make complaints against officers falsely claiming the officer physically attacked them, verbally used improper words, or planted evidence on them. These are done for a variety of reasons. But a full investigation into the complaints should be performed. If the officer acted improperly as the citizen alleges, then the officer should be punished accordingly. If the citizen was simply wrong or mistaken, then the officer is cleared and the case closed. But if the investigation determines that the allegations of the citizen are false, then the citizen should be charged with perjury, filing a false police report, or other charge as may be appropriate and authorized under state law. It would be the burden of the agency to prove that the allegation was false and the complainant knew it. This might be supported by the same type of evidence that might support the citizen's complaint. This could include eyewitness statements, video recordings, radio traffic, and time-distance information.

People that have a legitimate concern and complaint would not be dissuaded from filing a complaint. But others who were considering filing a false complaint might think twice about it if they knew they could be charged for making the false complaint. This type of policy and practice helps to protect the integrity of the system and reduces false complaints that could hurt an officer, the agency, or the community.

Recommendation 83: The agency should ensure that investigations are completed in a timely manner.

Performing investigations in a timely manner are beneficial to everyone: the complainant, the officer, the agency, and the community. The complainant is specifically interested in a timely investigation so they can be informed of the findings as to whether the officer acted appropriately or not. The officer is also personally invested in the investigation as it impacts their job, adds stress to their life, and they want the investigation to clear them (if indeed they acted properly). It is good for the agency and community to handle investigations in a timely manner so everyone understands the incident and appropriate decisions can be made based on the findings. It also builds trust and confidence in the agency if the investigation is competently investigated in a timely manner. There is no legitimate benefit in delaying or dragging out an investigation as it only breeds stress, contempt, and mistrust for everyone involved. It also delays the opportunity for everyone to take steps of corrective action if warranted.

Recommendation 84: The complaint investigation process should have certain notification characteristics. These include (1) the chief should immediately be made aware of all serious complaints, (2) the chief should be kept informed of the status of said investigations, (3) the chief or a reasonable designee should be made aware of the findings of all complaints, and (4) the commander of the internal investigations component must have direct access to the chief.

Complaints that involve criminal accusations, use of force involving serious injuries, or that threaten the public trust in the agency should be reported immediately to the chief. These types of complaints have the potential to generate a large amount of attention that could quickly escalate into protests, disturbances, political concerns, or rumors that threaten the work environment of agency personnel or the peace of the community. It is imperative that the chief be fully briefed on these incidents so that proper actions can be taken to maintain public confidence and peace. These actions might include advising community or government leaders, changing the deployment of officers, proactively disseminating accurate information, or interacting with the community. The goal is not to mislead the public nor to appease anyone. But rather the chief should strive to be aware of the complaint, ensure it is being fully investigated, and provide everyone with accurate information as can be provided. It also builds confidence in the agency if the chief can say they are aware of the complaint and monitoring the investigation. The chief should be briefed on the status of investigations involving serious issues on a regular basis, but at least weekly, if not daily, depending on the seriousness of the complaint. This ensures that the investigation is being handled diligently and enables the chief to speak intelligently about the investigation when asked.

It is important for the chief to be aware of complaints in general, including the findings of relevant investigations. Ideally, this should be before the complainant is notified so that the chief can be fully informed, and could even suggest, direct, or authorize additional investigation if warranted. Depending on the size of the agency, and how the investigative process is structured, the chief might be aware of the findings of all, some, or few of the various investigations. But certainly, in most agencies, the chief or a designee that oversees the investigative process should be informed of the outcomes of the investigations.

In some agencies, the chief may be the final decision maker regarding whether a complaint is sustained or not sustained, and may or may not be the final decision maker regarding corrective action and discipline. In other agencies, depending on the process, another level in the organization may make the decision regarding sustained or not sustained, and may make a recommendation regarding corrective action or discipline. There are many different processes regarding who investigates the complaint, who decides if a complaint is sustained, and who decides about corrective action including discipline. It might be a different entity or person for each decision, or one entity, person, or component may be responsible for many of the decisions to be made. Regardless of the decision-making structure, the chief should be aware of what is going on in the agency, how the public is viewing the agency, and how officers are performing.

In the vast majority of agencies, the internal investigation component should actually report directly to the chief. This ensures the chief can be fully informed regarding complaints, the status of investigations, and anything else the investigative component needs or believes is pertinent. In all but a handful of very large agencies, this occurs. It also prevents different persons from filtering information regarding investigations before it gets to the chief. But in some of the very large agencies, the internal investigative component may report to the second level of agency command or management. In no case should the component report to a lower management level. And in all cases, the commander of the internal investigative component must have the ability to go directly to the chief regarding investigations or issues of concern.

Recommendation 85: An annual statistical report should be prepared and published for public knowledge.

This report should be a quality overview of the complaints reported to and investigated by the agency for the previous year. It should include information such as number of complaints, types of complaints by title and type, outcome or findings of complaints, demographics of complainants and involved officers, type of call or activity during the complaint, and data such as day, month, day/night, component involved, and geographic area of all complaints. The report should not identify specific complainants or specific officers. It is meant to provide a detailed overview of all of the complaints filed against the agency. Providing this type of information to the public assists in keeping the community informed with accurate information, and building trust and transparency.

Recommendation 86: An annual review of all complaints should be written and submitted to the chief.

While this report would include all the information of the public statistical report, it would also contain additional information. Such additional information would include trend analysis regarding work teams, activities, areas of the community; multiple complaints against officers or work teams; specific discussions regarding bias, force, legal concerns, or moral/ethical issues; and issues involving the need for possible changes in or adjustments to equipment, supervision, training, and policy or procedures.

The intent is to provide the chief and the command staff with an analysis of all complaints so that information can be gained and decisions can be made regarding potential or needed opportunities for enhancement. Complaints should not be viewed as an individual occurrence but rather as part of the entire operation so that any patterns or trends can be identified as soon as possible, and then appropriate actions taken to reduce any concerns.

Chapter 12

Officer Wellness and Health

Policing is a very stressful profession physically, emotionally, and mentally. Numerous studies point out the impacts of policing on the human body and mind. Since officers provide services to citizens, oftentimes in crisis situations, it is imperative that the physical and mental well-being and health of officers be maintained at the highest levels possible. Any deficiencies could negatively impact the circumstances or outcomes of interactions between police and citizens. While this is especially true regarding sworn police officers, it also applies to support personnel such as communications technicians, crime scene personnel, and other positions that interact with the citizens.

The results of reduced health or well-being among police personnel can range from citizens being treated rudely, to officers charging people for minor offenses when not necessary or beneficial to the community, to increased use of force due to stress, unmanaged fear or anger, or poor physical conditioning. If the officer is having a "bad day" for whatever reason, they may conduct themselves less courteously or professionally. If they aren't in the best physical condition, then in a fight to overcome resistance or attack, they may need to resort to higher levels of force. While being as fit (mentally and physically) as possible may not prevent the necessity to use force, it can provide the officer with better options, and thus result in less injury to the officer or citizen.

In addition to these devastating service-related costs, there is the financial cost of poor mental or physical health. Officers suffer thousands of injuries each year including sprains, broken bones, concussions, stabbings, and shootings which can result in days off, forced medical retirement, and even death. All of these items have medical costs and/or pension costs in addition to the costs borne by the injured officer and their families. While there are costs to these programs, the benefits far exceed the costs. The results of not having a program can be tremendously more than having a viable and beneficial program. These programs are not new to government as some police agencies do have them. Most fire departments have fitness standards as part of a health and wellness program. The logic and reasoning of a firefighter program certainly applies to a police program, especially when the implications are so great. Keeping police personnel healthy is a benefit to everyone.

Recommendation 87: A mandatory physical fitness program should exist.

In an effort to keep the officer in a physical condition that reduces the likelihood of injury, all agencies should establish a mandatory physical fitness program. This should be a test very similar to the entry and academy level PAT as these tests are job related. While some agencies have fitness programs of various types, most agencies do not. Some existing programs are optional, with only a small percentage being mandatory. Generally, state and federal police agencies are more likely to have programs than do municipal or county agencies.

These programs should include job-related tests with reasonable standards, and include opportunities to maintain desired fitness levels. For newly implemented programs, there should be reasonable time frames included for personnel to build themselves back to the desired fitness levels. Just as it is inappropriate to mandate that all personnel have a Bachelor's degree in six months, it is impractical to require all personnel to meet new physical fitness standards in six months. Programs that enable personnel to build compliance are much better received than those that are unreasonable in the mandating of certain performance levels immediately. Agency personnel and other relevant individuals should participate in the design of these programs. These programs reduce officer and citizen injuries, reduce medical costs, and create a better work environment.

Recommendation 88: Counseling services and peer support should exist for all personnel.

The impacts of the profession on police officers are many. Officers are exposed to a variety of impacts and stresses on a regular basis. This includes verbal abuse and physical attacks by citizens, witnessing death and injury, and the general uncertainties of each call. Counseling services by professionals and peer-support programs offer a variety of methods in which personnel can talk with someone to help relieve and work through these many stressors. Trained and licensed professionals can provide services that might be useful, and should be made available to personnel as part of the benefits package without cost. Peer-support groups offer other services and have the advantage of utilizing people that understand the profession, as they also live it. They may even have endured similar critical incidents, and therefore can relate to what personnel are experiencing and can offer more focused and meaningful assistance. These services should be confidential unless there is a demonstrable danger to either the officer or others.

Recommendation 89: An Early Warning System (EWS) should exist.

These systems exist in various forms in many police agencies. Often times they are viewed as part of the disciplinary system, as that has been the focus of many programs. But they should also be closely linked to officer health and wellness. These programs watch for and look at various criteria to ascertain if a trend or problem is starting to arise. They are designed to give "early warning" of potential or possible concerns before they turn into problems. Some of the criteria used include traffic crashes, complaints, use of force incidents, injuries, rule violations, absences, and other criteria that might indicate deterioration in officer health, wellness, or capacity to perform.

The system generally has a threshold of a certain number of incidents of the various criteria within a given time frame. When a threshold is reached, the agency should require a review of the incidents individually and collectively, and discuss this with the affected person, to ascertain if these are just singular stand-alone incidents or if there is a trend and larger concern developing. The agency is basically asking the question, "Is there a pattern developing here that negatively impacts officer performance or officer health and well-being?" The reviewing supervisor should be required to submit a report of the incidents and their opinion regarding all the incidents to a higher level of supervision. This level then determines, either solely or with input from others, as to whether further action is needed. Further action may include a counseling discussion, training, or the offering or requiring of additional professional services. The goal is not to discipline or punish. But rather the goal should be to proactively ensure that agency personnel are still mentally, emotionally, and physically fit to perform the duties of the position.

Recommendation 90: The agency should utilize periodic psychological examinations or evaluations.

Most agency personnel participate in only one psychological evaluation in their entire career. Some will have additional evaluations if they are involved in a critical incident (officer-involved shooting, mass shooting response, etc.), are recommended for a fitness for duty exam, or apply to a special team such as SWAT, Bomb, or Hostage Negotiation, or others. The stresses of policing can be severe due to a specific incident, multiple incidents, or over the course of a career. Police officers are exposed to many horrors, injuries, deaths, cruelty, and inhumanity. This continuous exposure to incidents can cause trauma to the officer. Any or all of these can have a mental, emotional, or psychological impact on the officer, their well-being, and/or their ability to fully and properly perform the functions of being a police officer.

In an effort to understand, measure, and mitigate the impacts of the profession, agencies should at least provide, and really should require that agency personnel undergo a periodic psychological evaluation. All sworn personnel should participate in one probably every five to seven years. Some personnel should have these examinations on a more frequent basis depending on assignment and involvement in critical incidents. The psychology profession, members of the IACP Psychological Services Section, and the police profession should participate in setting guidelines for such evaluations. The agency should coordinate their own policy with input and participation from agency members, any collective bargaining entity, and the human resources group of their governmental parent (city, county, state).

The program and policy should be created based on the intent of protecting officers, citizens, and the agency. The goal is to ensure that all agency personnel are healthy and fit to perform the high stress role the community expects of them.

Part III

OPERATIONS

Chapter 13

Operations

Operations refers to the component(s), tasks, and activities wherein the agency and its personnel deliver actual services to the citizens. This service should be guided by good policy and procedures that are supported by and founded upon the Mission, Vision, and Values, core foundational beliefs and philosophies, professional standards, procedural justice, trust and legitimacy. All actions of the agency and its personnel must be legal, ethical, professional, fair, and impartial. Most of these services are provided by a patrol component with patrol officers, who respond to calls for service from citizens, provide proactive preventive patrol, and otherwise positively impact safety and quality of life by being visible and observing situations, circumstances, and violations. The patrol function may be supplemented by other components and functions such as traffic enforcement and crash investigations, canine, latent investigations (detectives), narcotics investigators, communications, and crime scene processing. Although sometimes these other components might be referred to as support, the reality is that they generally deliver services directly to the citizens.

The patrol function has often been called the "backbone" of policing since it is the largest component in most agencies, provides the most visible presence of the agency, and is the component that responds first to all calls for service. Virtually all investigations and reports originate in the patrol function. Some specialized investigations involving high-level drug activity, organized crime, and other offenses may originate with other components. But for the vast majority of offenses reported to or discovered by police, patrol is the first responding and originating component. This is also the component that most people will interact with and observe. They generally operate in a full uniform in fully marked police vehicles with highly visible markings, decals, and lights. Even though this component is where new officers start out, the importance of quality personnel with comprehensive skills, knowledge, and abilities cannot be overstated. The viability of investigations and prosecutions begins here. High-quality investigations, observations, and reports are critical to the operation of the rest of the criminal justice system, and to justice for citizens individually and collectively.

Community-Oriented Policing and Problem-Oriented Policing (COP/POP) should guide the police focus. Patrol personnel should know the community and citizens in the areas they serve. This enables the officer to assist citizens in resolving problems and getting the services needed. Examples include notifying appropriate entities of burned-out street lights, downed traffic control signs, potholes and nuisance situations that threaten the safety and quality of life in the area. Officers should also work with citizens to resolve various issues on a long-term basis. This is where the agency-wide philosophy of COP/POP actually becomes operationalized and implemented. Each officer should actively seek out ways to resolve problems and improve the quality of life for all citizens in their patrol areas. This also has the added benefit of building positive relationships between the officers and the citizens they serve.

Recommendation 91: Service and public safety should be the primary focus of all components and personnel.

Understanding Peel's principles, why police agencies exist, and providing various services that are focused on maintaining and enhancing public safety while improving the quality of life for everyone, should guide the actions, programs, and efforts of agencies and their personnel. How police officers view themselves, their role, and their purpose can greatly impact the manner in which they perform their various tasks and responsibilities. The debate over a "Warrior versus Guardian" mentality is part of the discussion about how police perceive themselves, and how citizens perceive the police based on the actions of the police. The agency should be taking steps to assist the community in becoming a better place to live, work, and enjoy life. Law enforcement should not be the goal or even the primary tool of the agency. Law enforcement should be used as little as possible and only when necessary and beneficial to enhance the overall safety and quality of life.

Recommendation 92: Identify repeat call locations and work to resolve the underlying issues.

Instead of responding to the same location numerous times for the same or similar type of calls, personnel should have the time to examine the reasons and causes of these repeat calls. There are locations in every community that generate police calls for service on a regular basis. The police respond, quiet things down, leave, and then after some period of time respond back to the location for the same issue or one similar to it. This is a tremendous waste of resources and generally reduces police effectiveness since the problem is never really resolved.

Officers should be given the time to work with citizens to identify the causes or issues that generate all the calls for service. If they can identify the underlying causes, then they may be able to fix the underlying causes, and resolve the need for continuous police responses that were actually ineffective in the bigger picture. Perhaps the cause of the repeat call is a neighbor disagreement wherein talking about the issues or even mediation might help both parties get to a point where they can tolerate each other. Maybe the location is a neighborhood park where kids make too much noise late into the night bothering area residents. Possible solutions might include timed lighting, additional recreational facilities, or other options. Maybe the issue is one that is much more difficult to resolve. But at least if the agency looks at the issues, they may help the community find a resolution that reduces the problems and enhances the quality of life for everyone.

Simply continuing to respond to repeat calls at a specific location does more harm than good. The officer gets frustrated with having to continuously respond for the same issues. Citizens, both those that call and complain, and those being complained about, become frustrated that either the problem continues or that they are being "harassed" by citizens and police. The police continue to expend resources and not have a positive meaningful outcome. Citizens on both sides of the issue may become frustrated and angry with the police thus causing loss of confidence, trust, and respect. If the officer tries, but cannot fully resolve the underlying issues, they at least tried and are no worse off for trying. Hopefully, they may have identified an issue wherein the government or other entities can begin working with the citizens on possible solutions. By trying to resolve the issues, the officer becomes a coordinator or facilitator of resources and solutions, instead of trying to use law enforcement as the universal solution.

Recommendation 93: All sworn personnel and all communications technicians should be Crisis Intervention Trained.

Crisis Intervention Training (CIT) is a training program specifically designed to enhance the skills, knowledge, and abilities of police personnel to recognize, understand, empathize, and interact with persons who are in crisis. It is not intended to make them mental health counselors, but rather to give them additional skills to de-escalate situations involving persons in crisis. This program has been around for over thirty years. Its primary goals are to increase officer and citizen safety and reduce the number of persons with mental health needs in the criminal justice system.

One of the current concerns about policing involves the police response to persons in crisis. Many argue that police are not properly trained for this situation and most officers agree. But currently there are no widespread options and mental health practitioners are rarely available to respond to the scene of an incident involving a person in crisis. Therefore, the task has fallen to police officers. Police officers have generally embraced this training but it is still not universally available.

Since it is impossible to predict when and where an incident will occur, it is prudent and beneficial to provide this training to all officers. While some have advocated against universal training, it is appropriate to have as many personnel CIT trained as possible. Even if there was to be a substantial shift in who responds to these types of situations, having officers that possess these basic skills, knowledge, and abilities can only be a benefit to everyone. Communications technicians should also receive this training as they often interact with either persons in crisis or their loved ones who are calling to seek assistance and help. By understanding the issues, communications technicians can ask more pertinent questions, gain more detailed information, and transmit it all to responding officers so they have a more complete picture of what is happening. Having all officers and other critical police personnel CIT trained can reap significant benefits to the officer, the citizen, and the community. It would reduce injuries, entrances into the criminal justice system, and have better outcomes especially for the person in crisis.

As discussed earlier, certified mental health practitioners should have primary responsibility for responding to and handling calls involving persons in crisis. Despite the difficulties in building such a program, it should be attempted. Until that time, and even when such a program is in place, most likely police personnel will still need to respond to protect and assist the practitioners. However, the practitioner would take the lead. Regardless of how the service is structured, police officers should still be trained in CIT to enhance their skill and knowledge levels, and to better serve the citizens.

Recommendation 94: All personnel should be trained in de-escalation techniques, and de-escalation should be a universal philosophy of the agency.

Many agencies have been training their personnel in de-escalation techniques for decades. However, more agencies have embraced this concept within the last several years. There have been very good outcomes in many situations. Even in those situations where the outcome was not as desired, it at least offered the opportunity to assist. De-escalation involves slowing things down, creating distance, reducing the stress and emotion as much as possible, and using verbalization skills to change the urgency and criticality of the immediate moment. These techniques can oftentimes enable officers to transform the situation from a high-stress, very emotional situation to a much calmer dialogue, wherein cooler minds come up with better options and outcomes.

De-escalation should be tried in almost every situation. But it must be realized that in some circumstances de-escalation may not work, or that any significant amount of time spent trying to de-escalate may not be appropriate. Examples of these situations include active shooters wherein citizens are in current and immediate danger. While de-escalation training is obviously essential for sworn personnel, it can reap benefits for all other personnel. Communications personnel can use it to calm down callers and to obtain more information to provide to responding officers, and might possibly calm the caller down a little prior to the officers arrive. All other personnel who interact with the public can use it to de-escalate situations that might arise in a police facility or over the phone.

Recommendation 95: Patrol personnel should have at least 40 percent noncommitted time.

Staffing and deployment plans are generally based on workload in an effort to provide relatively consistent patrol coverage throughout the community. Even though patrol areas or beats may be different sizes, the workload within each beat should be approximately the same. This is why various areas and beats are different sizes. As part of the planning process, patrol officers should have at least 40 percent of their available time as noncommitted. This means that the dedicated workload of an officer should not exceed 60 percent and should actually be less than that.

The workload for a particular beat includes the number of hours dedicated to call response and call handling, report writing, meal breaks, and other administrative duties. By having at least 40 percent noncommitted time, the officer has the opportunity to perform other tasks. These include proactive preventive patrol in areas where crime or disorder is high, traffic enforcement, follow-up investigations, and, most importantly, time for the officer to positively interact with citizens.

When officers are running call-to-call, they don't have time to be proactive, perform investigations of the highest quality, or have time to interact with citizens. Having time to perform these tasks enables officers to focus on prevention, and on proactive positive citizen interactions which result in better community awareness, enhanced police-citizen interactions, and a more effective police service.

Recommendation 96: Agencies should conduct periodic analyses regarding staffing, allocation, and deployment.

A police agency accomplishes its tasks through people. People, especially sworn personnel, are very expensive. Sworn personnel are generally more expensive than civilian personnel. This is predominantly due to the higher salaries, pensions, training costs, and equipment associated with sworn personnel. It is estimated that personnel costs, including salary and benefits, consume 80–90 percent of an agency's budget.[1] Some estimates put the personnel costs as high as 95 percent. All this indicates that personnel are extremely expensive and make up the vast majority of police department budgets.

Due to this cost, it is imperative that agencies make the best use they can of their primary resource, people. In order to do this, agencies should periodically review the complete use of all personnel. This includes the number of personnel overall, the type of personnel (sworn or civilian/support), and how all personnel are utilized. Where an agency places its personnel, can provide guidance as to what tasks, responsibilities, and roles it views as the most prevalent and the most important to handle and focus upon.

A review of staffing involves examining the workload of the agency and all its components. This enables an agency and community to understand the service demands that are going to be placed on the agency in the near and long-term future. This provides information regarding what staffing levels or numbers of personnel are and will be needed. As the role and workload of policing changes, it is appropriate to review the staffing levels. This review should provide guidance as to what types of personnel are needed, vis-à-vis sworn or civilian/support.

Allocation focuses on where will personnel be assigned within the agency. A good analysis should provide information as to how many personnel are needed in the various components of the agency. This includes patrol (which for most agencies represents the bulk of sworn personnel), investigations, specialty components of all and every type, and support functions. This information is generally derived by examining the workload of each component. For example, the type and number of cases that require latent investigative work will give insight into how many personnel should be assigned to the various investigative functions. It also requires an understanding of and consideration of the type of case. Since homicides are more serious and generally require a lot of investigative effort, homicide detectives will handle fewer cases per year, while larceny detectives will handle more cases. But the workload should be about equal. By understanding the workload (number of cases, severity, and hours per case), an agency can allocate personnel to the functions and components in a balanced manner.

Deployment generally refers to how the personnel in any component are assigned or scheduled to work. This is critical in the patrol function, as personnel are needed around the clock. But that does not mean they should be evenly deployed with one-third of the personnel working each of the three primary shifts of days, evenings, or midnights. Nor should the same number of personnel work during each day of the week. Based on the call load, and an understanding of the differences among different days and hours, personnel should be deployed to match call or workload. This might mean that more officers are needed on patrol during the afternoon or early evening shifts, and more officers on Fridays and Saturdays. It might even mean that more officers are needed in residential areas during evenings and weekends, and in commercial areas during the weekdays. Also, the agency must consider more than just the call load. Patrol officers need to have time for administrative activities such as vehicle fueling and maintenance; placing evidence into secure storage; and writing reports. Being in court also has to be planned for. One of the biggest items to plan and staff for is proactive preventive patrol. As previously mentioned, patrol personnel must have noncommitted time to accomplish other tasks and objectives. All of these items and their requisite time demands must be considered when staffing, allocating, and deploying patrol personnel.

Especially today, agencies must ensure they are being as efficient and effective with their personnel resources as they possibly can. While this is necessary just as a government leader and fiduciary, it is critically important today with all the tremendous scrutiny on the costs of operating police agencies. As communities and society in general review the amount of money spent on policing, especially against other societal needs, police administrators must ensure they are using their expensive personnel in the most effective and efficient manner possible. Besides examining what tasks, responsibilities, and role the police should be handling, the most fruitful opportunity lies in reviewing personnel staffing, allocation, and deployment.

Recommendation 97: Traffic law enforcement should be performed by sworn personnel for the enhancement of public and community safety.

The focus of traffic law enforcement (TLE) should be on public safety. It should not be a method to generate revenue for any level of government. Any fines generated should be used to offset the cost of the enforcement actions such as related equipment, salaries of enforcement personnel, and the provision of court services. No governmental entity should see a profit from TLE.

Many people believe that TLE is for the express purpose of generating revenue. There have been some examples wherein municipalities have used TLE to boost city revenues, and this is inappropriate. In some places, TLE revenue goes to school systems, court expenses, or a statewide training fund for officers. These are appropriate uses of revenues. It should also be understood that it is not the police agency that determines where the revenue goes, as this is set out by state law. It may be necessary and prudent to change the flow of TLE revenues via state law.

There is a bona fide public safety reason for TLE. First, violations of traffic laws are responsible for more death and destruction than any other cause in America. Recent years have averaged approximately 2 million injuries and approximately 35,000 deaths annually. The amount of property damage for all crashes is approaching $100 billion annually.[2] These are significant impacts. Second, complaints about traffic-related issues are the prime complaint to police agencies across the country. Virtually every police agency responds to numerous calls on a daily basis regarding traffic noise, congestion, blocking intersections, aggressive driving, speeding, and many other traffic-related issues. Traffic congestion impacts the quality of life for virtually all motorists. The number of deaths, injuries, property damage, and general traffic-related issues such as congestion and improper driving, unfortunately necessitates that the police continue to be heavily involved in general traffic law enforcement. Keeping the roadways safe is imperative.

Recently, there has been some movement toward removing sworn police officers from the task of traffic law enforcement. What is lost in this push for police removal from TLE efforts is the understanding of the purpose of and difficulties associated with TLE. Advocates claim that removing sworn officers from traffic law enforcement activities would eliminate the most frequent interaction between police and citizens, thus reducing conflicts, uses of force, disparate or biased actions, and other problems. They advocate that traffic law enforcement should be handled by unarmed traffic enforcement specialists, very similar to how some cities utilize non-sworn, unarmed parking enforcement specialists. Some argue that this would reduce arrests for minor offenses and eliminate government using traffic law enforcement as a way to generate revenues.

Another large issue with using non-sworn civilians to enforce traffic laws involves the attitudes of citizens themselves. There are already too many times when citizens refuse to stop for sworn police officers, and resist and assault officers who are merely trying to enforce the traffic laws and keep everyone safe. This is despite the repercussions of doing so. What makes people think these incidents will suddenly become less frequent, severe, or even disappear simply because the enforcement personnel are civilian? Civilian parking enforcement specialists are assaulted regularly. Many people simply do not want to comply with laws and societal expectations. There is no reason to believe they will do so just because the person issuing the citation is non-sworn. The arguments put forth by advocates for civilian traffic enforcement specialists simply do not match the reality of society, and will result in increased violence and a reduction in overall traffic law enforcement, which will lead to more death, destruction, and chaos on America's roadways.

Chapter 14

Use of Force

The use of force by police officers is one of the most critical and controversial aspects of policing in many ways. Using force can cause injuries to officers or citizens, and can cause considerable concern among community members. As has been seen recently, the use of force by police can result in negative public perceptions even to the point of protests and disturbances.

There is a considerable amount of misunderstanding and many myths regarding police use of force. In the vast majority of citizen contacts there is no force used. The use of force by police is actually rare and it is highly regulated. The National Police Foundation (NPF) indicates that a death resulting from the use of force by police occurs in about 0.0015 percent of all face-to-face contacts between police and citizens.[1] Even though the number of cases involving excessive force is statistically very small, it is too many and has great significance to those involved. Excessive force can take many shapes. It can be an unnecessary grabbing or shoving, unnecessarily taking someone to the ground, unnecessary or excessive striking, or the improper use of various tools, techniques or weapons. While these incidents are rare, they have tremendous impacts on individuals, officers, society, and societal perception of the police overall.

Most force used by police is used as a response to resistance, to overcome unlawful resistance or force used by citizens. The reality is that if citizens would comply with the directions of police officers, the use of force would be significantly less than it is today. Any use of force is not pretty. It is not how television or films portray it. When a citizen resists lawful police efforts, the police are authorized and required to use that amount of force that is necessary to overcome the resistance or force presented by the citizen. The existence of force usage or injury is not automatically excessive. A broken arm may not indicate excessive force whereas a significant scrape or bruise might.

It is all dependent on the circumstances. All uses of force must be viewed in the context of the specific situation. The type and level of force used by the police directly depends on that which is used by the citizen. Because of the vast ramifications involving any use of force, it is proper that all force use be regulated, documented, and reviewed.

The use of force can take many shapes. Types of force include moving a person by placing a hand on the shoulder or upper arm to guide them in a specific direction; grabbing an arm and pulling or pushing the person in a specific direction; taking the person to the ground; using authorized strikes to various parts of the body; using tools such as a baton, pepper spray, or CEW; or using a firearm in a deadly force situation.

Officers use more forceful techniques and tools based on the resistance encountered or the threat perceived. The force used by police is intended to overcome the level of resistance or force used by the citizen. In some cases, the officer may use force quickly to overcome one level of resistance and prevent the situation from escalating to another level. Oftentimes, several officers will use different low force techniques to overcome citizen resistance. In these situations, citizens often comment and complain about multiple officers struggling with one citizen. But the multiple officers are trying to gain control of the person, specifically their hands and arms. This is to more gently and quickly facilitate handcuffing. One officer can try to overcome the resistance, but there is a higher likelihood of injury to the officer and to the citizen.

Even Sir Robert Peel recognized that force should be used in limited situations and only to that extent necessary to gain citizen compliance. But he also acknowledged that the police should de-escalate situations as much as possible, as it is better to have voluntarily compliance with the law.

Recommendation 98: The agency must have a comprehensive, overall Use of Force policy that includes (1) stressing, requiring, and specifically stating that only that amount of force which is minimally necessary to accomplish the lawful task is to be used; and (2) stating that the sanctity or reverence of life is paramount.

Agency policy must set the standards, requirements, and expectations for everything, but especially regarding the use of force. Policy should specifically state that only that force which is minimally necessary to accomplish a lawful objective or task be used. Most agencies expect this with many actually requiring this. But based on how some policies and state laws are worded, officers may actually be allowed to use force necessary to overcome resistance, but not necessarily the minimum amount necessary. It is in everyone's interest to use the minimum amount of force necessary to overcome resistance and accomplish the lawful objective.

By stating that each life is important, the agency affirmatively points out that people should be treated with respect, and that deadly force should only be used when absolutely necessary to protect another person. It is not intended to be a religious statement or discuss abortion. It is intended to stress to the community, to the agency, and its personnel that life is precious and important. And the decision to use deadly force should be a last resort only to protect others or the officer. This type of statement points out officers should ensure that the use of deadly force is limited to those situations when it is absolutely necessary to protect the life of a person. It also indicates that life is more important than property.

Recommendation 99: Personnel should be properly trained in all tools, tactics, techniques, and weapons in which they are authorized to use.

Personnel should have comprehensive initial training before being authorized to use any tool, tactic, technique, or weapon. This training must be more in-depth than annual or periodic refresher training as this is the foundational training that the officer is receiving. The initial training regarding arrest and/ or defensive techniques is intended to give officers a basic skill level. In many cases, the techniques taught to officers are much more restrained than what recruits or citizens may have been exposed to previously. Police training is generally much less forceful, violent, or injurious than mixed martial arts (MMA). Annual or periodic refresher training must also be conducted to maintain and build the skill set, and to ensure that personnel are aware of any changes to law, policy, or how the tools should be used.

All relevant training (initial and refresher) should include a review of the agency's use of force policy and procedures, applicable laws and court decisions regarding the use of force, how each tool is allowed to be used, demonstrate qualification and proficiency with each tool, tactic, technique, or weapon authorized, and documentation of all such training. In order for officers to be more proficient in the various techniques, they need more than the usual 40 hours of training most basic academies provide. It is understood that this will be time-consuming and costly, but it is appropriate and necessary for such a critical aspect of policing and public concern.

Recommendation 100: All uses of force should be fully documented. This includes any use of force and when force, or higher levels of force, could have been used, but wasn't. There should exist a standardized form that is used by the agency to document all circumstances and situations regarding the use of force.

Any use of force should be documented. This includes placing hands on any person, pointing a weapon (CEW, pepper spray, firearm) at a person, using any impact technique (hands, knees, batons), and un-holstering of or display of a firearm. By fully documenting all uses of force, policing and society can have a better understanding of the actual facts surrounding the use of force. This includes how often various types of force are used, and most importantly the circumstances surrounding each and all uses of force.

While many agencies require most of these actions to be documented, many do not. Some have different thresholds of reporting wherein certain uses of force such as handcuffing, minor hand contact, or un-holstering a firearm are not required to be documented. But the severity of using force on a citizen, and the need to have full documentation of said force is so great, that complete documentation is warranted. And yes, this would be a tremendous amount of paperwork (written or electronic) that would be created, and therefore need to be reviewed. But the documentation process doesn't have to be over-burdensome. The value of full documentation greatly outweighs any inconvenience of reporting. Some argue that additional documentation could be a deterrent to using force when it is necessary, and might cause an officer or citizen to be injured. This is not and would not be the case. Officers are accustomed to documenting most uses of force and current documentation requirements have not caused hesitancy or injury. Also, if the officer follows their training, is compliant with law and policy, and believes the situation warrants it, they will use the tool, tactic, technique, or weapon as they believe necessary and appropriate. In those situations where an officer might stop to think about having to document his or her actions, then they probably don't need to do what they were contemplating. The incremental amount of additional documentation would not have negative impacts but would produce additional information of great value as it would give a much more comprehensive view and understanding of all force usage. All use of force should be documented.

Situations where force could have been used, or higher levels of force could have been used but weren't, should be fully documented. Documenting all uses of force is appropriate and necessary as this provides a great deal of information about the specific incident and use of force overall. However, if an agency only documents when force was used, there will be a lack of comprehensive and useful information. There will also be an inaccurate perception of force usage. To provide a more accurate understanding of force usage, it is necessary that documentation exists for when force could have been legally used but was not.

By documenting the circumstances of when force was not used, the agency (and society) can have a better understanding of why was force not used in this situation, and what techniques, tactics, or circumstances existed that allowed the situation to be resolved without the use of force. It is beneficial to know why the officer did not use force in a particular situation even though they legally could have. What did the officer see or comprehend about the situation that allowed them to resolve the situation in the manner they did? Was there something about the environment, the skills of the officer, or the actions of the citizen that caused the officer to act as they did? Why did the officer choose to use the particular level and/or tool or technique they used? Why did they use less force than might have been legally authorized? A wealth of information regarding training, individual officer skills and abilities, and even the effectiveness of various tactics can be learned if these situations are also documented and examined.

Another benefit of documenting when force was not used helps to put the overall use of force and related decision-making into perspective. It also shows how many times officers could have used force but did not. By examining when officers could have used force but didn't provide information regarding policy compliance. This is an important component of understanding the entire picture of police use of force. Simply having information about when force was used only gives limited information. By documenting all aspects of the use of force, including when force was not used, a better understanding of use of force can be realized.

To assist supervisors and investigators in completing a comprehensive investigation and report, the agency should utilize a standardized form, checklist, and process for the investigation of all uses of force. The form should have various sections including basic information such as date, time, location; personnel involved; citizens involved; type of force used; effectiveness of the tool or technique; injuries; nature of call; and other sections. A checklist can be created to ensure that all required investigatory actions are taken for each specific situation. It can serve as a reminder to the investigators as they proceed with the investigation. It can also be used to ensure that all tasks are completed, especially when there are multiple investigators handling various aspects of the investigation.

It is important that a standardized process be created and utilized for the investigation of force usage. The process (and forms and checklists) can and should be flexible to cover all incidents. The process should also allow for various aspects to be skipped if they are not relevant to the specific incident. But it should require the investigator or supervisor to specifically indicate that the section, activity, or procedure was not completed due to non-applicability. All supervisors should be trained in the complete process so they are familiar with it so it can be smoothly implemented when needed.

Recommendation 101: A supervisor should immediately be made aware of any significant use of force.

The agency should determine a threshold wherein the officer involved is required to immediately notify communications and a supervisor regarding the use of force that exceeds a defined and low level of force. This might include anything exceeding "soft hands" or handcuffing without injury or complaint of injury. If the use of force involves firearms, weapons, other techniques or tools, or results in injury or complaint of injury to citizens or officers, a supervisor should respond to the scene. This enables a supervisor to take control of the scene, request additional resources (medical, investigators, additional personnel, etc.), and to preserve the environment as may be necessary. It also enables the supervisor to have more information regarding the use of force and the overall circumstances, possibly identify witnesses, and to begin the documentation process. If the force used is significant or if a significant injury occurs, the supervisor can implement the proper level of investigation in a timely manner. If the immediate supervisor is involved in the incident, then another supervisor should respond to the scene. There simply is not a valid reason for not immediately notifying a supervisor, but there are numerous benefits to doing so.

Recommendation 102: Each use of force should be reviewed by the immediate supervisor and the next level of supervision.

The immediate supervisor should review all uses of force via the documentation required by the agency. This is to ensure that all relevant information is included and to make a preliminary decision regarding the propriety of such force use. The supervisor should ensure that the documentation is as comprehensive as possible including reference to any video (body worn, in-car, public or private area surveillance) that might exist. If relevant or beneficial to the investigation, the supervisor should request a copy of related radio transmissions and computer traffic. The supervisor should be required to document any comments they feel pertinent to the incident and should indicate their opinion regarding the necessity, appropriateness, and policy compliance of the use of force.

Having the use of force report reviewed by another level of supervision provides additional perspective that might be less connected to the officer who actually used force. It provides a more neutral and bigger picture review by someone who can provide continuity across individual squads or work groups. This level of review should also sign off on the report and indicate whether they believe the force usage was necessary and policy compliant. These multiple reviews of force usage indicate to the community and to agency personnel, the importance and regulation that the agency places on the use of force.

Recommendation 103: Each use of force report should be forwarded to a designated component that reviews all use of force reports and activities. The training component should also review all use of force reports.

There should be a central review, repository, and clearinghouse of all use of force reports and related activities. This component would review each individual report for appropriateness and policy compliance and would review all reports for general trend data and overall information. If this component determines the force was necessary and policy compliant, the report becomes part of the overall use of force database. If questions arise about the force usage, then it either directly or through the secondary level supervisor, requests additional information. If the reviewing component determines there is an issue, then it would be forwarded to the internal investigative component for investigation. At this point, a designated ranking official should be notified and decisions be made as necessary regarding officer status and other related matters. The incident should be investigated with input from the training component and relevant instructors regarding all facets of what was trained to the specific officer(s) involved. A decision would then be made regarding the appropriateness and policy compliance of the use of force.

The review of each individual incident should include the effectiveness of the tool or technique; how many different tools were utilized; and if multiple tools used, what was the order of use. This type of information can assist the agency and the training component in identifying trends regarding officer preference of which tool to use first, were the tools effective immediately, and other information that can assist in making decisions. This process and central repository enables a comprehensive review and report of all individual uses of force as well as a comprehensive review, analysis, and report of use of force collectively. This assists in making decisions regarding policy, training, and equipment. This can be a vital component of ensuring that all aspects of force usage are as desired.

In an effort to ascertain if training is effective and proper, it is necessary and prudent for the training component to also review all use of force reports. The training component would also review the annual report to have a larger picture of the trends regarding use of force. This review would focus on what tools, techniques, tactics, or weapons were used in what situations; was the item effective; was the item used consistent with training and intent; and are there opportunities or need to adjust training or equipment. This is being proactive to ascertain if the training is as effective and comprehensive as possible. It also helps avoid issues such as improper or inadequate training and reduces claims of negligent training.

Recommendation 104: If the use of force was found to be inconsistent with training, necessity, or policy, the matter would be referred to the disciplinary process.

An investigation consistent with the relevant policy, and appropriate to the level of force used should be conducted. It is simply not sufficient to document and review the use of force. The agency must make determinations as to the appropriateness of each use of force. And then the agency must take some kind of action for any and every situation in which force was not used consistent with policy or law. Failure to do so indicates to the community and to agency personnel that improper uses of force will be tolerated and not punished. This is an unacceptable position for the agency and its leadership to take. Once all the facts and information are compiled, the report, including any relevant opinions should progress through the established disciplinary process if a violation was found to have occurred. The chief or a command level designee (or board as set out by policy and procedure) would make a determination regarding the appropriate disciplinary action to be taken.

Recommendation 105: In virtually all cases of improper use of force, training should be required as part of any corrective or disciplinary decision.

If the determination is made that the use of force by any officer was unnecessary or inconsistent with training, policy, or law, then training should be part of the final decision. This would be in addition to any actual punitive discipline that might be mandated. Obviously if the violation is such that termination is warranted, then additional training would be pointless. But in any situation where the officer is to be retained, training must be part of the corrective action decision. Refresher or remedial training is necessary to ensure that the officer is fully aware of all relevant policies, procedures, laws, and directives. The officer should be required to demonstrate knowledge of all relevant directives and should be required to demonstrate actual proficiency in the proper use of the relevant tool, tactic, technique, or weapon. This training should take place before the officer resumes their role in the agency.

Recommendation 106: Following a determination of improper use of force, certain supervisory actions should occur.

Once a determination has been made that an officer used force improperly, that officer's immediate supervisor should be tasked with additional monitoring requirements. This should be part of the training, counseling, and developmental aspects of any corrective or disciplinary actions. For at least three months, but preferably for six months, the supervisor would be required to respond to the scene of any uses of force involving the specific officer; review all videos of any physical arrests or any force levels used by the officer; and provide a written review of the officer at the end of the defined enhanced review period. An additional review period of this nature is intended to be a proactive method of ensuring that the training and discipline were effective in adjusting the officer's skills and actions. It does not depend on the reactive nature of waiting for an additional complaint. This additional review and monitoring would verify that the officer is acting in compliance with applicable directives and expectations, while ensuring that the corrective action was sufficient and effective.

Recommendation 107: An annual use of force report should be completed and publicly published.

The community has an interest in and a right to know about the use of force by its police agency. Publishing a comprehensive document regarding the use of force informs the public so they have accurate information and can provide input as appropriate. The report would include statistical data with numbers of incidents, type of force used, precursor actions of citizens, injuries to officers, subjects, or bystanders, nature of call/incident, day of week, hour of day, work group (squad or component), beat or area of the community, demographics (age, sex, race) of involved persons, determinations of policy compliance, and corrective or disciplinary actions taken by the agency. This report would not identify involved citizens or officers. The report would provide information to the public and would be used by the agency to determine trends and ascertain if changes are needed to policy, procedures, training, equipment, or personnel. The public should be made aware of this report proactively and affirmatively.

Recommendation 108: Agency policy should severely limit shooting at or from moving vehicles.

Due to the many dangers and issues involved, agency policy should severely limit shooting at or from moving vehicles. Shooting from moving vehicles generally reduces accuracy which increases risk to others. Shooting at moving vehicles, even if successful, usually results in the still-moving vehicle crashing into something. Since there are circumstances and situations where it might be necessary to stop an active shooter or driver from intentionally injuring others, the agency should not fully prohibit such actions. Rather it should provide clear guidance to its personnel (and the community) regarding the risks, benefits, and limited situations in which such action would be warranted. The policy should prohibit officers from intentionally placing themselves in front of moving vehicles, and require officers to consider and use tactically safe positioning. However, it should also be understood that in some cases, a driver will intentionally try to strike an officer with a vehicle and the officer may not be able to get to safety. In these limited circumstances, the officer would be allowed to use deadly force to protect themselves. The policy and training would provide documented guidance.

Recommendation 109: The agency should recognize that there are numerous mechanisms and tools of deadly force.

In most cases, deadly force indicates the use of a firearm. However, depending on the circumstances, other tools and techniques can be deemed or considered the use of deadly force. Some tools that could be considered deadly force would be strikes to the head with a baton, or other objects. A vehicle very easily could be considered deadly force. This might include striking the person or even the use of various pursuit termination techniques such as the Precision/Pursuit Immobilization/Intervention Technique (PIT). Certain techniques such as various neck restraints could be (and recently more frequently are) considered as deadly force.

Agencies should provide guidance to their personnel that techniques and tools other than firearms might be considered deadly force. This all depends on the circumstances. The agency and the community must also understand that if deadly force is authorized and necessary, then the officer would be authorized to use any tool or technique to save the officer's life or that of a citizen. Just because the officer chose to use a tool or technique different than a firearm, does not indicate that the use of force was improper. An investigation should determine the circumstances of the incident. If the officer was legally authorized, and it was necessary to use deadly force, and the situation and circumstances indicated that the officer's actions were proper, then the tool or technique chosen by the officer would be appropriate. The use of a vehicle or generally prohibited technique alone should not be the deciding factor.

Recommendation 110: Officers must minimize injury and the risk of harm to all persons. Therefore, agency policy should require medical aid be provided and that citizens should be placed in positions and locations to minimize the risk of injury.

Agency policies and procedures must require officers to monitor and render or summon medical aid to any person in their care or custody. This is especially necessary for persons that have been the subject of use of force by the police. The agency must follow established protocols for monitoring citizens when certain types of force are used. Since officers cannot know the medical conditions of all citizens, they must actively monitor citizens. This is especially true for any police-citizen interaction involving use of force, aberrant behavior, or physical exertion. Someone may appear healthy but have a condition that manifests itself only after any struggle or resistance. This might include heart conditions, breathing conditions, neurological conditions, or any other condition. The person might have drug issues or other conditions that could cause an adverse reaction to any type or level of stress or physical exertion. While certain behaviors and appearances can indicate the possibility of excited delirium, it may also have a rapid onset that can be fatal. Therefore, it is imperative that police personnel monitor citizens for injuries, disorientation, breathing difficulties, loss of consciousness, or other medical issues.

Policy should require that medical aid be offered, rendered, and/or provided within the capabilities and training of police personnel. The provision of medical aid is regardless of the cause of injury and applies to traffic crashes, pure medical emergencies, use of force incidents and in-custody situations. Officers should render what aid they are trained to do if it can be done safely, and should also call for additional medical assistance. If the citizen appears injured or in distress beyond that which the officer can handle, then appropriate medical aid should be requested immediately with an expedited response also requested. While providing and/or requesting medical assistance should be a stand-alone policy guiding officer actions in all situations, it is necessary to specifically include this mandate in each use of force-related policy, including those dealing with deadly force and less than lethal force.

All officers must be trained in basic first aid at the very least. This includes CPR (Cardio Pulmonary Resuscitation) and basic first aid to stop bleeding. However, they should be trained to a higher level similar to Emergency Medical Responder (EMR)[2] as officers are frequently first on the scene of various incidents wherein these skills could reduce injuries or save a life. All sworn personnel should be trained in and be issued a tourniquet for personal use should the need arise. When officers have these skills and tools, they are better prepared to serve the citizens and protect themselves. And officers should be required to utilize these skills in the performance of their duties.

Once an officer has taken care and custody of a citizen, they owe that citizen a duty to minimize any further risk to them. The officer must monitor and assist any person in their care or custody, or in which they are interacting with or become aware of. The officer also has an obligation to minimize the risk of injury to citizens during encounters wherein the citizen is not in actual custody of the officer. This can be as simple as moving a person out of the roadway or from between vehicles during a traffic stop. It can also mean physically positioning a detained citizen in a position to avoid further physiological stress on the person. Positional asphyxiation and excited delirium are legitimate concerns and virtually all officers have been trained to recognize relevant symptoms and to take immediate steps to reduce these risks. Unfortunately, in some situations there might not be anything an officer can do to assist the citizen. But the officer should monitor the citizen and request a priority response from medical professionals at the first sign of significant concerns or problems. Training and policy should require that officers take prudent and appropriate actions to reduce the risk to all citizens, but especially those in custody.

Recommendation 111: When a use of force results in significant injury, an investigation should commence immediately.

If the use of force results in significant injury to a citizen, officer, or bystander, an internal use of force investigation team should respond to the scene. They would make a determination consistent with law, policy, and procedure as to guide the investigation; take it over, from the on-scene supervisor; or request an outside agency respond to conduct an investigation. Serious uses of force or serious injuries warrant an investigation beyond that of the immediate supervisor. This would be a very comprehensive investigation due to the serious nature of the force or injuries. Comprehensive investigations are beneficial to the involved citizen, the involved officer, the agency, and the community.

Recommendation 112: Some investigations should be conducted by an outside agency, or a regional multiagency team.

Due to the seriousness of some incidents, an outside agency should be called in to conduct the actual investigation. This might be based on the seriousness of an injury, an in-custody death, or the use of a firearm by the police. With very few and specific exceptions, all uses of firearms (or other deadly force mechanisms) by police should be investigated by an outside agency. The only exceptions to this are an obviously accidental discharge when not in contact with a citizen, compassionate euthanasia of an animal, or use of weapons on a range during training. But depending on the unique circumstances and outcomes of any incident, it might be prudent to have an outside agency conduct an investigation.

The intent is to have an independent entity conduct the investigation. While many agencies have excellent processes, procedures, and personnel in place to conduct very comprehensive investigations, the public perception of the validity of an investigation conducted by the agency that employs the subject of the investigation is oftentimes questioned or challenged. The question of an agency investigating itself or its own personnel is often raised. Even though most professions review and handle the actions of their own personnel, there remain concerns about the investigations. For significant investigations, having an outside entity conduct these investigations removes some of these concerns and can increase trust, objectivity, and transparency. In these specific investigations, the investigation can be handled by an outside agency such as the state police or state bureau of investigation. However, this places a significant workload on that agency and still does not alleviate the issue of who investigates the state agency personnel. Another very viable option is to have a regional investigative group conduct such investigations. This team or task force would be staffed with personnel from multiple agencies and would conduct investigations of regional personnel. This team could also work with the state agency and would investigate incidents involving state agency personnel. Depending on many issues (geographic size, number of incidents investigated, etc.), it might be advantageous for a state to have several regional teams. These regional teams may be the primary investigation components or work in a coordinated environment with the state investigative team.

This outside investigation must be independent and very comprehensive. Some agencies already do this and more are moving toward this process every day. Generally, only large agencies with well-trained "shoot teams" handle their own officer-involved shootings. Due to their size and experience, these internal shoot teams have developed highly skilled personnel. But due to recent concerns about who conducts these investigations and perceptions of biased investigations, it is better to have an outside agency conduct the investigation. On a side note, the concerns about biased investigations are not completely unfounded, but are not generalizable to the entire profession. Incidents of improper or biased investigations are extremely limited. But in order to be transparent and to maintain community trust, it is better to have an outside agency perform investigations regarding significant incidents.

An outside agency should conduct these investigations regardless of whether an individual was actually wounded by gunfire. In many situations, an outside agency will not respond to a request for investigation if no one was actually struck by gunfire. This is based on workload, but it is an inappropriate decision and policy. Most outside agencies respond to investigate an officer-involved shooting with the very narrow and specific mission of determining if the officer's use of force was lawful. They generally do not investigate the actions of the citizen involved except for the purpose of determining if the officer's use of force was lawful based on the circumstances. The investigation and any subsequent criminal charges against the citizen is left to the agency of the officer involved in the incident. But if the intent of an outside investigation is to determine if the officer's use of force was lawful, then whether the citizen was injured or not is actually irrelevant. The officer's use of force is based on the actions of the citizen, the perceived threats, and the laws of the state where the agency is located. The determination of whether such use of force was lawful has nothing to do with the level of injury sustained by the citizen. The officer's marksmanship should not be the deciding factor as to who investigates the incident.

In some cases, state law may need to be written or changed to not only allow but to require outside independent investigations. There may also need to be additional funding provided for resources and personnel to handle these investigations. But this is an extremely critical investigation with tremendous ramifications. It needs to be conducted by an outside agency in such a manner that the public has trust and confidence that a transparent, comprehensive, and independent investigation was conducted. It is suggested that a state level investigative agency or regional team perform this task. While there might be some outstanding local agencies with excellent officer-involved shoot teams in different areas, there generally seems to be more public confidence in state or multiagency teams than single agency teams. If an outside agency is desired, it should be an outside agency for every agency. Therefore, having at least two recognized investigative teams is proper. It could also reduce the workload on any one agency.

The agency that conducts the outside investigations should have highly trained personnel who are skilled in investigations, shootings, use of force, and interviews/interrogations. The teams should have resources including certified crime scene investigators, electronics specialists, and access to other specialists as might be necessary for any type of incident. The agency should develop a very comprehensive, yet flexible investigative protocol that covers all aspects appropriate for such investigations but allows for adjustments consistent with the specific circumstances of individual incidents. The Ohio Bureau of Identification and Investigation has an outstanding process with highly skilled investigators.

Recommendation 113: The investigation detailed above should be sent to the chief of the agency involved and the specified prosecutor.

Some states currently specify that an outside agency will conduct an investigation as specified above. In those states, the process is set up by either state law, or executive order of the governor or state attorney general. In other states, it is an option wherein the head of the agency involved in the incident must request the outside agency to conduct the investigation. For these states, there are different processes in place as to how the investigation will be conducted and to whom the final investigative report is sent. Some states require the report be sent to the designated prosecutor (local, special, or attorney general) upon completion. One concern is that the law or policy may not allow (and in some cases, prohibits) the involved agency head to receive a copy of the report. In some jurisdictions, the agency head may request the outside investigation but then cannot see the report unless the prosecutor decides to provide them a copy. This is simply unacceptable.

The head of the agency involved in the incident should be given a copy of the investigation when it is complete and when given to the applicable prosecutor. The chief has a need to see the full report so they can make various decisions such as officer status, training, issues raised, and responding to the community. The community has a legitimate interest in these critical investigations, and are usually asking the agency and chief about the investigation. The chief must be able to provide some amount of information to the community. It is not sufficient nor is it appropriate for the chief to respond to information requests by saying they are not conducting the investigation. The public wants to know what is happening. Also by providing some amount of information, the chief might be able to keep emotions down and preserve order in the community.

Recommendation 114: All aspects of the actual investigation should be recorded.

Best practice is to record all interviews in most criminal cases, especially interviews of key witnesses or involved persons. Since the outside investigation is centered on whether the officer's use of force was lawful, it is by nature and definition a criminal investigation. Interviews of witnesses, involved citizens, and involved officers should be recorded. While this seems to be standard, it is not; as some states and agencies do not record some of these statements. All interviews should be recorded. Recording all interviews and statements provides a record that is reviewable, verifiable, and subject to much less misinterpretation. It simply provides a much more accurate record than memory or notes.

Recommendation 115: The agency involved should conduct an internal investigation into these serious incidences.

While an outside agency should conduct an independent investigation regarding the lawfulness of the officer's use of force, the employing agency should be conducting at least one other investigation. This investigation should focus on the officer's actions relative to compliance with agency policy, procedure, and training. This investigation would look at matters including proper positioning by the officer, de-escalation techniques, compliance with all policies and procedures, and equipment and training issues. This enables the agency to have an understanding of what happened, how it progressed to the outcome it did, and what opportunities exist for enhancements of policy, procedure, equipment and training. Without this investigation, the agency misses an opportunity to examine agency-specific items related to the use of force and how the policy, training, and equipment impacted the outcome of the incident. It also allows the agency an opportunity to learn from each incident and to make beneficial enhancements. Additionally, it enables the chief to be able to make some comments about the incident so as to keep the community informed.

Recommendation 116: The state should decide which agency will conduct any criminal investigation into the citizen's actions.

The actions of the citizen have a direct impact on the actions of the officer involved in the incident. In most cases, the officer reacted to the actions of the citizen, and this makes it imperative to identify and analyze those actions. These citizen actions may be legal or they may be illegal. But some agency has to conduct the investigation. In most cases, the agency of the involved officer conducts this investigation, and then coordinates with the local prosecutor regarding the filing of any criminal charges. This investigation also generally provides sufficient information to determine if the officer's actions were lawful.

This investigation is different than the previously discussed investigation. The previous investigation focuses on the legality of the officer's actions and use of force. This specific investigation focuses on the citizen's actions. While they are related and linked, the focus is different. In this investigation, the actions of the citizen are examined to determine if charges should be brought forth against the citizen. It also serves as an indicator as to what precursor actions impacted the officer's decision to use force.

If the involved agency conducts the criminal investigation, there is the potential for the community to be concerned about the veracity, fairness, and independence of the investigation. The community may feel that the agency is seeking to charge the citizen for any number of improper reasons. While the question is rarely raised, it might be beneficial for the outside agency to conduct the full investigation. But this would have significant ramifications. First, it would place a considerable additional workload on the outside investigating entity. In effect, they would conduct two criminal investigations: one with the citizen as the subject and one with the officer as the subject. Second, it would most likely be subjected to some of the same criticisms since it is still one agency conducting both investigations. Third, the number of investigators may have to be doubled since it is two separate but related investigations. Also, the investigators would have to be aware of concerns regarding interviewing the officers, citizen, and witnesses for two separate investigations, each with its own focus. Fourth, the time frames may be significantly increased which would not be good for anyone. And fifth, if the employing agency did not conduct this investigation, the chief would have virtually no independent source of information with which to make various decisions and with which to inform the public. If this is done, then the agency needs to be kept fully informed of the investigation.

The decision as to who handles this aspect of the multiple investigations should be decided in advance. This, in effect, establishes a standard protocol or process that is known in advance. It reduces confusion when an incident occurs as the protocol is already in place. Whether it is a state agency, a regional team, or the employing agency, such decisions should be made in advance and documented either in law or agreements such as memorandums of understanding.

Recommendation 117: Holds and techniques that focus on the head or neck should be prohibited or extremely regulated.

Due to the risk of serious injury or death, various holds or techniques that focus on the head or neck should either be outright prohibited or very closely regulated. This includes placing weight on the head or neck area, grabbing the head or neck, and using holds that restrict breathing ("chokeholds") or blood flow (carotid restraint technique). These techniques should be completely prohibited or if allowed, allowed only under circumstances involving deadly force. If the officer is about to lose consciousness, or if the situation is otherwise a deadly force situation, then these techniques would be authorized. But any technique that is authorized should be trained upon. While this prohibition does not specifically include strikes to the face or head to cause temporary disorientation, these techniques should be reviewed with appropriate decisions made and trained upon. Essentially these holds carry a significant amount of risk and should only be used when the officer would be authorized to use deadly force. Some states and local jurisdictions have prohibited these holds, while many agencies have recently revised their policies regarding the use of these techniques. Recent adjustments to professional standards and guidelines call for prohibiting "chokeholds" but allow for "carotid restraint techniques" if properly trained.

Even though some holds involve the neck area, they can be very different types of holds or techniques. A "chokehold" involves grabbing the subject around the neck to either gain direct control of the subject or to cut off air flow and thereby indirectly gain control. This type of hold should be prohibited unless a deadly force situation exists. A similar hold, the "carotid restraint technique" involves the neck area but focuses on temporarily reducing blood flow to the brain, thereby causing the subject to lose consciousness momentarily. This is intended to cause the subject to stop fighting or resisting, allowing the officer to gain control and handcuff the subject. In the vast majority of situations, the subject regains consciousness very quickly without sustaining any injuries.

Part of the concern, however, is that both holds can appear to be the same, and cause public concern. The officer might use a "carotid restraint technique" but the public perceives it as a "chokehold." This can cause an escalation of issues at the scene and can result in numerous complaints. The "carotid restraint technique" has been taught for several decades and has been shown to be effective with minimal risk. This hold takes away the person's ability to resist or fight and ends the resistance quickly. Many other techniques focus on gaining compliance through the infliction of pain, which may or may not be successful.

One of the issues with these holds is that many agencies have trained on the use of these holds or techniques for several decades. They have been used to effectively control combative subjects without injury in the vast majority of situations. Therefore, officers have learned these techniques and may use them automatically as they get into a stressful force situation and their training kicks in. Agencies should provide immediate refresher training that includes specific statements regarding the prohibition of such techniques, and should provide training on other techniques that are a viable alternative. If an officer uses one of these prohibited holds, there should be a full investigation that examines the circumstances. If warranted, punitive discipline should occur but be accompanied by additional remedial training. If necessary and appropriate in the specific situation, with significant injury or intent, the officer should be terminated. Since these techniques have been authorized for many years, the officers need to be provided training and education to change the training they have learned.

Recommendation 118: Research on new tools and techniques should continue.

It is always prudent to research new methods, tools, weapons, and tactics to ensure that the policing profession is as efficient, effective, and humane as possible. While this is especially critical regarding the use of force, it applies to all aspects of policing. Research has provided additional tools such as CIT which has helped officers deal with persons in crisis; has provided tools such as conducted energy weapons (CEW/Taser); has increased knowledge about topics such as implicit bias; and has shown the value of tactics such as de-escalation. All of these have improved safety and outcomes for citizens and officers. Research that can enable police to perform their lawful role, tasks, and responsibilities with minimal risk to themselves and citizens benefit everyone. Private corporations, government, professional associations, citizens, academia, and police professionals should all be involved in researching modified or new tools to enable the police to better serve the citizens.

Recommendation 119: The use of Conducted Energy Weapons (CEW) should be expanded.

Conducted Energy Weapons (CEW) are commonly referred to as Tasers due to the dominance of Taser/Axon in the market. These devices provide a force option that uses controlled electric pulses to disrupt voluntary control of the muscles resulting in neuromuscular incapacitation. Basically, the devices lock up many of the muscles thus resulting in a loss of voluntary muscle control. In essence, the CEW takes away the ability to run, resist, or fight in most people. This generally results in the subject falling to ground and being incapable of further flight or aggression for a very limited period of time. This allows officers to gain control of the subject without using other force options.

While there has been some concern and debate regarding these devices, they are effective and reduce injuries to officers and citizens when compared with pepper spray, baton strikes, tackling, or physical confrontation. In most cases, the CEW takes away the actual ability to flee or fight which is better than other tools or techniques that rely on pain or direct injury to stop the resistance. The majority of studies indicate a very low risk of severe injury and an even lower risk of death. In the vast majority of cases, there are no injuries and even fewer long-lasting injuries or effects.

When the CEW is turned off, the subject generally feels like they have exercised heavily. But with other tools, the effects can last long after the subject is in custody. Pepper spray continues to irritate the eyes, nose, and mouth for approximately an hour or more. Baton strikes will leave bruises of various severity or broken bones, which leaves pain or injury for days or weeks. Tackling a subject can result in any number of injuries of various severity and duration to citizens and officers. Physical confrontations can result in a wide range of injuries with multiple levels of severity and can last any length of time. Detailed policies and procedures should exist regarding this tool (and all others), and annual refresher training should be required.

The policy should specifically identify circumstances in which the CEW might not be the best choice such as when the subject could fall from heights, when gasoline is present, or when the subject is obviously pregnant. It should also require monitoring for adverse reactions, the need for medical care, and require the summoning or provision of medical care should the subject begin to experience difficulties or a medical condition or emergency.

Recommendation 120: All officers present during the use of force should be required to submit a written report.

Most certainly any officer who uses force should be required to provide written documentation of the situation and circumstances surrounding the use of force. But any other officer present during the use of force, or arriving on scene shortly thereafter, should also be required to submit a written report of what they witnessed. This provides additional documentation from multiple perspectives and offers more information to understand what happened, what was perceived, and why the chosen options were selected. It also assists in identifying any and all officers present and understanding why witness officers either took action or did not take action. This is one more level of documentation and accountability that is good for everyone.

Recommendation 121: The agency should have a comprehensive procedure outlining the process when an officer is involved in a critical incident.

Being involved in a critical incident such as shooting at another human (whether that person is injured or not), has been shot at, or is involved in a situation that results in death or very serious injury to a citizen or officer (such as vehicle crash, resist arrest, or in-custody death) can have tremendous impacts on officers. It is imperative that the agency has plans and procedures for all aspects of such incidents. This includes procedures for how the investigation will be handled as well as how the officer will be treated. Aspects that should be considered in the policy and process include evidence collection, including all agency video, radio transmissions and the officer's weapon if relevant; testing of involved persons such as blood and/or breathalyzer; interviews of officers; making public comments or statements regarding the incident; transport of involved personnel; medical attention; notification of government officials, prosecutors, and union representatives if applicable; notification to the agency, family of involved officers, family of any involved citizens, and the media; and notification of outside entities including independent investigative groups.

Since these incidents are relatively infrequent, agencies and personnel may have limited experience in investigating such incidents. But, unfortunately agencies and their personnel will be involved in various critical incidents. Therefore, it is imperative and beneficial to plan ahead for these incidents and to create comprehensive plans and processes to deal with and investigate these incidents. Having existing policies, procedures, and processes in place before an incident occurs, provides a reference and resource so the incident can be managed in a calmer, consistent, and comprehensive manner. This planned response helps to ensure that all aspects of the investigation including professional and legal treatment of the officer are considered and will take place as expected. This is beneficial to the officer and the community.

Recommendation 122: When an officer is involved in a critical incident, certain processes should exist to assist the officer in recovering from the effects of the incident. These processes include (1) required participation in a psychological evaluation, (2) being placed on administrative duty status pending the preliminary results of the relevant investigations, and (3) participation in a modified training session relevant to the incident prior to returning to full duty status.

Critical incidents such as these can have tremendous impacts on officers. Before an officer is returned to duty, preferably even desk duty, the officer should be required to fully participate in a psychological examination by a trained and licensed psychologist or psychiatrist. The medical provider should certainly be fully licensed, but should also be trained and experienced in dealing with stress and trauma, but especially with police officers that have been involved in critical incidents. The provider should also be familiar with the role and tasks of a police officer as they should be required to provide a professional opinion as to whether the officer can return to full and regular duty. This is necessary to ensure that the officer can fully, competently, and safely perform all the tasks expected of them. It is necessary to ensure that any impacts on the officer caused by the incident are minimal and controlled. Eventually the officer will need to be out with citizens, carrying a firearm. It is imperative that the agency ensures that the officer can fully perform their role without negative residual effects of the prior critical incident. This type of examination helps protect the community, the agency, and the officer. The well-being of the officer is important for obvious reasons, but it can also impact their ability to perform.

Placing the officer who was involved in a critical incident on administrative leave and duty has many benefits. It gives the officer a chance to physically and emotionally reset. They may need time to recover from physical injuries and to mentally adjust to what has happened. They need to have time for the psychological evaluation to occur as discussed above. There will be at least two if not more investigations into the incident. This would include a criminal investigation into the actions of the officer, and would most likely be conducted by an outside agency. There would be an internal administrative investigation to ascertain if the officer complied with all agency directives and expectations. There may also be another criminal investigation into the actions of the involved citizen that led up to the officer's actions. It is possible there may be a federal civil rights investigation if the situation is controversial. And, almost certainly there will be a civil lawsuit filed by the involved citizen or their family.

In most situations, the officer will be placed on administrative leave with pay immediately following the incident. This involves the officer not performing any police-related tasks except those directly related to the investigation such as interviews, healing, and the psychological examination. Having the officer on administrative leave for at least a short period of time provides an opportunity for the officer to heal and recall more details about the incident. It also ensures that the officer is available for all interviews and activities associated with fully investigating the incident. It is not to be viewed as punitive, but rather as part of the investigative and officer well-being process. It also should not be viewed as a "vacation" as some citizens have referred to it. It is certainly not a reward of any kind. The reality is that a significant percentage of officers involved in a deadly force incident will not complete their career and will not retire on longevity. They will either quit the profession or retire medically. These incidents have a huge toll on the officers. It is also understood that the incidents can have a huge impact on the citizen involved, their family, and even the community.

The administrative leave should be at least three days, but should be long enough to allow for the officer to recover from any physical injuries or emotional impacts, and to accomplish the psychological evaluation. Once these conditions exist, the agency can consider placing the officer on modified administrative duty that does not require direct interaction with the public. This might be some type of support activity but definitely should not involve a full return to regular duty status. The administrative duty assignment should last as long as necessary to ensure that the agency has a good understanding of what happened in the incident at the very least.

Depending on the circumstances of the incident and the process used, the criminal investigation may take a few days or several months. If it is very clear cut and obvious that the officer's actions were lawful and necessary, this preliminary information may be such as to allow the officer to return to full and regular duty after the psychological evaluation has cleared the officer. This may occur even though the full official report of the investigation has not been completed, submitted, or reviewed by the prosecuting attorney. Since these processes can take months for the investigation, report writing, review, and final decision to be rendered, it generally is not appropriate for the officer to be in limbo and on administrative leave or duty status for that long. This is not to say that the report should be rushed, but it certainly should be completed in a timely manner. Also, if the investigation is complex, then it takes the time that it needs. But in many situations, it is clear to the agency and others that the officer's actions were lawful and necessary. And in those cases, it causes more harm than good to keep the officer off full duty status. While this is sometimes not a popular decision (returning the officer to full duty before the full final decision has been rendered), it is often better for the officer, agency, and the community.

It is important to remember that even though this is a criminal investigation (of the officer's actions by the outside agency), the officer has not been accused of any wrongdoing. It is the purpose of the investigation to ascertain if the officer's actions were lawful or if they were not consistent with applicable laws. Should the preliminary review of the incident indicate that there are serious questions regarding the officer's actions, or it appears that their actions were outside the law, then it is most definitely appropriate for the officer to remain on full administrative leave or duty for the duration of the investigation.

Prior to returning the officer to full duty status, the agency should provide and require the involved officer to participate in a modified training session that is relevant to the incident the officer was involved in. If the incident was a firearms-related situation, then a firearms-based session; if vehicular, then vehicle training; and if a different type of use of force incident, then training related to the situation. The purpose is to ensure that the officer can fully function if and when they are returned to full duty status. The agency and the officer need to be confident that the officer could perform as expected if a similar situation, call, or incident was encountered by the officer.

For firearms-based incidents, having the officer mechanically operate the firearm and respond to other incidents potentially involving a firearm is critical to the safety of the officer and other citizens. The officer should hear and feel the actual operation of the firearm. They should also be exposed to some decision-making scenarios (shoot don't shoot). If the incident was related to the operation of vehicle, the training should involve operation of a motor vehicle, possibly with emergency equipment operated. If defensive tactics, response to resistance, or arrest techniques were involved, the officer should go through some training related to the situation encountered. All this additional training should be scenario based and should have relevance to the situation the officer was involved in. It is intended to make sure that should the officer encounter a situation that is similar to what they were just involved in, they could competently handle the situation as the agency expects. This reduces the possibility of the officer failing to react, or not reacting in a way that leads to a more desirable outcome. It simply enhances officer and community safety.

Chapter 15

Peaceful, Compliant Protests

Citizens have the right to peacefully assemble, voice their concerns, and even air their grievances against the government or its components. Peaceful protests bring issues to a broader public attention; can send a powerful message to citizens, governments, agencies, and elected officials; and may result in positive change. That voice should not be limited or minimized. Peaceful public assemblies and protests that are compliant with law and public safety concerns are useful to society. Peaceful protests are protected by many laws and have a long history and tradition in America.

Violence, disturbances, and other activities reduce the power of legitimate voices and concerns. It also causes confrontations, injuries, and huge costs financially and emotionally. Citizens do not have the right to destroy property, commit violence against police or other citizens, and do not have the right to interfere with the rights of others including their right of movement and access. Unfortunately, peaceful protests are sometimes compromised by violence and destruction even to the point where the previously peaceful protest is stopped. By avoiding violence and destruction, citizens can help protect the opportunity to peacefully protest.

For discussion purposes, peaceful protests are characterized by compliance with laws; devoid of property destruction or damage; not interfering with movement of vehicles, trains, planes or other people; and free from violence of any and all kinds. It is necessary and beneficial to distinguish between peaceful compliant protests and protests which are not peaceful and compliant (disturbances, riots, etc.), as there are different police tactics and techniques which may be suitable for one type of situation but unsuitable for the other. This chapter focuses on the peaceful, compliant protests, while chapter 16 focuses on non-peaceful, noncompliant incidents.

Recommendation 123: The agency must have a written, comprehensive policy regarding peaceful, compliant protests.

To assist citizens in exercising their rights, each police agency must have a comprehensive, written policy that guides the agency's philosophy and response to peaceful, compliant protests. This policy must specifically recognize the right of citizens to peacefully engage in compliant protests. The policy should outline how the agency will prepare for protests, what techniques, tools, and actions will be utilized based on the circumstances of the protest, and how the agency will strive to keep protesters, bystanders, and officers safe during the protest. This policy should provide general guidance while at the same time detailing actions the agency will take and will not take. It should encourage working with the protesters to create a safe environment for everyone. This would include time, location, duration, actions by protesters, agency/officer actions, and basic guidelines for behaviors and conduct of all involved. It should also require that a specific plan be developed for each protest that provides details about the specific protest.

Recommendation 124: Police agencies should support and assist with peaceful, legally compliant protests. This includes establishing communications and open dialogue with protest leaders.

As previously mentioned, the Constitution of the United States enumerates various rights including the right to peacefully assemble and the right to petition the government. These exist because they are viewed as fundamental human rights that belong to the citizens, individually and collectively. Police agencies are expected to protect the rights of all citizens. In many situations, police protect citizen rights by keeping them free from the unlawful actions of other citizens. Police strive to stop crime, arrest criminals, and reduce the number of victims. In other cases, the police are expected and required to help citizens voice their concerns about various social and community issues. This support includes voicing concerns that might involve or be critical of government actions, including those involving the police. It is also necessary for the police to protect those involved in peaceful, compliant protests from others who might seek to limit the right of people who do not agree with their point of view.

The police, as a protector of rights, should develop policies and procedures that stress support for citizen rights. These directives should include a base philosophy of support for citizens expressing concerns, support, or displeasure regarding various issues. The agency should set out general guidelines that enable peaceful protests to safely occur. These guidelines should include flexibility regarding protests in general but also specifically regarding time limits and curfews if applicable. The agency should assist and help citizens to engage in peaceful, compliant protests, not just allow the protests to happen. The agency must help the protest to occur in a safe and meaningful manner.

The agency should attempt to establish communications and open dialogue with protest leaders. The intent of this communication and dialogue is to understand what actions the protesters want to take and where they want to protest. It is not intended to regulate the content or focus of the protest. This should include discussions with protest leaders so that police can help the citizens voice their concerns safely. It might include assistance with permits, road blockages, or ensuring that there are sufficient medical and sanitary facilities available. It should also include an analysis of threats against the protesters so the police can plan and prepare for others who might infringe upon the protesters' rights.

The discussions should also stress that protester actions must comply with applicable laws. This would include specific prohibitions against damage to property, throwing objects, and assaults upon or interference with officers. Other parameters such as duration and locations of the protests would also be discussed as might be applicable and beneficial.

Open discussion between police and the protesters can also inform the protesters of basic safety parameters, any governmental requirements such as insurance or permits, and what actions and items are allowed and what actions and items are prohibited. The police should encourage the group leaders to advocate for compliance and to separate any criminal actors from the group. These discussions should include time frames for the protests and location details such as where they will occur and specifically including any routes that might be traveled. Agencies should assist with route selection and route closures. Major highways and interstates should not be utilized or allowed to be closed. These types of roadways are designed to move large volumes of traffic at higher speeds. Closing them or allowing protesters to be on them poses significant threats to protesters, vehicles, and the occupants of vehicles.

All of these parameters are designed to ensure the safety of the protesters and the general community. The parameters or police activities should not have any focus on subject matter or content unless it advocates criminal actions or becomes criminal. All discussions before and during the protest should be documented for inclusion in the after-action report. By having pre-event discussions, the protests can be safer and more effective.

Recommendation 125: As long as the protest remains peaceful and compliant, solid, impact projectiles or tear gas should not be used.

If the protest is peaceful and compliant with general laws, and the lawful orders of police and/or government officials, there should be no need for any use of force. By definition, policy, and law, the use of force should only be used when necessary to perform a lawful function. If the protest is peaceful and compliant, there would be no reason, justification, or legal authorization to use force.

Verbalization should be the primary tool of the police for providing any necessary direction to the protest. Solid impact projectiles such as rubber bullets, bean bag rounds, wooden knee knockers, and similar projectiles should not be used for crowd control in a peaceful compliant protest. These devices are generally intended for use against individuals, not crowds. If the police and protesters have communicated before the protest, continue to communicate during the protest, and the protest remains safe, peaceful, and compliant, there should not be any need for the use of force against the group.

Several peaceful, compliant protests have been marred by vandalism or violence committed by very few participants. The police need to deal with these persons, who now are committing criminal acts. But they need to do so in a manner that allows the otherwise peaceful, compliant protest to continue. They should use individual-focused tools and techniques that have minimal impact or effect on other peaceful protesters. By doing this, the police can remove the criminal actors from the group, in a safe manner, and enable the peaceful protest to continue.

In some situations, tear gas has been used to disperse a group or crowd when the crowd has failed to act consistent with the parameters of the protest. This might include trying to block traffic outside police concurrence, moving into areas not within the protest footprint and plan, or extending the protest beyond the time frames. Tear gas, as with all tools and techniques, has its benefits and disadvantages. Police must carefully evaluate the situation should the protest become unreasonably noncompliant. Tear gas use can cause injuries as people flee the gas, and the reality is that people will flee in a direction they believe will allow them to escape the undesired effects or situation. This might aggravate a situation. Also, some people may be unaware of why tear gas was used and, therefore, have different perceptions about its use. If the protest remains generally and reasonably peaceful and compliant, tear gas should not be used.

Recommendation 126: The agency should exercise care and restraint in setting time limits and implementing curfews.

The setting of protest time limits and the establishment of curfews are often viewed as limitations on protests. Any limitations must have a reasonable relationship to community safety. Citizens should be allowed to protest in a peaceful, compliant manner, even if the protest is long. If the protest is in downtown or other business area, it might be allowed to go longer into the evening and night provided there are limited residential structures in the immediate area. If the protest is in more of a residential area, it might be restricted to earlier evening hours consistent with preexisting noise ordinances, and the rights of other citizens to be comfortable in their homes and to be able to sleep.

Curfews should be implemented only upon the affirmative showing of a public safety need. If people are in a downtown area, like a park or parking lot (with owner permission), there should be more flexibility with time frames. The location and environment does have an impact on the circumstances of the protests. Implementing a curfew just to end an otherwise peaceful and compliant protest is not good practice. If there are other reasons, based on public considerations, such as natural disasters, rioting, property damage, noncompliance with police directions, then a curfew might be appropriate.

The police should consult with their legal advisor, city attorney, mayor, city manager, and/or other authority when considering the implementation of a curfew. Agency policy should clearly guide how such curfew setting should occur, and how it is implemented. This provides guidance and pre-planning to everyone, so decisions are guided by law and policy, not emotions of a specific situation. Protesters should be made fully aware of the curfew or time limitations so they are aware and can plan accordingly. Also, it should be understood that if an event or protest is scheduled to end at the same time as a curfew begins, there must be a reasonable understanding that it will take some time for the participants to clear the area. The police should also exercise some discretion as to how quickly to end a protest. In reality, the police generally exercise great restraint, discretion, and flexibility when dealing with protests. But they can only allow the event or protest to be extended for relatively short periods of time. The reasoning for all limitations and police actions should be fully documented.

Recommendation 127: The agency must create policies and procedures regarding any recordings made during peaceful, compliant protests. Generally, the agency should record all protests including police actions and responses.

Even though it is recommended, prudent, and appropriate for the police to record various protests and events, the agency must establish very clear and comprehensive policies and procedures regarding what the police can and will do with the recordings after the protest concludes. There are many valid, legal, and appropriate reasons for police to record events and protests. These include documentation of citizen actions and activities, documentation of police actions and activities, and identification of persons who commit criminal acts. It also enables the police to document the full event and provide a more complete and accurate picture of what happened, than if only limited, redacted, or manipulated videos from individuals are released and used to depict police actions. It is not appropriate for the police to use the recordings in any manner that is inconsistent with these purposes or that is inconsistent with the law. This would include attempts to document or thwart the participation of persons in fully peaceful, compliant events or protests. It is proper and appropriate to record such events and participants, but the recordings should be destroyed in a reasonable time frame if no criminal charges, internal complaints, or other lawful purposes occur. By having policies that regulate the use of such recordings, citizens can be more comfortable with police recordings and that they will only be used for legitimate purposes.

Protests can be an emotional situation and crowds can change demeanor and behavior quickly. By recording the protest, there will be a full record of what happened, the order of events and activities, and the response by police. A complete and contemporaneous record of the events will enable all interested parties to more accurately understand what happened, and then to have any follow-up conversations that might be appropriate. Audiovisual records also offer the opportunity for after-action reports to be completed and can assist with any investigation that might be warranted. All body-worn cameras should be operating whenever an officer is in public contact or actively performing duties or tasks related to the protest or event.

Some people will be opposed to governmental recording of the protests for any number of reasons. The American Civil Liberties Union (ACLU) often complains about potentially inappropriate or illegal uses of police/government recording. And during the 2020 riots, at least one court had temporarily agreed with the ACLU, and had prohibited a police agency and government from recording protests and riots.[1] This issue has not been permanently decided and is inconsistent with other court decisions regarding recording in public places. But as long as the protests are in a public environment or are a public safety concern, recording is not only lawful, it is prudent, appropriate, and beneficial to everyone. Other entities and individuals such as bystanders, protesters, and the media will be recording it anyway. It is appropriate for police to record the event.

Recommendation 128: The agency should maintain a contemporaneous log.

A log should be maintained to document all aspects of event management. This log should be created at the time of the event and document activities as they transpire to enhance accuracy. The log should be comprehensive and include items such as dates, times, locations, equipment, orders given, personnel, tactics used, and a timeline of activities. It should also include any plans for handling the event, including any discussion or agreements with the event planners or protest leaders. This would be part of the permanent record of the event and assist in compiling an after-action report. It also provides a detailed contemporaneous record of the order of events and does not rely on memory. This log would assist in evaluating agency and officer responses and actions, enhancing policy and training, and responding to public concerns, questions, or complaints.

Recommendation 129: Officers should wear visible identification.

Police personnel who are in uniform generally, but especially during protests, crowd management, or civil disturbance situations, should wear visible identification. In some cases, this will be a name plate or name tag, while in other situations it may be a unique identification number. In recent times, with the advent of "doxxing" (ascertaining and/or publishing the names, addresses, and so on, generally on the internet, without their permission) of police officers, it is recommended that unique identification numbers be used instead of officer nameplates. This has become necessary to protect officers and their families. Regardless of the type of identification, it should be visible enough for citizens to read from at least three feet away. This enables any citizen to identify the officer while keeping citizens from getting within arm's reach of the officers. The identification must also be a unique identifier so citizens and supervisors can positively identify individual officers. This allows for complaints, concerns, or compliments to be accurately attributed to the correct officer.

Recommendation 130: The agency should carefully consider officer apparel for peaceful protests.

The operational plan for a protest should carefully consider what apparel, uniform, and equipment the officers wear and have. While it is appropriate for officers to be prepared for any eventuality, care must be exercised in determining the appearance of the officers. If the protest is perceived to be peaceful, and all available information and intelligence indicates it will be peaceful, then great consideration should exist to having officers working the event be dressed in normal everyday uniforms and attire. This will reduce any concerns that some people may have of the officers showing force or attempting to escalate the situation just by the uniform they are wearing and the equipment they are carrying.

However, it must be understood that the officers will be present in at least their standard everyday police uniform, equipped as a standard officer. This is necessary since the officer may be required to take action to stop a participant from committing a criminal act; the need to be readily identifiable as an officer; and the potential need to stop others from interfering with the rights of the protesters. It is also prudent, for officer and citizen safety, to have plans to immediately provide additional equipment and resources should the situation change or the need arise.

Chapter 16

Noncompliant Protests, Civil Disorders, Riots, and Looting

Actions and activities that are not compliant with public expectations, law, accepted societal norms, or involve active civil disorder, riots, or looting cannot be tolerated. Noncompliant actions include blocking major thoroughfares, highways, or interstates unless authorized and controlled by police authorities. Actions such as looting, burning, throwing objects at people, destruction of property, or defacing property, buildings, or statues are illegal, and cannot be condoned, allowed, or tolerated. Also included under assaultive behavior are new techniques crowds have begun to use such as flashing bright lights in the faces of officers and shining lasers into officers faces. These are intended to at least temporarily disorient or blind the officers, thereby putting them at risk. Each of these actions violates the rights of others and poses a danger to property, people, and society. The more destructive and violent a situation grows, the more appropriate more powerful tools and their use become to quell the situation. All the considerations and recommendations applicable to peaceful and compliant protests are still applicable here. But once a peaceful, compliant protest changes to a noncompliant, destructive, or violent disorder or riot, additional actions and recommendations are warranted.

Recommendation 131: Agencies should have detailed policies and procedures regarding response options to these types of situations.

It is imperative for the police to have a variety of plans available to deal with any type of disaster or disturbance that might be encountered and threaten the community. Since no plan can fully cover every type of incident in every location, the plans, policies, and procedures should speak in general terms. They should be flexible enough to cover any magnitude, event, location, or citizen actions. They should also be specific enough to give guidance to citizens, government, officers, and police commanders so that all have an understanding of what can be expected based on the situation. Agencies should keep the plans current and be part of the periodic review of policies to ensure they are current in all aspects. Agency personnel must train on these policies as part of the periodic refresher training cycle.

The bulk of the policies and procedures should be public and should have some public input into their creation. Specific tactical aspects may be restricted to protect officers and the effectiveness of the tactics. All relevant policies, procedures, and plans should be built on the core foundational philosophies of the agency, including service, protection of rights, using minimal force when necessary to accomplish lawful tasks, and treating people with respect. All agency and officer actions must be legal, ethical, professional, fair, and impartial.

Recommendation 132: Significant policies, such as the use of force policies should be included in the response to disorder plan.

Although police personnel should be familiar with the key agency policies such as the use of force policy, various policies and guiding principles should be included in the operational incident or response plan. This serves as a reminder to planners, commanders, and officers. The key policies should also be reviewed as personnel are assigned to specific duties during such events. Besides the use of force policies, other policies that should be reviewed and made part of the plan include, but are not limited to, bias policing policies and those related to fairness, professionalism, and ethics; de-escalation policies; discretion; and protecting the rights of all persons. By making these key policies and core foundational beliefs part of the response plan, the agency is reminding everyone of the importance and applicability of specific policies and beliefs.

Recommendation 133: Agency policy should require constant and continuous use of cameras.

Just as it is prudent to audiovisually record peaceful protests, it is even more prudent and imperative that incidents involving noncompliance, disorder, destruction, or violence be recorded in every possible manner. The agency should generally record these events just as in peaceful protests. But additional recording is warranted including constant and continuous use of body-worn cameras, in-car cameras, drones, aerial observations, and any other methods that might be available. As the volatility, violence, and destructiveness of an event increases, so does the need for additional recording.

The agency should ensure that it is fully compliant with all legal rulings, laws, and legal guidance. This area of the law is extremely active and additional court decisions, rulings, and actions should be expected for some time. By nature of this type of event (being noncompliant, violent, destructive, etc.), it is a criminal event by at least some of the participants. This makes it legally more appropriate to record as the recordings will be used for potential criminal prosecutions. But it is also appropriate to record the events when they have become criminal or noncompliant since the police will be taking actions beyond mere observation. The police will be making dispersal announcements, making arrests, and using various levels of force to protect society. It is imperative that accurate and complete recordings be made to provide full documentation for criminal prosecutions as well as after-action reports and investigations into the actions and responses of the police. Once again, the intent is to provide complete and accurate documentation of the incident, situation, actions, and responses of everyone.

Recommendation 134: Agency personnel should be uniformed and equipped consistent with the nature of the event.

As mentioned in the peaceful protest section, officers should be dressed consistent with the event that is expected. If the event is believed to be noncompliant or violent, or there is reasonable information or intelligence that violence might occur, then personnel working the event should be properly equipped. Officers may start out with regular uniforms and equipment, but should it be needed, other protective equipment should be immediately available.

In some situations, officers should be initially dispatched with additional protective equipment in order to protect themselves and the general public. This equipment might include helmets with face shields, gas masks, long batons, shields, flex-tie handcuffs, and/or additional body padding. All of this is intended to keep the officers as safe as possible so they can protect themselves, citizens, and property. It should be remembered that the appearance of officers in such uniforms and equipment might give rise to complaints or claims of the police escalating the situation, so care and balancing of needs should be exercised. Agencies should either take photographs of or visually record the uniforms and equipment used as this can provide additional documentation for any investigations and the after-action report. Comprehensive policies and procedures should guide uniforms and equipment. All decisions should be thoroughly documented.

Recommendation 135: Solid impact projectiles generally should not be used against the crowd as a whole except in extreme situations.

As previously discussed, these tools are not designed for general widespread use against crowds. They are designed and appropriate for use against individuals based on their individual dangerous, threatening, or assaultive behavior. These tools include rubber bullets, bean bag rounds, and wooden knee knocker rounds. They are designed to inflict pain in a less than lethal manner to convince the person to stop their actions.

If an individual is engaged in actions that are a danger to others, including officers, but does not rise to the need for deadly force, then these types of tools are appropriate. Policy should outline all authorized and prohibited uses. It may be appropriate to use these tools against persons who are assaulting officers in various ways, fleeing or resisting arrest for violent offenses or significant property damage. If the crowd or a number of individuals are engaged in such dangerous activities, then it might be appropriate to use these devices against the specific crowd or groups. It would also be appropriate to use such tools when innocent citizens are in danger, officers are in danger or the officers' position is in danger of being overrun. They should only be used within existing policy and only by personnel who have been trained in their use. Great care should be exercised to utilize these tools against persons who are a danger, and not against those who might be peaceful. The devices should be aimed at the torso or legs. Care should be used as the devices might not be as accurate as firearms and other persons might get into the pathway of the projectile. All use should be fully documented including documentation of every round. Medical care should be provided and/or requested as appropriate.

Recommendation 136: Tear gas should be allowed and regulated by policy.

Understanding that this event has turned destructive, noncompliant, or violent, it is necessary for police to have various tools available to regain control and stop the destruction, noncompliance, or violence. Policies, plans, and procedures should specifically indicate how and when various types of tear gas may and would be used. The plan may identify certain levels of command that are authorized to allow or order various types of gases or devices. Tear gas may be used in a variety of methods including personal officer use, large canisters, foggers (handheld or larger), thrown devices, and pepperball-type devices. Which device is used depends on the circumstances. Warnings should be given prior to use when feasible. Avenues of departure should be created and announced so that persons can disperse.

Tear gas devices are best used with individuals or crowds who are committing certain crimes or have become generally noncompliant. They should not be used against a crowd that is simply protesting or refusing to disperse from an otherwise peaceful compliant protest. It should be remembered that some tear gas mechanisms may be more susceptible to affecting unintended persons. The police should be aware of the mechanisms of various delivery methods and how narrowly focused or widespread each mechanism may be. This is necessary so that the tear gas is used against the intended targets and has as little impact elsewhere as possible. Medical care should be provided or requested as appropriate. All use should be documented.

Recommendation 137: Detailed directives should control the use of other devices.

Comprehensive policies, procedures, and plans should exist that specify when other tools, techniques, tactics, devices, vehicles, and weapons can be used. Each successively more severe level of force should be authorized by higher levels within the organization if practical. In some circumstances, the agency's standard policies and procedures would guide officer and agency response to resistance, and would not require specific approval. The event or response plan for the specific event or situation should include a list of the tools, equipment, and vehicles that are immediately available for use by event commanders. The event plan should consider which tools, tactics, or techniques will be utilized for various scenarios that might occur. As much preplanning and consideration for various scenarios should be considered so that advance thought and calm reasoning is used to develop response actions. Additional tools that might be appropriate in any given situation might include audio devices, individually directed impact weapons, and firearms.

Any tool, technique, tactic, device, or weapon that might be used in these types of events (or in any situation) should be regulated by comprehensive directives. All personnel authorized to use any tool should be trained in its use. This includes bicycles, barricades, and vehicles of all types. Any use should be thoroughly documented.

Recommendation 138: Agency plans should provide dispersal routes.

Agency plans should allow for protests and protesters to leave the area if they choose to do so or are directed to do so. If a dispersal order is given, there must be a pathway for the crowd and/or those individuals desiring to do so, to leave the area. The dispersal route should be repeatedly announced to event participants so they understand what the preferred routes are. The routes should be sufficient for the size of the crowd. Consideration should be given to what route is provided to ensure that the chosen route does not create more problems than keeping the crowd in its current location. The dispersal route should be safe for the crowd, the area, and agency personnel.

Recommendation 139: The agency should clearly announce all changes.

It is always much more desirous to have the crowd comply with the directions of the police. This applies to daily life and expected compliance with laws, and is even more beneficial when emergencies, events, or critical incidents occur. To comply with police directions and expectations, people need to know what the directions are, and how to comply. They should also be given reasonable time to comply with the directions. Changes in routes, status, legal declarations, and warnings should be clearly announced several times and in such a manner as to reasonably believe that the majority of the crowd and individuals have heard the announcements. The announcements should be made multiple times and should include desired routes of egress and so on. The primary goal is to get the crowd to comply with police directions. If the direction involves a dispersal order, the crowd can be more successful if they know the route and other relevant information.

Recommendation 140: A comprehensive after-action report should be completed and reviewed by the agency and other relevant entities.

Incidents such as these are generally rare, but have occurred more frequently in 2020 and 2021. These incidents are extremely dangerous and have huge ramifications for officers, chiefs, agencies, and communities. An after-action report is critical for concerned parties to learn about the incident. Learning opportunities exist throughout the event, including, pre-event, during the event, and post event. Topics that should be reviewed and analyzed include intelligence, communications (internal and external), planning and plans, tactics, equipment, contingency plans and options, training, and personnel issues such as numbers, relief, and support.

All reports and video should be compiled and included in the report. Reports and input from other agencies should also be requested, discussed, and considered. The after-action should be a document wherein the lead agency and other entities can understand what transpired, how events migrated or changed as they did, and how a better outcome can be realized if possible.

Chapter 17

Pursuits

The International Association of Chiefs of Police (IACP) defines "vehicular pursuit" as "an attempt by an officer in an authorized emergency vehicle to apprehend a suspect who is actively attempting to elude apprehension while operating a vehicle as defined by applicable law."[11]

People have tried to flee from police (or their counterparts) for centuries. Pirates used their ships to flee from naval authorities, robbers and horse thieves fled from lawmen on horseback, and people have fled from the police on foot forever. It all stems from the desire to commit a crime or rule violation, and to avoid being caught and held accountable for their actions. Virtually every person who commits a crime or violates one of society's norms hopes to avoid detection and get away with the offense. While this section focuses on vehicular pursuits, pursuits of any manner should be covered by policy. This includes aircraft, all-terrain vehicles, bicycles, and even foot pursuits. This is for the safety of all concerned.

As motor vehicles began to appear, they became popular mechanisms for criminals to use in committing many of their crimes. They used them to get to the scene, carry away the fruits of their crimes, to flee the scene of crimes, and to flee from police. Society and governments began providing vehicles to police agencies so they could patrol larger areas with a single officer instead of multiple foot beat officers, could respond quicker to citizen calls for service, and to enable police to catch criminals who fled. Police also began using vehicles to enforce the newly created motor vehicle laws that were and are designed to protect citizens. This led to the inevitable motorized pursuit of criminals, rule breakers, and suspects by police as they attempted to avoid detection, capture, and ultimate responsibility for their actions. As time and technology has progressed, virtually every mode of transportation have been used by criminals to flee from police. This includes bicycles, motorcycles, skateboards, motorized boats, jet skis, snowmobiles, parachutes, and various types of aircraft.

Vehicle pursuits, the pursuit of one vehicle by another, have become an important topic of discussion in society and in the police profession. They have become relatively frequent, very popular, and sometimes deadly. Many people like watching police pursuits. This is partially evidenced by the number of car chases (police or not) in TV shows and films. It is also demonstrated by the number of police chase videos that fill the internet and how popular live broadcasts of police pursuits are on television. Over 95 million people watched as the police chased O.J. Simpson as his white Ford Bronco refused to stop for police on June 17, 1994.[2] He was wanted pursuant to arrest warrants for the murder of two people.

Some of the latest official data shows the prevalence and impact of police pursuits. The 2017 report of the Bureau of Justice Statistics "Police Vehicle Pursuits, 2012–2013"[3] is the most recent official report. It estimates that state and local law enforcement agencies conducted approximately 68,000 vehicle pursuits in 2012.[4] It is an estimate since the number is based on a survey of a nationally representative sample of agencies that covered approximately 92 percent of full-time officers.[5] This number includes pursuits that were brief and long durations and those that were short or lengthy in distance. The report also highlights that from "1996 to 2015, an average of 355 persons (about 1 per day) were killed annually in pursuit related crashes."[6] This is a lot of pursuits and a lot of deaths. The majority of deaths (65 percent) in police pursuits are to occupants of the pursued vehicle, with innocent citizens, those not involved in the pursuit, accounting for 33 percent of the fatalities.[7]

It is, therefore, appropriate that there be significant discussion regarding vehicular pursuits. But this discussion must be more than whether police should pursue or not. It must look at society's expectations to comply with societal expectations overall (not committing crimes); its expectations regarding responsibility of the criminal who chooses to flee; when should police pursue; and ensuring that excellent policy, procedures, and training exist for when police do pursue.

It must also be remembered that the person who has the most control of a pursuit is the driver of the fleeing vehicle. They have the option at all times to stop their flight and surrender to lawful authority. Many people choose to blame the police for pursuing, and they want to hold the police accountable for anything that goes wrong. This is a largely flawed position. Yes, the police have a responsibility to conduct their activities, including pursuits, in as safe a manner as possible. But to hold the police accountable for another person's decision to unlawfully act (flee) is shifting the blame and responsibility from the unlawful to the police. The argument that some use that the attempt to stop the violator by police caused the violator to flee is misplaced. Society expects people to comply with the law and lawful authority of the police. There is no right to flee. Police must be reasonable, but generally they should not be held accountable for the actions of the law violator or criminal as they flee to avoid their own responsibility.

Recommendation 141: Every agency should have comprehensive policies and procedures covering all aspects of vehicle pursuits.

It is imperative that every police or law enforcement agency have a policy and procedure that comprehensively guides and regulates police pursuits of and with vehicles. The agency should also have a policy regarding foot pursuits as they can be dangerous, and are more so for officers than citizens. Fortunately, most agencies do have pursuit-related policies as over 96 percent of state and local agencies have written pursuit policies.[8] But due to the issues surrounding pursuits, each policy must be comprehensive and provide great guidance to officers, supervisors, and the agency. A good policy with excellent guidance and high levels of compliance can be safer for citizens and officers.

A comprehensive policy should cover certain key items. The most important is arguably when and when not to pursue. This is the foundation of the policy as it determines when pursuits are authorized and when they are not. Pursuit policies can be generally classified into one of two types: restrictive or discretionary. Although the classifications are somewhat subjective, restrictive-type policies impose more restrictions on when a pursuit is authorized, how it is conducted, and when it should be terminated. Discretionary-type policies allow the officers and supervisors more discretion in deciding all aspects of a pursuit. Discretionary pursuit policies provide guidance to officers, but leave more decision-making abilities to the officers and supervisors. There are also versions of each type with "permitted, but subject to supervisory approval and review" being a version of a discretionary-type policy, and "prohibited" being an extreme version of a restrictive type policy. It really is a matter of control and specificity in the policy.

At a minimum, the agency should have a policy that covers the following aspects:

- Pertinent definitions
- Value of human life, balancing needs to apprehend versus risks of pursuit
- When is a pursuit authorized, what offenses and situations
- When should a pursuit be terminated
- Environmental, vehicle, driver, and radio conditions
- Radio protocol
- Role of officers, supervisors, communications, air service
- Methods and techniques of pursuit terminations

- Legal aspects and considerations
- Leaving agency jurisdiction and/or assisting other jurisdictions
- Documentation and review of pursuits

The policy should be as comprehensive as possible to supply as much guidance as possible to the officers, supervisors, and agency. It must be consistent with any applicable state laws and court decisions. It must also direct the officers and supervisors to constantly weigh the need for immediate apprehension versus the risks the pursuit generates to uninvolved and innocent citizens, the occupants of the pursued vehicle, and the officers involved in the pursuit. The agency should consider consulting the IACP's model policy[9] and its related documents as it provides excellent guidance. CALEA accreditation also requires agencies have a policy regulating police pursuits, and it has fourteen different aspects that need to be considered to be compliant with standard 41.2.2.[10] A comprehensive pursuit policy is not only imperative, it is beneficial to citizens, officers, and society.

Due to the highly mobile nature of vehicles, and the proximity of one jurisdiction to another, the pursuit policy should address the issue of other agencies pursuing vehicles in the agency's jurisdiction. Typically, this occurs when a vehicle fleeing one agency leaves that jurisdiction and enters another jurisdiction. But it can also occur when an agency with concurrent jurisdiction (such as a sheriff's office or state police) or limited jurisdiction (university, some federal agencies) within the agency's jurisdiction is involved in a pursuit. The agency's policy must address how and in what circumstances its personnel will assist another agency that is involved in a vehicle pursuit.

Some agencies, especially those with very restrictive policies, will not assist the other agency. Other agencies may only assist the pursuing agency if the reason for the pursuit is consistent with and authorized by the agency's own policies. Yet, some agencies take a broader view of the issue, and will render assistance to the pursuing agency, with most having additional guidelines in place.

While all the issues surrounding pursuits impact this specific situation, one of the key concerns actually centers on the safety and the nature of assisting another agency. Too many agencies view the issue only from the perspective of a pursuit. This is a limited and unsafe perspective. When an agency enters the jurisdiction of another agency, the entering officers generally have less knowledge of the area. They are trying to broadcast pertinent information, but especially information focused on their location. This location information is critical for many reasons. It enables other officers to try to assist the pursuing officer, allows other agencies to assist with traffic control, and offers the opportunity for other officers to assist when the pursuit ends. When the pursuit ends, the entering officer will need assistance. This might be general traffic and/or crowd control, medical or crash assistance, or assistance with detaining the subject(s) in the pursued vehicle. If the agency with primary or concurrent geographic jurisdiction is not close by, the situation can deteriorate, putting people at risk.

All police agencies will generally assist another agency, whether it is with traffic or crowd control, making arrests, helping with investigations, or delivering messages to people. Pursuits, however, have become the one area where some agencies limit their assistance. To some degree this is understandable. Agencies want to limit risk and liability from pursuits. But agencies should also consider the risks of their not being involved in pursuits within their own jurisdictions.

A good policy can protect everyone and make situations safer. The agency policy should look at this issue from a perspective of assistance to the other agency and general safety to the public. The policy should authorize a limited number of units to assist the other agency in the situation. This generally means that the responding agency allows its units to assist the other agency in specific ways. They might allow one or two units to engage in active pursuit behind the other agency. This provides immediate location and other information to the responding agency allowing that agency to make decisions that can protect others. This might include taking control of intersections ahead of the pursuit so that innocent vehicles don't enter the path of the pursuit. It might also enable the responding agency to utilize different methods such as tire deflation devices to terminate the pursuit. At the same time, the responding agency should try to ascertain the nature of the charges against the fleeing vehicle so they can make other decisions.

However, in these circumstances, the responding agency should be a support element of the pursuit and should not become the lead unit unless the initial pursuing agency becomes incapacitated and the violation is pursuable under the responding agency's policy. If the initial agency voluntarily terminates the pursuit, the responding agency should not automatically assume the pursuit unless it meets the responding agency's pursuit criteria. If the initial agency involuntarily stops pursuing (vehicle damage, etc.) then the responding agency should evaluate the charges and abide by its own policy.

The responding agency can and should also provide support to the initiating agency by being aware of the pursuit and trying to position themselves around the pursuit area so they can be in the immediate location to offer assistance. They can try to "parallel" the pursuit but must do so safely and within their own agency guidelines, specifically those dealing with pursuits, assistance to other agencies, and emergency response. This supports and assists the initiating agency without putting the responding agency into active pursuit.

Since these situations occur with some frequency, the agency must address the situation in its policy and provide guidance to its personnel. It cannot wait until the situation occurs and make policy and operational decisions on the fly. For officer safety, it is best to have the responding agency provide some type of close assistance to the initiating officer. For public safety, it is good for the responding agency to be involved at least to the point of helping to minimize risk to the innocent public. It would be beneficial for area agencies to coordinate their policies and assistance protocols so every agency understands the reasons why each agency might pursue, and understands the assistance they can expect from other agencies.

Recommendation 142: All pursuits should be thoroughly documented. This specifically includes pursuits that occurred, when pursuits are terminated quickly, or when pursuits are never started due to policy compliance.

Every pursuit should be thoroughly documented, and it is strongly recommended that a specific form or format be used. A standardized pursuit report helps to ensure that all the desired information is captured. The pursuit should be documented in a criminal or incident report as is necessary to support any relevant criminal charges against the fleeing driver. But a stand-alone pursuit report offers the agency the opportunity to capture much more in-depth information relevant to the pursuit and how it was handled.

The pursuit report should include as much information as possible. This allows for reviews and decision-making regarding the appropriateness of the pursuit, and whether it was compliant with policy. Specific items that should be included are:

- Date, time of initiation and termination
- Reason for pursuit initiation and subsequent charges
- Initiating officer, secondary officers, assisting officers
- Road conditions, including traffic density, area types (residential, highway, etc.)
- Weather conditions
- Speeds including most common, low, and high
- Distance traveled
- Supervisors involved, aware, or notified
- Information regarding any crashes, injuries, damages
- How, why, and by whom pursuit terminated
- Complete, detailed description of entire pursuit
- Any other information pertinent to the incident

The policy should require that the primary officer originate the main report, but should also require every officer that did anything related to the pursuit complete a pursuit report that documents exactly what they did. This provides additional information that the originating officer may not be aware of. It also documents all who were involved so the agency can constantly review its policy and procedures, and compliance therewith. The primary officer should submit the report to their supervisor prior to the end of the current shift.

All supporting materials should be collected specifically including radio tapes, computer messages, and all video from in-car and body-worn cameras. These items should be collected from every officer that responded to or assisted in the incident in any way. If applicable, video from traffic control systems, general area surveillance, aerial video, and private sources should be collected. This enables the agency and the community to have a more comprehensive view of how the pursuit progressed and the actions of the fleeing vehicle and the officers. The report should be as comprehensive as possible.

As mentioned, most agencies have pursuit policies and the vast majority of them require some type of report to be completed for each pursuit. These generally do a great job of documenting pursuits that occur. However, many agencies do not require a report when the officer otherwise fully complies with the policy and did not originate a pursuit. These are generally described as situations when a suspect or vehicle operator flees from the police and the officer does not engage in a pursuit. In most cases, this occurs for traffic violations. The officer witnesses a traffic violation, activates their emergency equipment directing the vehicle operator to pull over and stop, but the driver does not stop and decides to flee the officer. If the policy does not allow pursuits for traffic offenses (and most policies prohibit pursuits for minor traffic offenses), and the officer does not engage in a pursuit, but discontinues all efforts to stop the violator, then they have fully complied with the spirit and intent of the policy.

The problem is that many agencies do not capture this information. And this is some of the most important information to capture—when officers comply with the policy. If the agency does not compile this information, then it is only capturing information when pursuits occur. While important, it is not the full picture of officer behavior and policy compliance. It is imperative that this type of information be compiled so that a comprehensive picture of pursuits and officer behavior can be realized. Even though technically no pursuit occurred, the easiest manner to capture such policy compliance is through the pursuit report. The report should indicate that no pursuit occurred but should capture as much detail as possible regarding the incident. This allows the agency and society to have more information regarding pursuits, citizen behaviors, and officer actions.

Recommendation 143: Pursuit reports should be reviewed through a prescribed chain of command, and by the training component.

Reports are important mechanisms to document specific events, incidents, crimes, or activities. They are important as stand-alone records of what occurred and what the agency did regarding the incident. But reports are equally important when they are read and used to review an incident, or pattern of incidents. Each individual pursuit report should do more than just document a single specific pursuit. It should progress through the chain of command so that each level can review the pursuit and add value to the review and analysis of the pursuit. Each reviewer should add their input regarding the appropriateness of the pursuit and if they have any suggestions for how the specific pursuit could have been handled better, or if they have suggestions for pursuits and pursuit management overall.

The first review of the pursuit report should be the immediate supervisor of the officer who initiated the pursuit. This first-line supervisor should review the report for completeness, accuracy as they might know of it, and ensure that all related reports and documentation are completed. Since multiple officers may have been involved, each individual report should be reviewed by their immediate supervisors and then all reports and documentation should be combined into a single pursuit package. Each immediate supervisor should sign the report and indicate whether they believe the pursuit was in compliance with the policy and agency expectations. They should be able to make any comments they feel are relevant or appropriate regarding the incident.

The next level in the chain of command, the supervisor over the first line supervisor of the originating officer, should review the entire pursuit package. They should seek additional clarification or information as they determine appropriate. After they have the information they need, they should indicate their views and opinions regarding the pursuit overall. They should make any recommendations they believe are beneficial. If the agency has procedures that require further review, then the package should progress accordingly. These might be related to any injuries, crashes, or special considerations resulting from the pursuit. If not, then the report should be forwarded to the training component and the component designated as the central repository for all pursuit packages. If there are concerns regarding policy violations, then the package should progress to and through the disciplinary process as outlined by the agency. Each pursuit should be viewed as a learning opportunity for the officers and the agency.

All pursuit packages should be reviewed by the training component to ascertain if the agency's training is sufficient. Training should examine the pursuit in its entirety to determine if the pursuit was handled in a manner consistent with training; to identify any deficiencies in training; and to identify any opportunities for enhancement in pursuit-related training. If each incident (whether pursuit or other type of incident) is to be used as a learning opportunity, those responsible for training should be involved in the review process.

The training component should not only look at the vehicle operation aspects of the pursuits, but should also review all facets of pursuit management. This would include the actions of all personnel including officers, supervisors, and communications personnel. They should examine if agency policies and procedure need to be reviewed to enable the agency to better respond to such incidents. Some of the information they may glean might result in recommendations for changes to training, equipment, and/or policy. An example might be how radio communications are handled agency-wide during pursuits; more training regarding pursuit intervention techniques; or if additional or different equipment is needed. Based on what the training component finds, they can make changes or recommendations for changes so that future pursuits can be managed in a more efficient and safer manner. This process helps to ensure that the police agency is truly a continuous learning environment.

Recommendation 144: Agency personnel should be trained in emergency vehicle operations generally, and pursuits specifically.

All agency personnel that operate an authorized emergency vehicle (as defined by applicable laws) should be trained to operate the vehicle in emergency response or driving situations. This includes a wide range of situations including, but not limited to, emergency response (using warning lights and/ or sirens) to calls for service, initiating traffic stops, blocking roadways, and pursuits of other vehicles. Most states have laws which define an authorized emergency vehicle, and what equipment is needed to be in operation for the vehicle to fully designated as an emergency vehicle. Some states also have laws that regulate the use of such equipment and have requirements for how the vehicles can be operated. This might range from the ability to stand, park, or drive irrespective of signage and general motor vehicle laws up to and including the ability to travel in excess of posted speed limits. But in most cases, states require the emergency vehicle operator to operate the vehicle in a safe, and non-reckless manner.

To meet these requirements, and to protect the safety of the community and agency personnel, it is imperative that officers and other appropriate personnel be fully trained in emergency vehicle operations. This training should include legal aspects (laws and court decisions), vehicle dynamics, agency policy, and actual practical hands-on training operating vehicles in an emergency response condition. Some agencies have driving simulators that can be very effective in training the basics of emergency vehicle operation. But even with simulators, the officers should have time in a real vehicle where they can experience the real-world dynamics of operating a vehicle in emergency conditions.

This practical training should include slow speed and highspeed operations so the student can understand the dynamics of the vehicle and its systems (especially steering and braking) when operated in various manners and conditions. They should have practical hands-on training that allows the student to corner, brake, make sudden decisions, and to understand stopping distance requirements at various speeds and in various weather conditions. They should experience real-world situations in a controlled learning environment where it is safer, before they actually have to operate a vehicle out in the community. The student should be required to pass a written test and a practical skills test before they are authorized to operate a vehicle in emergency status. Every officer drives, and at times must utilize emergency equipment and emergency operations driving skills. It does not only happen in pursuits, but it is imperative that officers have the requisite skills before the agency puts them into a situation where the skills might be necessary.

Pursuit training is an extension of the basic skills associated with emergency vehicle operations. It builds on the basic skills, but is more intensive and focused. It requires the vehicle operator to control the vehicle in a more challenging and changing environment than daily or call response driving. In most cases, the vehicle operator who is using emergency equipment to respond to a call for service, knows the route they will travel and can easily control the speed of the response. They can plan a little ahead and anticipate some of the circumstances which they will likely encounter. There is still uncertainty, and hence the operator must be ever vigilant and well skilled.

But pursuit driving adds more uncertainty, and usually more speed. It is more uncertain since the officer probably does not know the route they will be traveling since the fleeing person is picking the route they will travel. This adds uncertainty and stress to the officer. The speeds are generally set by the fleeing person, with the officer maintaining a reasonable speed and proximity to the fleeing vehicle. During the pursuit, the officer will also have to utilize the radio more frequently to keep other units informed of the locations, direction, and speeds of the pursuit. This increases the number of tasks that the officer will have to perform simultaneously. This is all in addition to the usual skills and awareness needed to drive normally or even in general emergency operation. The officer must continually observe their surroundings to watch for innocent vehicles and persons, to watch the movements and actions of the fleeing vehicle, and to monitor the actions of the fleeing vehicle's occupants. All of this adds stress to the officer.

To ensure compliance with applicable laws and agency expectations, and to ensure public safety, officers who are authorized to engage in pursuits must have specific pursuit-related training. Just because someone has a driver's license and has driven a car for some amount of time does not mean they can safely operate a vehicle in a pursuit. It is true that many of the people who flee from the police do not have training beyond a basic driver's course. And in many incidents they drive well and often times are successful in eluding the police. But they are not held to the higher standard of operating their vehicle safely. They are expected to obey traffic and other laws, can be charged with violations, and can even be charged criminally and sued civilly for their actions. But in most cases, they receive relatively light punishments for their actions, and are rarely in a position to pay damages in a civil action. Officers are held to a higher standard and generally suffer stiffer penalties for situations that occur when they operate vehicles in emergency situations, including pursuits. As previously mentioned, the public generally seeks to condemn and blame the officer for anything that occurs in a pursuit. This is true when the fleeing vehicle strikes an innocent vehicle and the police vehicle caused no damage.

For these reasons, personnel should be trained in actual pursuit driving. This should include classroom and general knowledge training regarding laws, court decisions, and agency policies. It must specifically include in-depth training regarding the agency's pursuit policies. One of the key aspects of the policy training must be the requirement to constantly evaluate the need for immediate apprehension of the suspect versus the risk to the officer and the general public. More serious criminal violations carry more weight than less serious, minor traffic offenses. Also the ability to positively identify the suspect and the ease of capturing him/her later without additional risk to the public must be considered. Understanding the pursuit policy and the key foundational beliefs and values of the agency are critical.

But pursuit training must include practical hands-on training and experience in actual operation of a motor vehicle in a pursuit situation. The officer must experience the focus and multitasking that is required in a vehicle pursuit. They must experience what it is like to operate the vehicle in a pursuit situation, and, at the same time, be aware of their location and surroundings, while operating the police radio to keep others informed of the status of the pursuit. They must understand and experience the actual dynamics of the vehicle as they change direction, accelerate, decelerate, brake, and make various vehicle movements to avoid items, while staying in reasonable proximity to the fleeing vehicle. They must also know when and how to terminate the pursuit by either ceasing their attempts to stop the vehicle or using any approved intervention techniques. The officer must also be able to safely, calmly, and professionally take the subjects into custody if the situation allows that.

If the agency authorizes any type of intervention techniques to terminate the pursuit, the officer must be fully trained in such techniques. They must have practical hands-on training and experience in these techniques. Such techniques might include the use of rolling or stationary roadblocks, boxing-in, precision/pursuit immobilization/intervention technique (PIT), tire deflation devices, and other techniques. If these are authorized, the officers must understand the issues, dangers, limitations, and advantages of each technique. They must be trained and experienced in each technique that they are authorized to use.

Pursuit training should be a combination of classroom and practical hands-on training that focuses on developing skills, knowledge, and abilities related to pursuit driving. Officers must be tested on all these aspects and must successfully pass all aspects of the training before they are allowed to engage in a pursuit. There must also be periodic refresher training to maintain the desired skill and knowledge levels. This additional training will reduce the number of pursuits, and enhance the safety of officers and citizens.

Recommendation 145: The agency should complete an annual analysis of all pursuits.

The agency should conduct a meaningful and comprehensive analysis of all pursuits on an annual basis. This analysis should be much more than a simple numerical count of pursuits with minor statistical data regarding day, time, and reasons for the pursuits. It should provide useful information to the chief and the agency so they can make decisions regarding the nature of pursuits in their community. The analysis should provide comprehensive information regarding the reasons for pursuit initiation, how long they lasted and how far they went, speeds, how terminated and by whom, and data regarding injuries and damages.

The analysis should provide sufficient information for decision-makers to consider the total costs of pursuits in the community. Citizen complaints and concerns, as well as any media articles regarding pursuits (especially in the specific community) should be included in the analysis. This helps to add public input and perspective into the review and decision-making process. It should provide them with information regarding their specific pursuit policy, their pursuit training, management of significant incidents, equipment, and larger policy implications. The analysis should also include the latest research regarding pursuit management, and any new tools, techniques, laws, or procedures that could enhance overall safety. This recommendation for a meaningful annual analysis is also consistent with CALEA standard 41.2.2.[11] The agency can only make meaningful decisions regarding pursuits by examining the overall nature of pursuits within their community. A comprehensive annual pursuit analysis is the mechanism for the agency to accomplish this necessary activity.

Part IV

EQUIPMENT

Police officers and agencies have a variety of tools and equipment available to enable them to accomplish the tasks and missions required of them. This is no different than any other profession. Some of these items are relatively common in policing and to the public such as marked patrol vehicles, handcuffs, and uniforms. Other items are specialized such as rescue vehicles, battering rams, helicopters, and weapons of various types. Due to technological advancements, policing today utilizes a significant amount of computers, software, communications methods, and cameras. Every tool and piece of equipment serves a purpose. Nothing exists in the inventory of agency-authorized tools, vehicles, or equipment that does not assist the agency and its personnel to better serve the citizens in a safe, efficient, or effective manner.

Over time, the types and variety of police equipment has changed. Policing started on foot with a whistle and lantern. Then vehicles were added to enable the officers to be more mobile. Batons and then later firearms were added to enhance the safety of officers and citizens. Firearms were used by early marshals and rangers in the "Old West" to meet the firearms used by outlaws, who resisted lawful arrest. Some of this evolution was due to changes in society overall, but also included technological advancements. Other changes or additions were due to changes in the nature of crime and how the peace and order of society was being threatened. But every tool, vehicle, or piece of equipment that policing has implemented, or uses today, exists to meet the threats from criminals and the challenges presented by keeping society and citizens safe. There are some items that cause concerns with some of the public, and there is considerable misunderstanding regarding some of these items. This part of the book will focus on major items, items that cause concern, and special items.

Chapter 18

Military Surplus and
Specialty Vehicles

An issue of considerable recent concern and focus involves the practice of using surplus military equipment and what some call the "militarization" of police. This term originated from some people who were concerned about local civilian police agencies acquiring surplus military equipment. The term has been expanded to include the attitudes of police, especially those who have military surplus equipment. The two concepts really should not be confused or intermingled as they are two different issues. One focuses on equipment, while the other focuses on attitude and mindset. There are some who advocate that equipment and appearance can positively or negatively impact attitude and mindset. In other words, some claim that having military surplus equipment and/or dressing in military-style clothing will cause the police to act more militaristic than if equipped and dressed differently. While there is some validity to this argument, one does not automatically lead to or produce the other.

Under federal law, surplus military equipment is made available to local governments for their use. The National Defense Authorization Act (NDAA) of 1990/1991 authorized the Department of Defense (DoD) to transfer excess property to federal, state, and local law enforcement agencies.[1] In 1997, the NDAA granted the Secretary of Defense the permanent authority to transfer DoD materials to law enforcement agencies. This occurred in section 1033 of the 1997 NDAA, hence the commonly used name of 1033 Program.[2] In June 2020, approximately 8,200 agencies participated in the program.[3] This represents less than half of all federal, state, and local law enforcement agencies in the United States. The primary users of this program are police agencies. The intent of the program is to provide equipment that is no longer useful to the military to state and local governments and agencies at greatly reduced costs. These items have generally outlived their cost-effective useful life and are being disposed of by the military. Police agencies can acquire many of these items at very low cost, thereby saving the citizens and communities considerable sums of money. The process involves the agency either finding the desired equipment on their own through a dedicated website or asking the state "point of contact" to find what the agency is seeking. Each state has a designated point of contact (POC) that is the coordination point for the transfer of any equipment. The POC helps find items, coordinates transfer, and tracks the items for a small administrative charge paid by the agency. If the item is located and the request is approved, the agency must make all arrangements for acquisition, transportation, and making any and all necessary repairs to the item so it can be useful and operational.

The primary reason the program exists is to continue the usefulness of surplus equipment. Taxpayers have already paid for this equipment. And if the item can have a second life by a government to help service the citizens, it is an economical benefit to everyone. Agencies utilize the program because it saves considerable sums of taxpayer funds. For example, a small armored vehicle purchased new from a civilian manufacturer generally costs $250,000–$350,000 or more. These vehicles are similar to vehicles used by banks and cash transfer services to protect cash and other valuables in transit. A military armored vehicle generally costs approximately $2,000 to acquire through the state POC. Transportation, mechanical repairs, and paint will cost the agency anywhere from $2,000 to more than $20,000 depending on the location and condition of the vehicle. So the local agency can put into operation an armored vehicle from the military surplus program for roughly 1/10th ($22,000 versus $250,000) the cost of purchasing a new civilian made vehicle. In many cases, the military surplus vehicle may be larger than the civilian vehicle but it still serves the same purpose of keeping officers and citizens safe during critical incidents. None of the vehicles come with weapons mounted on them.

Other items besides armored vehicles are available including helicopters, clothing, rope, generators, non-armored vehicles such as pick-up trucks and 6×6 trucks, fencing, and many more items. Knives and guns are available but in very limited supplies and are strictly regulated. According to a National Police Foundation (NPF) June 2020 report that reviewed acquisitions from June 2019 through May 2020, most agencies requested clothing items such as jackets, boots, shirts, and pants.[4] Mine-resistant vehicles (armored vehicles) were requested by 169 agencies during this review period.[5] Regarding the 1033 Program, the NPF stated:

> While some agencies and states continue to receive military equipment such as mine resistant vehicles, rifles and associated parts, the vast majority of equipment transferred during this period consists of clothing, personal protective

equipment such as gloves and facemasks, and basic infrastructure needs such as wiring, tools, generators, etc. States and local communities save hundreds of thousands of dollars through the program. The Foundation encourages those considering policy changes to examine the data and respond in ways that don't diminish the appropriate uses and value that states and local communities receive.[6]

These items, especially armored vehicles, have been used by police agencies for decades. They are generally used as rescue vehicles, to rescue officers or citizens who are injured or under attack. They can also be used to stop active shooter threats and end barricaded subject situations. In many cases, they act as a deterrent to using force since the officer can be safer in the vehicle as they rescue citizens or officers. The vehicles can also be used as a method of de-escalation in that the appearance and presence of the vehicle has sometimes convinced the armed and dangerous subject to surrender without additional injuries to anyone.

The fact that these items come from the military does not automatically impact, change, or modify the attitude or mindset of the agency or its personnel. These items are simply tools to resolve dangerous situations, rescue officers or citizens, or transport people when they are or may be subjected to gunfire. The items are acquired to handle and respond directly to threats that actually exist to the community and the officers. And the equipment saves lives while saving the taxpayers hundreds of thousands of dollars annually.

Recommendation 146: Agencies should have comprehensive policies and procedures regarding each type of specialized vehicle in their inventory.

For each type of specialized vehicle in the agency's inventory, there should exist comprehensive policies and procedures regarding the use of each vehicle. These policies and procedures should include why the vehicle is in the inventory, what is its purpose, and how does the vehicle help fulfill the mission of the agency. The procedures should also specify when the vehicle may be used, what are any prohibitions against its use, and the specific details of how it will be used. Other aspects that should be included in the policy include what training is required to operate the vehicle, who and how can the vehicle be "checked out" and utilized, and who and how the vehicle will be maintained. It should also be defined as to what equipment will be stored on or in the vehicle.

The term "specialized vehicles" is purposefully and generally very broad. It is more than just military surplus vehicles. It can include trucks, various types of motorcycles, off-road vehicles, bicycles, snowmobiles, various types of watercraft, crime scene vehicles, prisoner transport vehicles, mobile command posts, ice-cream trucks, and aircraft. It basically includes anything other than a standard passenger car, whether fully marked and equipped, plainclothes, or civilian transportation. Since these various specialized vehicles exist for special or unique situations, there should be comprehensive policies regulating their use.

In order to maintain proficiency with any specialized vehicle, certified operators should operate the vehicle at least monthly. This helps to maintain the skills, knowledge, and abilities of designated personnel to competently operate the vehicle. Depending on the vehicle, the operators should drive or operate the vehicle consistent with its intended use so that in critical situations, the operator is very comfortable and competent in operating the vehicle.

This monthly operation of the specialized vehicle also allows the vehicle to be checked out and inspected so as to ensure it is functionally operational and capable of performing its intended duties. Vehicles cannot and should not be allowed to sit unused for months at a time, with the expectation that they will be capable of fully performing in critical incidents. The operator should fully inspect the specialized vehicle to ensure that all fluids are at appropriate levels; that all key systems (electrical, starting, lights, communications, and braking) are functioning properly; and that any equipment is ready for immediate use. The inspections and periodic operating sessions should be fully documented. Any deficiencies should be reported and fixed immediately. Any specialized vehicle that is not maintained in operational condition or that cannot be safely and competently operated is of no use to the agency or the community.

Recommendation 147: The use of armored vehicles should be carefully regulated. Such vehicles should be shown to the public.

Armored vehicles exist to protect officers and citizens. Unfortunately, some citizens view the mere presence of such vehicles as an escalation by the police. The reality is that these vehicles are defensive, not offensive. They are designed to transport personnel into or out of a dangerous area. They do not and should not have firearms mounted on or attached to them. In reality, these vehicles very much resemble armored vehicles used by banks and armored car companies to transport money and other valuables. However, understanding the perception that some have regarding such vehicles, the visible presence of these vehicles should be a consideration in how the vehicles are actually used. But if the situation warrants the use of such vehicles, then they should be utilized responsibly and within existing policies. Each situation will be different and the use of armored vehicles should be based on the specific situation encountered. This is no different than any other tool.

Armored vehicles are most likely to be used in situations involving barricaded subjects, hostage situations, active shooters, or rescues. The vehicles primary purpose is to protect people from gunfire. It can allow officers to get closer to incidents in which firearms are being used. What the officers do from there is dependent on the specific situation and the actions of the citizen(s) involved in the incident. They might be able to negotiate, deploy smoke or tear gas, or provide medical or food materials as appropriate to the situation. The vehicle might enable officers to rescue an injured citizen or officer without placing the rescuing officers in an unprotected position during the rescue.

Understanding the perception of these vehicles, they generally should not be upfront or highly visible in peaceful protests. In noncompliant or violent events, it is appropriate to have the vehicles in operation. This provides the opportunity for everyone to be aware that the event has turned away from being peaceful and the vehicle's presence does signal that additional tactics are warranted and may be used by the police. It also provides protection for officers from thrown objects and would allow rescues of officers and citizens to take place. How these vehicles will be used should be part of the police operational plan for the event.

It is also recommended that these vehicles be made visible in various community events such as parades, National Night Out, and other events of a positive nature. This can be part of community outreach, community interaction, or general information efforts by the agency. By letting the community see and understand the nature and use of these vehicles, there will be less misinformation and misperception about them and their use. Any use of the vehicle should be completely documented in reports. It is also suggested that the vehicle be equipped with video cameras so its use can be fully recorded for later review.

Hiding armored vehicles, military surplus vehicles, or rescue vehicles from the public only adds to the negative perceptions, fears, concerns, and suspicions. If the vehicles are generally hidden from view, and only used in certain situations, there is more of a likelihood that some will dislike the vehicles or mistrust the police use of them. The vehicles should be shown to the public when acquired and placed into operation. Ideally, the acquisition of the vehicle was publicly known so it isn't a surprise when it arrives. Besides being used in police-community events, the vehicles should also be used in natural disasters like floods, and can be used to help locate missing persons in bad weather or rough terrain. By being transparent about what the vehicle is and what it isn't, the agency can help reduce negative concerns and build trust and support.

Recommendation 148: Any surplus military vehicle acquired by the agency should be repainted prior to use.

Understanding the perceptions surrounding military vehicles in civilian use and possibly confronting citizens, it is beneficial for the agency to remove the military appearance from the vehicle. Yes, the size and actual construction of the vehicle will not change. But repainting the vehicle from a military paint scheme can have tremendous effects and benefits. It takes away that initial shock of seeing a military vehicle on American streets. It must be remembered that due to immediate news and social media, people have seen these vehicles in wars, in armed conflicts, and in foreign countries. By repainting them to a nonmilitary and non-camouflage paint scheme, some of the edge, complaint, and comparison can be reduced or eliminated. It also serves to reduce the applicability of the argument regarding the officer/agency mindset from moving toward a militaristic view. The paint scheme can be white, blue, black, or match the general paint scheme of agency vehicles. The cost of repainting should be included in the total cost to acquire, repair, and place the vehicle into operation. The agency should repaint the vehicle before it is placed into operation or displayed to the public. But changing it from the military paint scheme can have sizable benefits for everyone.

Recommendation 149: Specialty vehicles should not have firearms affixed to them.

Specialty vehicles should not have firearms affixed to them, especially those that are military surplus vehicles. It is not practical to have firearms affixed to vehicles in the civilian environment, as firearms are intended as individual weapons, not group or crowd-focused weapons. Affixing firearms to vehicles will certainly appear to be more militaristic and will most likely inflame people's views and perceptions about the vehicles themselves.

The vehicles may have firearms in them, or transport personnel with various firearms depending on the mission and purpose of the vehicle. In this sense, these vehicles are no different than marked police vehicles. Some optional equipment that is appropriate for vehicle mounting includes gas/smoke dispersal systems, water systems, and various sensors. These enable gas/smoke to be dispersed into buildings or violent events. The water systems enable the rescue vehicle to put water on fires that involve barricaded shooters and on other fires that a fire truck might not be able to safely reach. If the vehicle is equipped with a water nozzle, very detailed policies and procedures should exist regarding authorized and unauthorized uses. This should specifically include direction as to if and when the water function can be used in crowd control efforts. Whatever equipment is part of any specialized vehicle must be covered by comprehensive policies and procedures that govern their use, documentation, and related training for operators.

Chapter 19

Helicopters, Airplanes, and Unmanned Aerial Vehicles

Aircraft, especially airplanes, have been used by police agencies for decades. The original use was to help with traffic flow in major urban areas. Over time, the uses expanded as did the different types of aircraft. Some agencies are able to utilize various types of aircraft to accomplish the mission of keeping the community safe. Police aircraft have saved countless lives (suspects, officers, and citizens), assisted in call response, found lost or missing persons, and provided tremendous amounts and types of information. These tools act as a force multiplier, can move more quickly to scenes and calls, and can greatly assist in routine calls, investigations, emergency situations, and disasters. They have been particularly helpful in vehicle pursuits, locating fleeing suspects, checking large areas, and locating and rescuing lost and injured persons.

Unmanned aerial vehicles (UAVs), or drones as they are sometimes called, have become increasingly popular, useful, and cost effective. These small remote controlled vehicles can provide an aerial view of crash scenes, crime scenes, fires, disasters, events, or general areas. They send a video to various receivers that enable command personnel to make more informed and more timely decisions about dynamic situations. Their cost-benefit ratio is outstanding, and they can greatly improve officer and citizen safety.

Recommendation 150: Any agency utilizing any type of aircraft or unmanned aerial vehicle must have comprehensive policies and procedures regarding their use.

Policy and procedure must exist for every type of vehicle, tool, technique, tactic, or weapon used by a police agency. Aircraft are no exception and actually are one of those high liability areas that require very comprehensive directives. Due to the complexity of aircraft, the risks associated with flight, and citizen concerns regarding aircraft use, it is imperative that all aspects of aircraft operation be regulated and controlled by comprehensive policies and procedures. The use of aircraft is also governed by additional laws, rules, and regulations promulgated by states and federal agencies including the Federal Aviation Administration (FAA). Various state and federal courts have also heard cases and issued decisions regarding the use of aircraft. Agency directives must consider and be compliant with these laws, regulations, and rulings.

These policies, procedures, and directives should include the purpose and mission of the aircraft, safe operation, operator certification, maintenance, and parameters of use. The protection of citizen rights and safety must be a high priority in any aircraft operation, and these must be affirmatively dealt with in the policies. The agency should have its own requirements for who can operate any type of aircraft, but these requirements must include proper certification by the FAA and any other entity that has lawful jurisdiction over the aircraft. FAA certification as might be applicable should be the absolute minimum requirement with the agency supplementing its additional requirements as they deem appropriate.

The operation of occupied aircraft is generally complex in the best of circumstances. But operating an aircraft for police purposes, in the expected circumstances, is even more complex and difficult. It is strongly recommended that the agency require two occupants to be present in aircraft being operated for police purposes and tasks. This is especially true in helicopter operations. A pilot is needed to operate the helicopter, monitor its systems, and use the radio as necessary. A trained flight observer, typically referred to as a tactical flight officer (TFO) has the primary responsibility of carrying out most of the police-related duties. They coordinate information between the helicopter and ground units and/or the communications center. They handle the spotlights, infrared, and camera systems while the pilot flies the helicopter. Some agencies have used and some continue to use a single pilot to do all these tasks, but this should be discouraged due to the magnitude of handling all these tasks simultaneously. It is best and safest to have two personnel present to handle the amount of tasks expected of a flight crew.

The policy should clearly identify the weather and environmental conditions in which the aircraft will operate with the intent of ensuring the safety of the public, the operators, and the aircraft itself. The aircraft should always be operated within the operational parameters and limitations of the specific aircraft type. Maintenance should be at least compliant with manufacturers recommendations and FAA requirements. The agency should identify how and when the aircraft should be utilized for situations such as for pursuit, so the grounds units can "back off" close pursuit if the situation warrants and allows it. The policy should specifically address agency-added equipment including infrared, spotlights, cameras, and anything else the agency adds.

This is to ensure that the agency has thought about all aspects of the many issues of aircraft operation. Clear and comprehensive policies and procedures will enhance the overall operation, but specifically the protection of citizen rights, and the safety of the community, the operators, and the aircraft.

Recommendation 151: All operators must be appropriately trained and certified.

While there should be detailed agency policies and procedures regarding aircraft use and operation, and operator training and certification, there are additional regulations that apply to aircraft operation. The FAA has authority over aircraft including those operated by civilian police agencies. The agency directives must require full compliance with all FAA regulations. This includes pilot or operator training and certification, operational guidelines, and equipment standards and maintenance.

The agency should require full FAA certification and licensing in the type of aircraft that is operated by the agency. It should also require additional time operating the specific agency aircraft in the agency's operational environment. The agency should have its own internal training program that exceeds FAA requirements. This would include familiarization with the area in which the aircraft and pilot will operate in, handling the aircraft systems and relevant police equipment, and ensuring the pilot has a sound understanding of policing. In most cases, the pilot should be a police officer, so they have the basic, practical understanding of what information would be helpful to the officers on the ground. Even though some agencies hire and utilize non-sworn pilots, there are additional operational advantages to having a pilot and flight crew that understands policing. Having just the basic FAA certification is not sufficient for operating a police aircraft in various circumstances.

Personnel that operate UAVs should have all relevant and available types of FAA certification for emergency and routine situations, including out-of-line-of-sight operation. Since this is a relatively new field, operators must keep informed of pending rule changes, best practices, and changes in equipment and technology. They should immediately comply with new recommendations or requirements as they are implemented. All air service personnel (pilots, tactical flights officers, drone operators, mechanics, and commanders) should keep themselves current on regulations, safety standards, best practices, and equipment issues. They should belong to relevant professional organizations such as the Aviation Committee of the IACP[1] and the Airborne Public Safety Association (APSA).[2] This provides ongoing professional education as well as access to various resources, reports, and relevant information.

Recommendation 152: Aircraft and UAV should be equipped with video capabilities.

In an effort to document what the operator and aircraft did, how the aircraft was utilized, and for future investigative and prosecutorial processes, all aircraft should have video recording capabilities. It is best to have the capability for live downlink to various receivers so other personnel including commanders can have real-time information to assist in decision-making. These recording capabilities enable the aircraft to be fully beneficial, document activities, and respond to complaints.

There is and will be concerns by some of the public regarding privacy issues. These concerns are magnified with the increased use of drones by government agencies, specifically police agencies. The agency should be aware of these concerns, new laws, and any relevant court decisions. As legislatures and local governments consider laws, rules, or regulations governing the use of aircraft and cameras, recording, or surveillance from any type of aircraft, police professionals and agency leaders should be involved in these considerations. They should be knowledgeable regarding the current state of regulations and be capable of discussing how such systems and equipment are and would be operated. The agency should have comprehensive policies in place prior to placing any such equipment into operation. There should be comprehensive policies and procedures that guide how video will be used, when it will used, and the maintenance of all video.

Recommendation 153: The public should have knowledge of these resources.

All police resources exist for the purpose of assisting the agency in delivering services to the public and keeping the public safe. The public should be aware of what resources the agency has; and should have input into the acquisition and use. The agency should announce what equipment it is desirous of acquiring, and then there should be reasonable discussion about it. The agency should be able to identify what the resources are, why they are needed, how they will assist in maintaining order, keeping the public safe, and serving the public. The agency should also be able to answer questions regarding any concerns the public may have regarding the use of these resources.

This does not necessarily mean that the public should approve each item, but rather that the public should be informed and knowledgeable of police resources. The reality is that in most communities, virtually all police requests and resources are publicly known or the information is available. This is generally due to the budget process applicable to most agencies. These require that the applicable governmental board (council, commission, etc.) must approve the budget of police agencies. An informed public that has had opportunity for input will be more knowledgeable about the agency and the agency will be more transparent.

Chapter 20

Cameras

Video documentation has become more available, cost-effective, commonplace, practical, and expected. Virtually every police-citizen encounter and every police action is now recorded in some manner. Citizens driving down the street, walking, or shopping that happen to see police officers engaged in some kind of activity are recording officer actions, predominantly in hopes of recording the officer doing something wrong or being involved in a force situation. In many cases, these videos are livestreamed to the world.

Many agencies have cameras of various types. Some have in-car cameras that begin recording when the emergency equipment (lights or siren) is activated. Some systems record when certain speeds are reached, or there is some type of impact to the vehicle. Officers can also activate the cameras manually. These in-car cameras are predominantly dash cameras that look forward through the front windshield, but some systems also record the interior areas of the police vehicle where detained persons sit. A growing number of agencies have more recently begun using body-worn cameras (BWC). These cameras provide additional information, documentation, and understanding of police actions, activities, and interactions. This is a positive benefit for the profession, the community, officers, and citizens.

There have been numerous studies regarding body-worn cameras. Some question the usefulness since the cameras in the study did not document police misconduct or lead to a reduction in complaints or use of force as many expected.[1] But the cameras did work and serve a purpose as they showed that the vast majority of officers do the job legally, ethically, professionally, fairly, and impartially. Other studies indicate that the use of force and complaints were reduced when body-worn cameras were utilized.[2] BWCs have also documented hundreds of incidents and situations wherein questions, concerns, or complaints were raised, with the vast majority of times the cameras were able to prove the officer acted appropriately. In some cases, the cameras showed the citizens to be the aggressive, improper party. Cameras also offered opportunities to observe officers performing heroic acts, saving lives, and acting with great restraint. Overall, police agency cameras, especially body-worn cameras are beneficial to everyone.

It must be understood that cameras of all types may not record everything that occurs or that is relevant. Citizens sometimes either accidentally or intentionally don't record an entire incident. When that video is viewed, it can provide an inaccurate perception of an incident and can lead to community concern or anger. Admittedly, in rare cases, officers have failed to use the cameras as expected. In these cases, the officers are usually disciplined, sometimes severely, and appropriately so. But even when used as expected, police cameras may not record everything that is pertinent, desired, or relevant. This is due to a variety of factors including where the camera is pointed, environmental conditions, user issues, and the nature of technology itself. It is also quite possible the camera recorded something the officer did not see or recognize, or that the officer saw something that the camera did not see and record. Because the cameras are technology, they can suffer breakdowns or be damaged. The camera itself may malfunction, or a cord may break. It also frequently occurs that the camera is knocked off of the officer and either is damaged or doesn't record the relevant actions. For these reasons, cameras, especially BWCs are not a panacea. But they are definitely a beneficial tool.

Cameras and the related recording and data storage systems have considerable costs. Costs have certainly dropped for the cameras themselves, but the cost is still significant depending on the camera type, accessories, and configuration of the overall activation system. The reality is that currently the camera, especially body-worn cameras, are not the most expensive part of a system. Storing all the videos in some kind of data storage system is the largest cost of operating cameras. Some agencies use systems that store the videos on their own servers while some of the more popular systems store the videos "in the cloud" using a vendor's storage system. The systems for storage and retrieval must allow for the videos to be stored for long periods of time, be searchable using various search elements or criteria, and allow the videos to be accessed by various persons. It must also provide security measures that document when the videos were made, contain various information about the video, and prevent the videos from being altered. While it is costly, the benefits far outweigh the costs.

Certainly one of the primary reasons for cameras, especially BWCs is to document the actions of officers as they interact with citizens and they perform the numerous tasks expected of them. Cameras can be quite helpful in most situations to ascertain what really happened and can, therefore, be used to show that the officer either did or did not perform as expected. They can be extremely helpful in critical incidents like use of force situations. Another important use for cameras focuses on training, skill development, and review of policies and equipment. By observing officer videos, an agency can determine if the officers individually and collectively are abiding by policy especially regarding legal issues, use of force, and demeanor when interacting with citizens. They can ascertain if there are training issues that need to be refreshed or revised, and they can help ensure that agency personnel have the right equipment to carry out their functions and tasks.

Recommendation 154: Comprehensive policies and procedures must exist that cover all aspects of the police cameras. This policy must specifically require full compliance by all personnel.

These written directives must detail every aspect and concern regarding police cameras and systems, especially body-worn cameras. Regarding BWCs, these procedures must specifically address when they will be worn, activated, and shut off. The policy should also guide how the cameras will be worn by the officers, and inform the officers of any restrictions regarding their use. The policy must consider all legal guidance including state laws, court decisions, and guidance from agency legal advisors. Legal guidance must be kept current to ensure that officers and the agency fully comply with all current legal expectations and restrictions. The policy must be as comprehensive as possible and include all the recommendations in this chapter. The policy must also stress that any deliberate interference with the cameras will result in disciplinary action.

Any activity involving a call for service, traffic stop, pedestrian stop, response to priority calls, and situations in which an arrest, ticket, or charge is likely, must be recorded. These are the types of incidents and encounters that are most likely to cause questions or concerns, so it is best to record all such encounters. It is recommended that all citizen interactions (except those that are purely positive and nonenforcement) be recorded.

Written directives must clearly and comprehensively identify when cameras, especially BWC, are to be worn and operated. While this would be part of the overall policy regarding cameras, this aspect is critical. If the cameras are not worn and operated as expected, then they will be counterproductive. The public will lose faith, trust, and confidence in the police whenever they believe that officers intentionally did not comply with the policy and failed to have the cameras operating. Many will believe the police are deliberately hiding their inappropriate or even illegal actions. Failure to fully utilize the cameras deprives everyone of knowledge and opportunity. Everyone misses out on potentially important information that could have been gathered if the camera was operating. Failure to operate the camera deprives the officer of the opportunity to have additional documentation of what happened. This loss of opportunity and information also applies to the agency, the involved citizen, and the entire community.

The directives should specifically state that deliberately turning the camera off, deliberately failing to activate it when required (and circumstances allow), or deliberately interfering with the camera operation, is a serious violation and would result in severe discipline such as suspension or termination. Accidentally, turning the camera off or not turning it on as required when the camera program is first introduced would be a training issue. Repeat instances of violating the policy or procedure should result in suspension unless unusual and exigent circumstances exist. It is also likely, that in a critical sudden, unexpected situation that the officer may not have time to turn the camera on if manual activation is required. An investigation into the circumstances would prove that exigent circumstances either did or did not exist. It should be made crystal clear to all personnel that cameras are to be worn and operated consistent with policies, and that failure to do so will result in severe discipline.

Recommendation 155: Initial and periodic refresher training must be mandated regarding the operation of all cameras especially BWC.

Prior to an officer wearing a BWC, they must participate in and successfully complete initial training. This training should include all aspects of the relevant agency policy; a discussion of the purpose of the cameras; the benefits and limitations of the cameras; how and where the cameras are to be worn; when the cameras are to be activated and deactivated; documentation of camera presence in reports; maintenance, functionality checks, and inoperability documentation; and how the cameras are activated and deactivated. The training must include practical exercises and demonstration in proficiency regarding the activation of the cameras. At the conclusion of this initial training, the officer should be comfortable with and competent to operate the equipment as the agency desires.

At least annually, the agency should hold refresher training regarding the use of cameras, especially BWC. This should include a review of the agency policy; any legal changes; examples of beneficial camera use; issues with camera failure, including operator error; and any other discussion that would be beneficial for enhanced operation of the cameras. It is imperative that agency personnel are utilizing the cameras as intended, so that their full benefits can be realized.

Recommendation 156: All patrol personnel should be issued body-worn cameras, and be required to use them pursuant to policy.

Patrol personnel are the ones that will respond to most calls for service and will have most of the contact with citizens. It is imperative that they be issued BWCs and that the cameras are activated according to agency policy. In today's operational environment, and consistent with public expectations, BWCs should be considered standard equipment and a cost of doing business. Having only some personnel wearing BWCs may save some money since fewer cameras are being operated. But no one is smart enough to know which officers will be involved in incidents where a camera would have been beneficial. Also, the small cost savings realized due to fewer cameras will be dwarfed by the damage done by not having a camera in a controversial or significant incident.

Recommendation 157: All police personnel should be required to wear and use body-worn cameras anytime they are making arrests, serving search warrants, conducting any type of enforcement actions, or involved in certain other activities.

Non-uniformed personnel who are involved in search warrants, making arrests, conducting high-risk activities such as active shooter, barricaded subjects or hostage situations, and other high-risk activities as designated by the agency, should be required to wear and operate BWCs. The logic for this is the same logic why uniformed officers should wear and operate BWCs. The use of force, arrests, and many other activities often cause concern with the involved individual or the community. Having additional documentation and video of what happened can quickly clear up any concerns. It is the nature of the activity that is concerning to many, and having video documentation offers an additional piece of contemporaneous, independent information that can be quite useful in determining exactly what happened.

Just about the only time BWCs should not be worn is when the nature of the activity (an undercover operation) or the identities of undercover personnel might be compromised. For the actual investigative parts of such operations, it would be prudent to not have cameras as that would compromise the investigation. But when it comes time for the serving of arrest and search warrants, cameras should be worn and operated. In some cases, it would be recommended that supervisors wear and operate BWCs as it would provide documentation regarding directions and decisions. This would be very useful for after-action reports and future training situations.

Recommendation 158: Body-worn cameras should be tested at the start of each shift.

A defective camera is of no value, and in many cases, actually causes more concern than not having one at all. By testing the camera at the start of the shift, the officer is acknowledging that the camera was working then. If it is tested and found to be defective, inoperative, or not fully functioning as expected (audio and video), then the officer should be required to immediately notify an on-duty supervisor. The supervisor should examine the camera to ascertain what the issue is and if it can be remedied at that time. If the camera cannot be made fully functional, the officer and supervisor should remove the camera from service, document and process it for repairs, and then acquire a working camera for the officer. If the officer cannot secure and use a fully functioning camera, it should be documented so all are aware that the officer does not have a camera. It is imperative that this documentation be completed before the shift, in a timely manner so as to avoid legitimate questions or concerns regarding the actual functionality of the camera. This protects the agency and officer should that officer become involved in a situation wherein the video would be useful. It helps to negate accusations that the officer didn't activate the camera or broke it before or during the call.

Recommendation 159: Policy should specify how and where the body-worn camera is to be worn.

Agency policy should provide clear and specific direction regarding how the body-worn cameras will be worn, used, and operated. The policy will be impacted to some degree by the specific camera being used by the agency. Most cameras are designed to be worn high in the center of the chest. Some can be worn on the shoulder while others can be worn on the head near one ear or the other. Some of the decisions regarding placement are tied to manufacturer while other decisions are tied to cost. Depending on make and model, some agencies allow the officers the flexibility of choosing where to wear the camera within limitations.

Camera placement is important as it can only record what it can "see." Having the camera located in the center of the officer's chest is the most common placement location. It allows the camera to record most activities that occur in front of the officer. But it can be easily blocked by the normal hand movements of officers as they perform various tasks. In the most critical situation, the use of firearms, the officer's hands will likely be raised in front of them, thereby effectively blocking the camera from recording almost anything except the officer's hands. This is not very useful for after-action reviews and determinations regarding what happened. Therefore, placing cameras in the center of the officer's chest is not the optimal location.

Having the camera mounted on one shoulder or the other eliminates many of the problems associated with center of chest mounting. However, it would have a tendency to move more with the movement and actions of the officer, especially their arms. This location may not provide as much useful information as desired or possible. In some cases, a chest or shoulder-mounted camera will record what is in front of the officer. But if the officer has bladed themselves (turned sideways for protection), is behind cover, or is looking to one side or the other, then the camera will not record what the officer is seeing and reacting to.

The best, preferred, and recommended location for mounting body-worn cameras is on the head at eye level. This can be on the front brim of a cap, or on the dominant hand side of the head. Some manufacturers have multiple head mounting options that include the brim of a cap, on glasses/sunglasses, or on a brace that wraps snugly around the back of the head allowing the camera to sit right near the temple. Wearing the camera on the dominant hand side of the head near the temple or on a cap brim directly in front of the officer provides maximum visibility for the camera. It is not easily blocked or compromised by hand or arm movements. Being mounted on the dominant side of the body also enables the camera to see what the officer is doing with his dominant hand and also reduces the likelihood of being blocked by any object that the officer is seeking cover behind. Being located on the head, at or near eye level, in the front or on the dominant hand side of the head allows the camera to see almost everything that the officer sees. And the officer generally is watching what is important and reacting to what they see. By having the camera track as nearly as possible the movements of the officer's head, the camera now sees more accurately what the officer is looking at, and, in most cases, what the officer is reacting to. Body-worn cameras can be of great assistance and benefit to everyone. But they must be able to record what is pertinent, relevant, and important. For maximum effectiveness and benefit, cameras should be mounted to record what the officer observes and reacts to.

Recommendation 160: Camera systems, especially body-worn cameras should be synchronized.

All of an agency's cameras, whether body-worn or in-car cameras, should be synchronized to provide the most comprehensive documentation possible regarding any type of incident. With some manufacturers this is already technically feasible and is offered as an additional service. The ultimate synchronization and coordination would be to have all cameras activated whenever any activation parameter occurs. If an officer activates the emergency equipment of their patrol vehicle, the in-car camera usually activates, but the body-worn camera does not. In the ideal system, once the in-car camera activates, the body-worn camera also activates. Some systems allow for automatic activation of body-worn cameras whenever a firearm is unholstered or if a CEW is powered on. Also, when any individual camera is activated, all other cameras (whether body-worn or in-car camera) in the immediate area should activate.

This type of automatic activation and coordination offers many advantages over independent systems requiring manual activation. With these coordinated systems, once any camera is activated, all others are automatically activated. This removes the need for individual officers to manually activate any camera, thus removing an opportunity for the camera not to be activated when desired or beneficial. This type of automatic coordinated system would provide substantially more video and documentation of any scenario or incident. It would provide more video since more cameras would be activated and they would be activated earlier and automatically. Video would also be available from many different perspectives, locations, and vantage points, thereby providing a more comprehensive view of the entirety of the situation.

However, it should be remembered, that with this enhanced documentation of what happened, any individual officer may not have seen what all the cameras recorded collectively. It would include the response of the officers, and more of what they actually encounter as they arrive and make early decisions regarding how to address the situation. Once again, while this increases the cost of the systems, additional video and documentation are a great benefit to the officer, involved citizens, the community, the agency, and the profession.

Recommendation 161: Videos should be randomly reviewed.

While there is value in the videos that would be recorded, the greatest value occurs when the videos are actually reviewed. In many cases, videos might only be reviewed for court presentation or when complaints occur. Certainly videos involving any complaint, use of force, and significant arrests or incidents should be reviewed by the agency. While the video is certainly helpful in these situations, there is much more value available. Videos should be randomly reviewed on a regular basis by various persons and entities. The purpose is to proactively ascertain if officers are performing as expected. These random proactive reviews can observe if officers treat citizens with proper dignity and respect; if they comply with agency procedures, policies, and expectations; if officers perform exceptionally; if agency policies and procedures are proper or need revision; if agency training needs to be modified; and if equipment is appropriate for the tasks. The benefits and proactive nature of these regular random reviews cannot be overstated as there is so much that can be learned. These random reviews act as an additional accountability and training tool.

First line supervisors cannot be on every call with every officer under their supervision. By reviewing videos, the supervisor can have a better, more complete and accurate picture of how the officer performs. This assists in evaluation, training, and development of the officer. First line supervisors should review at least three but preferably five videos per officer per month. This would supply a tremendous amount of information and would not be overly burdensome on the supervisor. On a random basis, other supervisors, managers, or entities should randomly review videos of agency personnel. The reasons for these additional reviews are the same as previously stated.

But having additional random reviews increases the number of videos that are reviewed which allows for more information to be gained by the agency. Having different persons and entities review the videos allows the videos to be reviewed from different perspectives. Some of these additional reviews might include Internal Affairs and Training, with each looking at the videos for individual and trend information.

Recommendation 162: State laws regarding police-related video should be reviewed.

Each state should review their laws regarding privacy and open records as they relate to police and government video. Many laws were written before the use of cameras, especially body-worn cameras by police. There is a very wide difference in how video, especially BWC video, is handled from state to state. In some states, agencies have decided not to wear body cameras specifically because of the applicable state laws. In other states, access to or the release of police video might be restricted due to it being considered part of an ongoing investigation or part of a personnel record. Some states allow the video to be released, but also allow it to be restricted. Some states require a court order to allow release.

The intent of a review of applicable state laws would be to allow and require publication of police video in critical incidents or other specified situations in a timely manner. The release of a video might help reduce public concern, outrage, rumors, and even protests or civil disturbances. By showing the public what the video indicates, there is an opportunity to inform the public about what happened and allow for a calmer and more beneficial dialogue. Now in fairness, in some situations, the video might aggravate the situation or inflame the public. But at least the public would have more information that is accurate. Regardless of what the video shows, there is the opportunity for accuracy, transparency, and explanation.

It is recommended that each state bring together involved persons to discuss how police video should be handled, and then make any beneficial adjustments to applicable laws. Some of those who should be involved in these discussions include police professionals, prosecuting attorneys, defense attorneys, citizens, collective bargaining units if applicable, legislators, citizens, and various interest groups. Part of the discussion should also involve retention periods for video as this would create some consistency. It would also impact storage costs depending on whether the retention period is shortened or lengthened. While it is important to release video when possible, there must be provisions to restrict access to videos if there is a legitimate concern that an active investigation might be hindered. Laws should require video to be released within five days unless there is a specific, articulable reason not to. If it is believed that releasing the video is not appropriate for whatever reason, the agency should be required to appear before a court of competent jurisdiction and explain the reasons, with the court making the final decision regarding release. This presumes that the video will be released, but it can be restricted for a specific reason with court approval. By presuming that the video will be released, there is more likelihood that the video will be released and the presumption of release is good for the public. This issue is one that is ripe for either federal or professional guidelines to be created so that there is some consistency across the country.

Chapter 21

Uniforms

Police officers have worn uniforms virtually since police agencies were created with full-time paid officers. The United Kingdom saw their police in uniforms starting in 1828. In 1854, NYPD became the first U.S. municipal police agency to issue uniforms to its personnel.[1] Other agencies quickly followed. Many officers were concerned about wearing uniforms as they thought it might expose them to ridicule or assault. Even today, uniforms are the subject of much debate among officers, the agency, and the public.

The primary reason police officers wear uniforms is so they can be easily identified by other officers and citizens. This helps other officers know it is an officer that is approaching, assisting, or making a request of the officer. It informs citizens that an officer is present and that it is an officer who is taking the actions they are taking. It also signals citizens that an officer is nearby and they can seek assistance from that officer. Wearing a highly visible uniform provides notice to everyone that an officer is present and this serves to deter crime and disorder in many cases. Uniforms provide a variety of purposes, including standardizing the appearance of the police force.

All aspects of a police uniform serve a functional purpose. Even the police hat. It is intended to enable people to find and identify a police officer in crowds. This too assists in helping to deter crime and disorder, while signaling to citizens that assistance can be found from the officer wearing the hat. There have been changes over the years in uniform appearance with colors, materials, types of jackets and hats, and with virtually every part of the uniform. Each change was and is intended to enhance the ability of the officer to perform their tasks.

But not all police personnel or even police agencies wear a recognizable uniform. Many investigative agencies wear a less identifiable uniform. In many cases, this consists of civilian-type clothes with only a badge indicating

their status as a police officer. Some agencies even opted for blazers or suits
for their personnel, even those performing regular patrol functions. Many
agencies today have some personnel in "polo"-type shirts in an effort to
soften the appearance of police personnel. But the general standard is that
most police officers (officers, sheriffs, troopers), especially those performing
regular patrol and call response functions, wear a standardized police uniform
that readily identifies the wearer as a police or law enforcement officer.

Agencies and police personnel must be aware of the public's perception
of how an officer looks. The public makes initial determinations about the
professionalism and competence of police based on their appearance. This is
a natural reaction with all people when they view others, especially when they
expect a profession to be clothed in a certain manner.

Recommendation 163: The agency should have comprehensive policies identifying and regulating all authorized uniforms.

Since appearance is important and can impact how the public perceives
police personnel, the agency must have detailed, comprehensive policies
regarding all aspects of the uniform. The agency should identify various
types of uniforms that it authorizes. This might include different uniforms for
various components such as patrol, motorcycles, marine patrol, SWAT, and
K-9. These different uniforms should only be authorized if the functions and
tasks of each component are different. For example, it is understandable and
practical that SWAT, K-9, and other components might be different from the
standard uniform of patrol personnel. They generally perform different tasks
so the uniforms should match the tasks. Components should not be allowed to
have different uniforms just because they are a different component though.
But each authorized uniform should have some common elements such as
agency patch, badge, and officer identification.

The uniforms should be functional, appropriate for the mission, consistent
with civilian policing in a democratic society, safe, and durable. Uniforms
should allow the officers to be identifiable to each other and citizens, but at
the same time should not unnecessarily highlight officers at night. Policing
requires a balance of allowing officers to be identifiable, but safely so. The
uniform should not make them an easy target, especially at night. The uniform material should be comfortable for the officers to fully function for the
duration of their shift, but also be durable so replacement costs are minimized. The uniform of each specific agency should be matched to the weather
and environment in which the agency operates.

Because of concerns regarding a military appearance, agencies should be
aware of these concerns and perceptions. Uniforms should not directly mimic
standard military uniforms. But for some functions (such as SWAT), camou-
flaged uniforms may be appropriate. The agency must strive to have a balance

among many competing concerns including public perception, functionality, safety, durability, cost, and wearability.

How a uniform looks is more than just the actual articles of clothing. What accessories are attached to the uniform can have a large impact on perception and safety. Public perception and hence support can be enhanced or reduced based on what accessories the agency allows and what accessories officers wear. Items that refer to television or films (e.g., *The Punisher*) that are anathema to policing should be prohibited. Items of clothing that include a reference to a political party or view, or popular comments on social media (e.g., inappropriate hashtags) should also be prohibited. These can cause concern among different members, groups, or segments of the public or give the impression that the officers might not be completely neutral in their actions. This can damage relationships, support, and trust.

The policy must identify what accessories are part of the uniform. It should include what accessories must be worn, and those that may be worn as optional items. The agency should control all aspects of what goes on the uniform as it can impact appearance, perception, and hence the ability of the officer to perform as expected. If the agency allows temporary or non-essential items on the uniform (such as ribbons or pins supporting different causes like breast cancer awareness), it must specifically authorize such items through a written directive of some kind. It should specify what can be worn, where it is to be affixed to the uniform, and the durations allowed. The agency should carefully consider approving such items as it does send a message to the officers and to the community. And inevitably, the question will arise regarding if that item and cause, then why not this other one. Deliberate care should be exercised regarding all aspects of the uniform and its appearance.

Recommendation 164: The agency should supply all uniforms and accessories.

A police uniform is standard equipment for police officers. Since the agency expects officers to appear professional and appropriately attired, the agency should provide the required uniforms, accessories, and equipment. This also ensures that officers are standardized in their appearance and equipment, and that they are professionally presentable. Most agencies do this with most supplying virtually everything. In many agencies, the only thing the officers are responsible for are underwear and socks. Some agencies provide funds or reimbursement for shoes while some do not. This is acceptable and understandable. But the shoes must meet agency specifications, and the overall appearance must comply with agency expectations and requirements.

It is understood that this can cost a considerable amount of money. But the benefits of standardization and professional appearance outweigh the financial costs. Even though it does not completely eliminate the situation, having the agency provide the uniforms reduces the likelihood of people pretending to be police officers by independently acquiring the uniforms. The agency should also provide for the replacement of uniform items that become unserviceable during the officer's tenure. Uniforms become dirty and stained, fade, and become tore due to the tasks and situations officers become involved in. The agency should have a mechanism to replace such items. This can be either through the agency's acquisition of replacement items or through the officer purchasing the items using a periodic clothing allowance. Some agencies purchase the items for the officer based on an approved requisition. Others provide officers with a stated amount each year and that money is supposed to be used for maintaining a professional uniform. Either method works and allows the officers to have appropriate presentable uniforms while enabling the agency to monitor, regulate, and mandate that the officer is properly attired and looks professional.

Some sworn personnel do not wear a regular patrol-type uniform on a daily basis. This might include undercover personnel, plainclothes personnel, and various levels of management. For these personnel, many agencies provide an annual clothing allowance. This enables personnel to be properly attired, consistent with their primary duty assignment while the agency bears the costs. And the benefits of these programs are the same as for uniformed officers. The plainclothes personnel may still damage their clothing in the performance of their duties or they become less professional looking. By providing the funds for these items, the agency is able to mandate that agency personnel still look professional and can take steps should someone not look clean and professional. The main concern is that officers perform various tasks that can damage their clothing. The agency should provide the clothing, within reason, so that its personnel look professional, and the agency can hold them accountable for their appearance.

Recommendation 165: The agency should designate which uniform version will be worn for various events.

If the agency has different versions of its main uniform (and most do), then the agency should designate which uniform will be worn for various types of events. In most cases, the regular duty uniform will be the appropriate uniform. This regular duty uniform would be the one worn by patrol officers during regular assignments and shifts. By its nature, it is the most appropriate for most events. The agency should allow for some officer flexibility regarding which standard, regular duty uniform is worn. A short sleeve uniform may be good for daytime, but some may prefer the long sleeve version at night. As long as the uniform is a standard regulation uniform, the agency should provide the officer with limited choices.

However, for some events and activities, other uniforms may be designated. Such an example would include special services such as funerals, memorials, and possibly dignitary visits. For these events, it might be appropriate for personnel to wear either a dress uniform or a more formal uniform. Sometimes it might be appropriate to wear long sleeve shirt and tie, but not necessarily the full dress uniform. The nature of the event should guide which uniform is most appropriate.

For some events, it might be appropriate for various components to wear their regular uniform, while other components wear a different uniform. But for other events, it might be best that certain components change into the standard regular duty uniform of the patrol group. For example, it might be appropriate for the bike patrol to wear their standard bicycle uniform with shorts for various events. But for other events, they should be in the regular duty uniform with long pants and standard duty shirt.

For protests that are expected to be peaceful, having the bike patrol present to assist can be very beneficial. It allows for close contact and interaction with protesters, enables more dialogue to occur, and can facilitate officer movement among and around the crowd. It would be appropriate for the bike patrol to wear their standard uniform of shorts and "polo"-type shirt. This can assist in presenting a more supportive and assistive image, than the regular uniform which might be perceived as more authoritarian. However, for protests that might turn noncompliant, the bike uniform with shorts might not be appropriate. While citizen perception needs to be considered, it should not be the deciding factor. The nature of the assignment, keeping officers safe, and ensuring officers are prepared and equipped to keep the community safe should be the deciding factors.

Since the nature of police work is characterized by change and uncertainty, all sworn personnel should be required to keep a standard regular duty, patrol-type uniform immediately available. This means that detectives, managers in plainclothes, and units that have other uniform types should keep a full standard patrol-type uniform available for use. This could be in a vehicle or in the office, but it should be available should the need arise to have additional personnel in uniform.

Situations that might necessitate additional personnel in uniform would include natural disasters, sudden storms, unexpected disturbances, unplanned special events, requests for assistance from other agencies, or any situation where additional personnel in uniform are needed. By having a full uniform available, agency personnel can change and respond as needed. Even though plainclothes and personnel in other uniforms can respond, having them respond in standard duty uniform reaps all the benefits of being in full uniform.

Recommendation 166: The agency should provide body armor to every sworn person, and have a policy that mandates its use.

Unfortunately, it has become imperative and appropriate for officers to need and wear body armor. This tool helps to protect officers from gunshots of various characteristics. The type and caliber of the bullet that can be stopped or significantly slowed depends on the specifications and designs of the body armor. The thicker (and heavier) the body armor, the more types (larger caliber, faster, etc.) of rounds it will be able to stop. Body armor is not a guarantee, but it does work. At least sixteen officers were saved by their body armor in 2020 alone.[2]

Due to the risks to police officers, every sworn officer should be issued body armor. Patrol officers serving in the regular patrol function should be mandated to wear the body armor at all times. Other personnel should be mandated to wear the armor when they are performing various activities. These would include serving search or arrest warrants, participating as a backup officer in undercover operations, responding to critical incidents such as bank robberies and active shooter situations, and other situations where the possibility of firearms exist. Detectives, management, and other plain-clothes personnel do not have to wear it in the office environment. However, it would be wise to do so based on the increased number of attacks on officers and police facilities. But they should be required to wear body armor when they are engaged in the various types of activities that involve high risk. All personnel should be required to keep their body armor immediately available.

The agency should ensure that all personnel have body armor that is current. Most manufacturers only certify their armor for certain periods of time. This is to meet liability and insurance requirements, and to ensure that the body armor is capable of doing what it was designed for. Weather, sweat, and other factors can start to impact the strength of body armor over time. The agency must ensure that all sworn personnel have and use body armor that is within the certification period. This is to ensure the safety of all officers.

Recommendation 167: The agency must mandate that all uniforms have the officer's identification clearly readable.

It is imperative that each officer has visible identification on their uniforms. Historically, this has been the officer's name, either an initial and last name or just the last name. Recently, some agencies have moved to having a unique number as the officer's identification instead of the officer's name. This is generally used in protest situations and due to recent "doxxing" attacks on officers. Many police in other countries wear identification numbers instead of names, and have done so for years.

In most American police agencies, officers in uniform wear identification that has their last name clearly visible. This is the general norm. In most situations, the agency should prefer the use of the last name of the officer as it is a much friendlier and more personable type of identification than a number. But regardless of whether the identification is a name or number, it must meet certain criteria. This includes that it must be accurate. The name or number must match the wearer and it must be capable of positively identifying the wearer. This is so complaints or compliments can be attributed to the correct person. The identification must also be legible. A citizen should be able to read the identification of the officer relatively easily. Historically, American police had a small nameplate on their uniform. The name was clear but it required the citizen to get fairly close to the officer to actually read the name on the nameplate. Generally, they had to be within about three feet of the officer. For many peaceful encounters, this is not a large concern. But as situations have changed in society, most officers are not comfortable with people getting that close to them, especially when they are taking any type of enforcement action.

As uniforms have changed and now possess less metal and fewer pins, cloth name strips have become commonplace. These have several benefits in that they are more durable (don't break like metal nameplates) and they are generally larger than the metal nameplates. This larger size makes them easier to read, including easier to read at greater distances. Regardless of the method of identification, uniformed officers should have unique identification clearly visible.

Plainclothes officers generally do not have clear unique identification on their apparel. But if they are going to be involved in crowd situations, they should change into a patrol-type uniform complete with visible proper identification. If they or any police personnel are asked for their identification, agency policy should mandate that the officer professionally provide accurate identification when it is safe to do so.

Recommendation 168: Agency policy should require periodic inspections of personnel, uniforms, and equipment.

In order to ensure that agency personnel are properly equipped and attired, the agency should conduct regular inspections. These inspections can be brief or lengthy, general or specific, and be limited or comprehensive. First line supervisors should conduct daily observations of their personnel to ensure they are professionally attired and equipped. On a regular basis, they should conduct more formal inspections of the officer's personal equipment, attire, and appearance. This is to ensure that each officer meets agency expectations as they prepare to perform their duties and serve the public. In a formal but more infrequent basis, the supervisor should inspect all equipment assigned to their personnel. This is a more comprehensive and longer inspection as it is intended to ensure that all equipment is present, accounted for, and fully operational. These inspections should also verify that only authorized equipment is carried by police personnel. The inspectional process should be a standard part of an agency's preparedness and professionalism efforts.

Part V

WEAPONS

Unfortunately, police are required to be armed and equipped with a variety of weapons. Weapons are any tool used by the police including batons, CEWs, pepper spray, hands, and firearms. While some point out that police agencies in other countries are less armed than those in America, these comparisons fail due to vast differences in societies, history, and laws. In those other countries, the societies have progressed and developed differently in many ways including issues, beliefs, rights, and the prevalence of firearms. With the prevalence of firearms, and the number of assaults on police officers, including those killed in the line of duty, it is impractical and unrealistic to disarm American police. This is truly unfortunate.

Chapter 22

Firearms

Virtually all sworn officers that possess the ability, power, and responsibility to make arrests are authorized to carry firearms. This includes federal, state, and local police, agents, troopers, and sheriffs, regardless of title or jurisdiction. This authority is governed by federal and state laws, and in some cases, local regulations. The use of firearms is closely regulated. The most common firearm carried by police personnel is the sidearm or duty weapon, which is typically worn on the duty belt, around the waist. Depending on assignment it may be worn visibly, concealed, or even on other parts of the body.

Today, virtually every law enforcement agency utilizes a semi-automatic handgun as its primary duty weapon or sidearm. These firearms carry more rounds that are fed into the barrel via a magazine that is generally housed in the handle or grip of the weapon. Depending on caliber and manufacturer, semi-automatics generally hold six to thirteen rounds or more. They are also easy and quick to reload if necessary. The revolver, which was the primary type of police duty weapon for decades, generally holds six rounds. It took longer to reload and had to be reloaded more frequently than most semi-automatics. For these reasons, semi-automatics have almost universally become the weapon of choice by police officers and agencies. Police agencies use a variety of calibers in their authorized semi-automatics including 9mm, .40 caliber, and .45 caliber. Other calibers were used at various times, but these three have dominated the market.

Other firearms that might be available to police personnel include shotguns and/or rifles. Sometimes, rifles and shotguns are collectively referred to as long guns or long weapons due to the longer barrel on each. These firearms provide additional reach and standoff distance in circumstances that do not allow the officers to approach a threatening subject. Each type of firearm has intended uses, specific purposes, and benefits and disadvantages.

Unfortunately, these different firearms have become necessary to protect officers and citizens. Shotguns are medium range weapons that carry various types of rounds. Examples include slugs, 00 buck, bean bag rounds, and disruptor rounds. These have various purposes such as longer range use, defeating barricades, incapacitating individuals, and interrupting electrical circuits on explosive devices. Shotguns have been used by police agencies for many decades.

Rifles of various types are used by many police agencies. Their use has greatly increased in recent years directly due to the threats that police and the community have faced. More and more persons are using rifles to attack crowds, schools, coworkers, and law enforcement. In several incidents, officers who responded to bank robberies, drug deals, and active shooters were severely outgunned. One well-known incident demonstrated that the police needed more than just their sidearms. On February 28, 1997,[1] two individuals attempted to rob a Bank of America location in North Hollywood, California. They were armed with high-powered rifles and hundreds of rounds of ammunition. Most of the officers were equipped with only .38 caliber revolvers or 9mm pistols.[2] Surprisingly only the robbers died, but twenty officers and civilians were injured.[3] Some officers borrowed weapons from local gun stores to defend themselves, protect innocent citizens, and stop the shooters. This incident led the Los Angeles Police Department to acquire 600 M-16 rifles from the Pentagon.[4] It is these types of incidents that have caused police agencies around the country to enhance the power and variety of the weapons they have available.

Traditionally, only SWAT teams were issued or allowed to have rifles. But recently regular patrol personnel have been authorized to carry full rifles or "patrol" rifles. The patrol rifles came about since the patrol officers are generally the first responders to high-threat situations such as active shooters. The increased popularity of rifles, and negative attitudes toward police, have increased the risk to citizens and officers, thereby requiring officers to be equipped with rifles. These rifles sometimes have a smaller caliber round than other rifles, with 9mm being popular. In many cases, this is very similar to what the officer's carry in their primary firearm (pistol). It provides more accuracy at a greater distance, enabling the officer to neutralize a threat from a longer, safer distance. In some cases, higher-powered rifles are authorized such as the .223 caliber. These provide additional accuracy at even greater distances. The intent has been to provide additional response options to patrol officers who are the first to respond to critical incidents thereby giving them better options to protect themselves as they protect and/or rescue citizens and stop active shooters.

SWAT teams have utilized high-powered rifles for many decades. These firearms are designed to provide increased accuracy and stop threats and incapacitate persons even if behind various materials or at longer distances. They are typically used in active barricaded shooter and hostage situations. These firearms are generally found in .308 or .336 calibers and they provide a high degree of accuracy. Due to the nature of rifles and shotguns, additional policies and procedures must be in place. When it comes to firearms, all prior discussions regarding use of force are especially pertinent and applicable.

Recommendation 169: Comprehensive policies and procedures must exist regarding all aspects of firearms use.

Agency policies and procedures should very clearly, comprehensively, and strictly regulate the use of firearms. Written directives should include material regarding legal authority and parameters, when firearms may be used, when they cannot be used, reporting and documentation requirements, and training-related items. The legal authority will predominantly arise from state law (since most police agencies are local and operate under state law), but such authority is also impacted by federal court decisions and agency directives. Agency policy should very clearly cover all aspects of firearms use, including what weapons and ammunition can be carried. The firearms policy should reference the agency's use of force policy, especially sections that discuss and regulate deadly force. This policy should also discuss the sanctity of life, and using deadly force only as a last resort to protect the life of the officer or the life of another.

Recommendation 170: All personnel authorized to carry a firearm must be trained. This includes initial training, periodic refresher training, and remedial training.

Before personnel are authorized to carry a firearm, they must be trained. This training must be standardized, documented, and conducted by specially trained and certified instructors. The training must include a review of applicable state law and various agency policies, but most especially those directives governing the use of force and deadly force. It should include the need for de-escalation, cover, and tactical positioning to enhance officer safety. In some cases, being physically fit or good tactical positioning may reduce the need for the use of a firearm. The initial training of police personnel must include in-depth training regarding the technical functioning of the weapon, how to safely handle the weapon, and must include demonstrated proficiency in the handling of and marksmanship with the firearm.

The initial training must also include decision-making and de-escalation training as an integrated component of the firearms training. It is simply not good enough to teach the technical aspects of firearms use. It all must be integrated so that even during firearms training, there is an emphasis on tactical positioning, de-escalation, verbalization, and time management.

Decision-making tools such as simulators are critically important to training officers. These tools have multiple benefits such as tactical positioning, verbalization, weapon selection, de-escalation, and a reduction in implicit biases. All firearms training should focus on legal and necessary use, while providing the technical skills for real-world situations, including effectiveness.

Periodic re-qualification and refresher training should occur at least annually, although more frequent re-qualification is strongly suggested. Due to the severity and impact of the use of a firearm, more frequent refresher training, such as semi-annually or even quarterly, is recommended. This would have increased costs, but more frequent training is certainly appropriate because of the issues surrounding the use of a firearm. Currently, some agencies train only annually, with a few training even less often. This is simply unacceptable. The periodic refresher training must include skill refresher, review and testing on the agency policy and legal aspects of the use of force, and actual re-qualification. The re-qualification should be on an approved, specifically designated course, and should require a proficiency of 80 percent. While some agencies require 80 percent proficiency, most require 70 percent. And once again, due to the severity of using a firearm, 80 percent proficiency is more appropriate.

For some firearms, qualification and re-qualification requirements and standards should be higher due to the increased power of these weapons. Shotgun qualification should be at least 80 percent if not 85 percent, and this includes all authorized ammunition but specifically both slug and 00 buck ammunition. Patrol rifle (9mm and .223) qualification requirements and standards should be at least 90 percent. The qualification standards for high-powered marksman rifles should be at least 90 percent if not higher. These are all based on the power of the involved firearm. Personnel that have the high-powered rifles and/or are designated as marksmen should train quarterly and should keep complete documentation of every shot. They should also practice with "cold bore" shots and fully document all activities and accuracy. These higher standards and more frequent qualification requirements are appropriate due to the nature of the firearm, its capabilities, and the greater distances that are likely to involved in their use.

The re-qualification should include day and night courses and must be completed with the firearm that is actually carried by the officer. Officers must re-qualify with all firearms that they are authorized to carry. This includes any off-duty or backup weapons that are authorized and carried.

As discussed in chapter 9, "Training," the agency must have a general remedial training policy and program. This training is intended to rebuild competency in the use of any tool, technique, tactic, weapon, or firearm. However, a firearms remedial training program is critical due to the nature and severity of firearms use. Remedial training is required should any officer fail to qualify at the standard level with any assigned or authorized firearm. An officer cannot be allowed to return to full duty status if they fail to qualify.

Remedial training must be offered that seeks to enhance the officer's skills. This is not simply another qualification attempt. It must be actual training, that is documented, and it must occur before any additional re-qualification attempts. The type and breadth of remedial training can be flexible depending on the level of failure and type of firearm, but it must have some standardization and must be fully documented. If after remedial training the officer still fails to qualify with their basic sidearm, they should be placed on restricted duty status with their firearms and authorization to carry and use firearms suspended. If they fail to qualify with additional firearms (shotguns or rifles), then their authorization to possess, carry, or use such firearms should be suspended or revoked. The agency policy should direct how authorization to carry and use such firearms may be reinstated. In some cases, this might necessitate participating in and successfully passing the basic course for the specific firearm. The remedial firearms policy should outline future steps which might include additional training and discipline, up to and including termination.

Recommendation 171: Agency directives should specify several aspects regarding firearms and ammunition. This should include (1) what firearms and ammunition are authorized for official use; (2) specific documentation of all firearms that are authorized, issued, or carried; and (3) maintaining the ballistics of all firearms authorized, issued, or carried.

The agency should clearly define what firearms its personnel are authorized to carry and use. This includes the manufacturer and caliber of the firearm, as well as the ammunition that is authorized. The agency may have very few authorized firearms or may have several. Agencies cannot allow officers to carry any weapon they desire or to utilize any ammunition they prefer. The firearms and ammunition must be selected based on many factors, including officer and citizen safety. What firearms and ammunition are carried should be based on studies regarding effectiveness of police-carried firearms. But it is incumbent upon the agency to clearly identify what firearms are authorized. This provides more uniformity, and ensures that only authorized firearms and ammunition are carried. It also provides increased safety for the general public, as only firearms and ammunition are used that have been selected to reduce the risk to non-intended targets.

The agency should also maintain records of the specifics of each agency owned or issued firearm, and all other firearms that the agency authorizes its personnel to carry. This would include specifics such as make, model, caliber, accessories (lights, pointers, etc.), and the serial numbers of all firearms. The agency should also track, document, and periodically inspect the firearm to ensure it is authorized, meets agency requirements, and has not been improperly modified. Specifically this would include any adjustments to the trigger mechanism including pull weight.

Each firearm has its own ballistic characteristics and markings. Some characteristics, such as caliber and barrel twist (lands and grooves) are common or class characteristics that are similar in firearms from a specific manufacturer. Other characteristics and markings such as nicks in the barrel are individual to a specific firearm. It is these class and individual characteristics that enable forensic examiners and scientists to ascertain and determine that a certain bullet was or was not fired by a type of weapon or even a specific individual weapon.

Each agency should have a complete record of the ballistics and individual markings for each agency owned or agency authorized weapon. This enables the agency to determine which firearm fired any particular round, which can be helpful and possibly critical in situations where multiple rounds are fired by multiple officers. This is especially true if the agency provides the firearm as all would have the same caliber and class characteristics. Being able to identify which round was fired by which officer can be helpful when a citizen (suspect or bystander) is struck, when rounds damage property, and of course when multiple officers are involved. It can assist in identifying which rounds caused what damages or injuries, which can be helpful in investigations and lawsuits. It can also assist in verifying which officers fired their weapons, which officers did not fire weapons, and whether in fact it was an officer that fired a specific round. If the agency authorizes officer-owned firearms to be carried on duty, the agency should have the complete ballistics profile and description on file.

Recommendation 172: The agency should provide the primary firearm.

When the agency provides the primary firearm, typically the sidearm, it enhances uniformity. It is more cost-effective when considering the cost of the firearms, the ammunition, holsters, magazine holders, parts, and so on. If one firearm is supplied and carried, the agency only has to stock one set of supplies for it. But if the agency provides different primary sidearms, then it must supply multiple types of firearms, parts, holsters and all related supplies and equipment. This standardization also allows for magazines and ammunition to be shared among officers should the need arise. It also makes inspections easier and ensures the firearms are consistent with agency specifications, and are carried as the agency mandates.

Some agencies allow officers a choice of what firearm they can carry. If it is based on assignment (uniform versus plainclothes), then this is appropriate. If the agency allows officers their choice, especially in the uniform patrol group, then the agency must either provide the variety of firearms, or allow officers to purchase and carry their own. This has the coordination and uniformity issues previously discussed, could increase agency cost, and could lead to devastating results if an officer cannot be resupplied with ammunition. It also has the concern of issuing the officer another firearm should their firearm need servicing or if they have been involved in an officer-involved shooting and their primary firearm is held as part of the investigation. Having the agency supply the primary firearm costs the agency more money, but it is appropriate for the agency to provide the necessary equipment for its personnel to competently and safely perform their expected tasks.

Recommendation 173: The agency must have a policy regarding the carrying of secondary or backup firearm.

It is imperative that the agency completely regulate what weapons, especially firearms that officers can carry and utilize, especially when on duty. The agency must specify in its firearms policy if officers are allowed to carry a secondary firearm on their person. This is generally referred to as a "backup" weapon. This is not the same as the officer being authorized to have a shotgun or rifle in their vehicle. For this specific discussion, a secondary weapon is carried on the officer's person, generally in a concealed manner. It is intended as an officer safety weapon should the officer's primary weapon become unavailable to or unusable by the officer. Hence the characterization as a "backup" weapon.

The agency can make its own decision regarding whether such a firearm is authorized. If they decide to authorize secondary or "backup" firearms, they must regulate it as strictly as they do the primary firearm. The agency should specify all the characteristics of the weapon, including caliber, approved manufacturers, ammunition, and how carried. Regulating these matters helps to ensure that the agency has reviewed the issues and made an affirmative decision. It also helps control what firearms officers will have on them while performing their duties. If an agency allows these firearms, they should also mandate periodic qualification with and inspection of the firearm. The agency should also document who is authorized to carry what weapons and keep an accurate record of all such weapons.

Recommendation 174: The agency should mandate safe storage of all agency weapons, especially firearms.

In order to ensure that agency weapons, especially firearms, do not become involved in unintended incidents or are stolen, it is necessary for the agency to provide mandatory directions to its personnel regarding the safe storage of all weapons. The policy should mandate that all weapons be stored in a manner to reduce the likelihood of theft and the likelihood of falling into the hands of children. The policy should include directions for safe storage at home or when off-duty. The agency has an interest in this matter and mandating that agency weapons be securely stored is appropriate. The agency cannot be silent on this issue.

Recommendation 175: Comprehensive policies and procedures must exist regulating all aspects of the use of shotguns and rifles.

Agencies that utilize shotguns or rifles in any capacity must have detailed directives that govern all aspects of these weapons. The directives should identify which firearms are authorized, including manufacturer and caliber, and what ammunition is allowed. This applies to shotguns, patrol rifles, and high-powered rifles. Only those weapons that match agency specifications and only authorized ammunition should be used and carried. Policy must also specify the type of initial and periodic training that is required. Due to the appearance and perception of the firearms, policy should address the display of such weapons.

While a general firearms policy can provide much of the basic guidance regarding any firearm, the agency must either have a stand-alone policy that covers these types of firearms, or specifically discuss these firearms in the general firearms policy. These firearms require additional training, regulation, and monitoring due to the nature and perception of these firearms. There is a different public perception when these long weapons are displayed. The public is very accustomed to see officers with sidearms, and the vast majority of times that sidearm is holstered. But these long weapons are more conspicuous because they are larger and are carried in a more open manner. The agency policy should address how these firearms are carried, stored, and secured in vehicles; how they will be handled and displayed when in potential use; and when it is appropriate to utilize these firearms. While they are a different type of firearm, their appearance, perception, and power make it important for agencies to address them specifically.

Recommendation 176: Officer-made adjustments to firearms should be prohibited or greatly restricted.

The agency should prohibit or greatly restrict and control any adjustments that officers make to their firearms. This applies to agency-owned weapons issued to officers and to officer-owned weapons that the agency may authorize officers to carry. These adjustments include a wide variety of possible adjustments, but most importantly any changes or adjustments to the trigger pull function. The pressure needed to pull the trigger on any firearm can be adjusted. Agencies should set these measurements and pull weights and should prohibit any adjustment to them. If the agency does allow such adjustments, they should only be allowed for specific documented reasons. Allowing officers to adjust the pull weight or pressure necessary to fire the weapon could result in accidental or inadvertent discharges, causing serious injury or death. This regulation of weapon characteristics applies to sight systems, lights, holsters, and so on. The agency should regulate any visible markings on the firearms or holsters and should prohibit any markings that could interfere with firearm operation or that might be controversial. Any adjustments that are allowed should only be made by certified personnel and should be reviewed by competent agency personnel. All adjustments, additions, or changes, including why the changes were authorized by whom should be fully documented.

Recommendation 177: Agency policy must address sights, scopes, and optics.

The agency must determine what types of sights will be required or authorized on various firearms, but especially rifles authorized to different persons. This is necessary due to the additional training requirements and maintenance issues associated with different sight systems. It may be prudent to have iron sites on patrol rifles used by patrol personnel, and then allow other optics for other weapons. Actual scopes might be limited to SWAT or similarly designated marksmen due to the issues associated with these devices. Either way, the agency should make advanced decisions regarding these attachments and tools. The agency must document in policy what equipment is authorized and what equipment is prohibited or limited. The policy must require periodic maintenance on any equipment and the equipment must be part of the periodic training requirement.

Recommendation 178: The agency must have a comprehensive directive that regulates non-training discharges of a firearm. This should require that any non-training discharge of a firearm be immediately reported, and that all such discharges must be fully investigated and documented.

Due to the multitude of issues involved with the discharge of a firearm, any and all discharges must be immediately reported. This reporting should be accomplished by radio if at all possible so that other officers are aware of the situation and so that communications can dispatch additional resources to assist with the situation. It also enables a supervisor to be aware of the situation and to begin the agency-designated process regarding any discharge of a firearm. By providing notification via radio, it also creates a contemporaneous record of what is happening and this has numerous benefits to the officer, the agency, and the community. If the officer does not have immediate radio contact (a detective or undercover officer possibly), the officer should make immediate notification to communications or an on-duty supervisor by the quickest method possible. Calling an off-duty supervisor, even if it is the officer's immediate supervisor is not acceptable.

Discharges that occur on a training range, during approved training sessions are not included in this immediate notification requirement, unless an injury occurs. The types of discharges that are covered include accidental discharges, especially if in contact with or in the presence of citizens, an intentional discharge directed at a human being, and the euthanizing of injured or dangerous animals. All of these situations warrant immediate notification and apply whether the officer is on or off duty. There should be no delay in reporting these types of firearms discharge. It is a public safety issue, is of great concern to the public, and every discharge must be reported in a timely manner so it can be fully investigated.

Any discharge of a firearm that does not occur as a planned part of a training session must also be fully investigated and documented. An agency's use of force firearms discharge team (shoot team, etc.) can investigate certain incidents. These would be incidents involving the euthanasia of an injured or dangerous animal. It is imperative that even these incidents are fully investigated and documented. Any time a firearm is discharged, it should be considered a serious incident. Shooting at an animal may cause a citizen to be unintentionally injured or might place a citizen in danger. If the animal is a family pet, then the family will probably be upset. It is imperative that a full investigation be completed and documented. As mentioned previously in the "Use of Force" chapter, an independent outside agency or combined regional team should investigate discharges that are intentional or accidental if a citizen is present.

Chapter 23

Less than Lethal Weapons

Less than lethal (LTL) weapons are those weapons and tools that are designed and intended for use in non-deadly force situations. These weapons are designed to be less than lethal, but are not guaranteed to be nonlethal. They are intended to provide an alternative option between hands/physical force and firearms/deadly force. These types of weapons are not generally appropriate for use in deadly force situations. But they can be used in potentially deadly force situations if the officer using the LTL weapon is covered, supported, or protected by another officer with deadly force immediately available. For example, in some situations it might be feasible to use a CEW, rubber bullet, bean bag, or pepperball, when a subject is armed with a knife. In rare situations, it might even be possible to use an LTL with a subject with a firearm, if another officer is ready with deadly force should the LTL not be effective. The most common LTL weapons include batons, pepper spray, CEW, rubber bullets, pepperball, and bean bag rounds. New tools are being experimented with and include nets, shields, and wrapping rope devices.

Recommendation 179: Agencies must have comprehensive policies and procedures regarding all less than lethal weapons authorized by the agency.

The agency must have detailed written directives that govern all aspects of LTL weapons. These policies and procedures must include a description of the weapon, what training is required to carry and use the weapon, who can carry such weapons, and when the use of such weapons are authorized and prohibited. The agency should specify that if one tool, technique, or weapon is ineffective, then other tool, technique, or weapon should be tried. If several uses of a specific tool have not accomplished the desired results, then continuing to use that tool becomes pointless. The amount of times any specific tool, technique, or weapon is used depends on the specific tool and the circumstances. This proviso should be included in all use of force policies. The procedure must also require the provision of medical aid as necessary and relevant to the weapon. Because any use of force can become a significant issue, it is necessary for the agency to provide comprehensive guidance and direction to agency personnel regarding the use of any force weapon.

Recommendation 180: A written directive must detail, regulate, and require training regarding less than lethal weapons. This directive must require (1) initial and periodic refresher training, and (2) that should an officer fail to successfully complete any relevant training, the specific tool should be removed from the officer.

Before any officer is allowed to carry any LTL weapon, they must be appropriately trained by an instructor who is certified to teach the specific weapon. The initial training must cover technical aspects of the weapon, how it works, what situations are appropriate and inappropriate for use, and any precautions or limitations that exist regarding the specific weapon. This training should also include a review of the agency's deadly force and use of force policy, including applicable state law and court decisions. It must also include a requirement to directly observe the subject after the weapon has been used to ensure that the subject is not having any adverse reactions. The officer must be required to demonstrate proficiency in the authorized use of the weapon and all training must be fully documented.

Refresher training should occur at least annually and should cover the agency's deadly force and use of force policies. Applicable state law and recent court decisions should be reviewed. A general refresher on the weapon itself should occur before the officer is required to demonstrate proficiency in the authorized use of the weapon. De-escalation techniques should also be discussed and rehearsed in practical exercises. Only those personnel that pass the training, including a demonstration of suitable proficiency, should be allowed to continue carrying the weapon.

If any personnel fails to successfully complete the training course, including attaining the required scores or levels on written tests or proficiency qualifications, that officer should be prohibited from carrying that weapon and it should be immediately removed from them. Only personnel that demonstrate sufficient skills, knowledge, and abilities should be allowed to carry and use any tool, technique, tactic, or weapon. The officer must be required to participate in a structured remedial training program that ensures the officer has reacquired the necessary knowledge and proficiency levels before they can be reissued the weapon. If the officer fails to qualify with the LTL weapon, the agency must decide if it is appropriate to allow the officer to remain on full duty status, or to be placed in an administrative duty status. This is necessary as just removing one LTL weapon from the officer's available choices may place the officer in the situation of having no or only one LTL option. This might result in the officer resorting to deadly force more quickly than if they had had multiple LTL options available to them. This and all training should be fully documented.

Recommendation 181: Agency directives must regulate and mandate the carrying of less than lethal weapons. The directive should specifically require that (1) all uniformed personnel carry at least two different types of less than lethal weapons, and (2) detectives and non-undercover plainclothes personnel carry at least one type of less than lethal tool.

In recent years, there has been a tendency for agencies to allow personnel to remove items from their duty belts, and hence from their available options. Reasons for this include studies that show certain LTL tools are being used less; to reduce weight and stress on the officer's back; and to allow room for other items on the belt. However, this has resulted in some officers removing tools from their belts leaving them with only one LTL option available. This is problematic and unwise. Having only one LTL option reduces the options available to the officer. In some cases, a specific LTL may be inappropriate, prohibited, or ineffective. In such situations, the officer would only be left with verbal skills, physical force, or deadly force. Therefore, officers must have multiple LTL options available. Otherwise, the officer may have to resort to increased force levels, including deadly force if the only available LTL is ineffective. Requiring two types of LTL weapons increases the likelihood and chances that at least one will be appropriate and effective in any given situation. It would also substantially reduce the possibility of having to resort to deadly force.

Often times detectives and other personnel in plainclothes attire (sworn personnel in administrative/office assignments, and higher-level management personnel such as executives, etc.) only carry a firearm with some carrying a set of handcuffs. This greatly restricts the options available to these personnel. Without any LTL option, the plainclothes personnel is left with verbal skills, physical force, and deadly force. This is unacceptable. Having an LTL option reduces the likelihood of injury to the officer and citizen, reduces the possibility of using deadly force, and is beneficial to both the officer and the citizen. Therefore, plainclothes personnel should be required to carry at least one type of LTL weapon. This does not apply to undercover personnel who are involved in immediate or long-term undercover operations (which is different than plain clothes personnel such as detectives).

Recommendation 182: If a specific less than lethal tool is ineffective, then other tools or techniques must be considered.

Since no tool or technique is effective in every situation with every citizen, officers must consider the other tools they have available. Repeat or continuous use of a specific tool that is not effective is inappropriate since it has been proven to be ineffective in accomplishing its purpose in this particular situation. This does not mean try once and change to another tool. It means that if a tool has been proven ineffective after reasonable and appropriate attempts for that tool, then another tool or technique should be tried. If the probes of a CEW have made full contact, it can be tried twice. If the CEW is used in drive stun mode, and the desired results are not realized after three attempts, then the use of a CEW should be discontinued. Similarly, if a baton has proven ineffective after several strikes (depending on the situation and circumstances), then another tool should be tried. Once it appears that any particular tool or technique has proven ineffective in a specific situation, another tool or technique should be considered and attempted. One tool that should always be considered if another is ineffective is momentary disengagement if it is appropriate for the situation. In those situations, where momentary disengagement is appropriate, doing so might give the subject the opportunity to think about what is happening and enable them to decide to stop resisting. In all cases, the citizen should be afforded the opportunity to surrender and voluntarily cease their resistance. Officers should constantly be giving verbal commands as to what the officer wants the citizen to do. This gives the citizen the opportunity to comply at any point. As previously mentioned, this concept of constant evaluation of tool effectiveness should be included in every use of force policy and procedure. It is important enough to be discussed as part of a comprehensive policy but also specifically itemized here and in all relevant policies.

Recommendation 183: Any and all uses of less than lethal tools should be thoroughly documented.

Due to the issues associated with the use of force, any time police personnel use force, including a LTL tool, the use and circumstances should be completely documented in the appropriate report. For some situations, like when soft hands or handcuffs are used, the use might be documented in the incident report. For LTL tools and firearms, a specific use of force or response to resistance type report should be used. The specific use of force type report is preferred as this will enable all use of force incidents to be fully documented, tracked, and analyzed. Any and all use of force is worthy of reporting, documenting, and being reviewed.

Part VI

ROLE OF OTHERS

Improving police services will involve more than just the police. And it should not be accomplished by the police alone, or without the police. Others have a role, obligation, and responsibility to participate in these processes and efforts. And participation can take many forms. It could include criticism (constructive or negative); filing complaints and compliments when appropriate; voting; making voices heard (peacefully); working with police and others; providing input and guidance; understanding policing and procedures; appropriately funding for the new tasks, roles, and mission; and cooperating and complying with officers as they perform their tasks and duties. Some of the groups that must be involved include unions, elected officials, police professionals, various interest groups, and most importantly citizens. Agencies, entities, and citizens should engage in civil dialogue to identify common ground and discuss what changes should be made, and how policing can be enhanced. There should be conceptual and focused discussion, and action, regarding what role policing should play in society.

This process must be undertaken diligently, and based on the current concerns regarding policing, it must occur immediately. But immediately does not mean quickly, without discussion, or under threat of disturbances. These issues, especially how all related services will be delivered, require deliberate thought and planning. Making snap, knee-jerk decisions will not be beneficial to anyone in the long run. It won't be easy, and there will be disagreements over the paths taken and the decisions made. But all groups and persons should come together in a respectful and peaceful manner to enhance policing and the overall quality of life for everyone.

Chapter 24

Elected and Appointed Officials

For municipal entities and jurisdictions (cities and towns), policing represents an extremely large investment in many ways. These include monetary/financial (budget), political, economic (business health), quality of life, and visibility. In most cases, policing is the component that is either the largest or one of the largest budget items. It is also operationally the most visible and active component of local government. Unfortunately, especially recently, it is the most visible and controversial activity which will have huge political ramifications. As we have seen recently, policing can have tremendous impacts (positively and negatively) on a community and how the community is viewed by itself and others. Lawsuits, injuries, and even protests, disturbances, and riots can result from police action, inaction, or even the perceptions of how they acted or reacted.

Elected officials exist to provide leadership and make good decisions for the community as a whole, and its citizens. Just as with a police chief executive officer, elected officials (mayors, governors, city/town councils) and appointed officials (city manager, county administrator) will be required to make decisions that not everyone will be happy with or support. The fact is that every decision made will result in some dissatisfaction. But an elected or appointed official is put into the position to make decisions that are best for the community and its citizens. Most do a great job in making appropriate decisions.

Recommendation 184: Elected and appointed officials should make decisions that are the best for the community and its citizens. They should not make decisions or comments based on the heat, pressure, or sudden public opinion of the moment.

While this may seem like a given, it unfortunately is not. There have been too many examples of elected and appointed officials making decisions for purely personal or politically expedient reasons. Some decisions are made to reduce or minimize the heat on the official, or are made to keep them in power or in their position. This does not help the community. Elected and appointed officials are put into their various positions in order to oversee the operation of local government, and to make decisions that are in the best interest of the community and citizens as a group. The actions and decisions of such officials should be legal, ethical, professional, fair and impartial. This is very similar to how police, judges, and others in positions of trust must act. Decisions that benefit the official or friends at the expense of the community are inappropriate, unethical, and in many cases outright illegal. Officials should live by the oath of office (if any), and make decisions for the collective good of all citizens.

All decisions by elected and appointed officials have significant ramifications. This includes decisions regarding hiring and retention of department heads, budgetary funding, and broad policy issues. Because of the importance and long-term impacts of most of these decisions, they should be made after careful deliberation and based on input from a variety of sources. Examples of recent impulsive reactions include very quick and sudden decisions to cut police agency funding ("defund the police"), and to pass various laws and ordinances regarding various police techniques, tactics, and equipment. No doubt there is a need for change. But these issues should not be brought up suddenly, without full discussion, and changed within a matter of weeks under pressure of civil disturbances and riots. Major decisions should not be made based on the loudest voices, or solely the views of those few present at one or several council meetings. Most city council chambers can only hold a very small number of citizens compared to the population of the community. It should be remembered that the previous decisions that have led to our current status and nature of things were made over time and based on much discussion, review, research, and input. These issues should be thoroughly discussed so that everyone can understand the ramifications of any decisions, and implement the best decisions possible.

Recommendation 185: Elected and appointed officials, including city councils, should gather all the facts and information possible.

Once again, the decisions of elected and appointed officials have long-term implications for the community and its citizens. Officials should take time to gather as much information as possible, from as many people and entities as reasonably possible, and to hear from the public. Decisions should be based on law, information, and democracy, not mob rule. Oftentimes, and especially recently, an issue will generate a degree of public concern.

Sometimes, city councils react to a vocal minority of the overall community. Most city council and county commission chambers hold only 50 to 250 people. Sometimes, the governing body of officials will listen to and vote based on the voices present in the chambers at that moment. But those present are only a small fraction of the entire community, in most cases less than 1 percent of the entire community. For issues related to policing, community safety, and quality of life, the police chief and agency should be consulted and involved. They are the professionals and their input can be very helpful especially regarding critical issues such as policing and public safety. They should at the very least be one of the entities at the table discussing the issues and providing input. Councils should not act on limited information or what view is making the most noise at the moment.

Recommendation 186: Police chiefs should be insulated from the political process as much as possible.

In the vast majority of situations, police chiefs are career professionals that understand the community and are extremely skilled and knowledgeable regarding the police profession and public safety. Their tenure and service should not be decided based on political party or affiliation, or issues that become politicized or emotional. Elected and appointed officials should decide issues surrounding the police chief based on valid information, leadership, and success in serving the public. The concept of "a new mayor means a new police chief" or "he's a good man, just not my good man" should have no place in determining who is or is not the police chief. A chief's tenure should not be continued or shortened due to political expediency.

This does not mean that police chiefs should not hear, understand, or respond to public voices and criticism, because they most definitely should. And they should be responsive to and build excellent working relationships with all elected and appointed officials. But just as with elected and appointed officials, not everyone will like every decision a police chief makes. But police chiefs should be empowered and allowed to make the tough decisions that need to be made for the sake of public safety. And making those tough decisions that are for the greater good should not jeopardize their position. Having police chiefs, and other department heads selected, retained, and terminated based on cause and good reason is beneficial to the agency, the government, the community, and the citizens.

Recommendation 187: Elected and appointed officials should strive to understand policing.

Being that policing is so important to any community (financially, economically, quality of life, and visibility), it is important that elected and appointed officials make good decisions regarding policing. One of the most effective ways to do this is to understand policing and its professional concepts and expectations as much as possible. It is important to understand what police agencies, officers, and chiefs can and cannot do, and what they should and should not do. Some of the actions that are commonly asked of police are based on the personal desires of citizens or officials. A lot of this involves quality of life offenses, moving people out of sight or the area, voiding tickets, or writing tickets to increase governmental revenues. Officials should not expect, ask, or demand that agencies perform actions, activities, or tasks for political or revenue generation reasons. These actions are not professional or ethical, and in many cases may be illegal.

There are many ways for elected and appointed officials to learn about policing so they can make more informed decisions. They should ask for regular briefings from the chief of police on various topics, especially any issue that is either up for public discussion or that is a concern in the community. They should ride along with officers, and request the chief to ride with them around the city or their political subdivision. They should ask for position papers, thoughts, suggestions, and views of various relevant topics. They should avail themselves of the various management and administrative reports that agencies produce on a regular basis. If there is a Citizen's Police Academy or similar type of educational program for citizens, elected and appointed officials should participate in as much of the program as possible. All of these and many more activities can provide a wealth of knowledge and information to help elected and appointed officials make better decisions for the agency and the community.

Recommendation 188: Elected and appointed officials should support continued enhancements and innovation in policing.

Policing cannot be a static profession. Especially now, there is a constant need for continuous research, improvement, and change. This covers all aspects of policing including personnel matters (hiring, retention, discipline); training; policy and procedure revision; reexamination of the police mission; and constant review and innovation regarding tools, tactics, techniques, and equipment. Officials, especially those with input regarding policing in general and funding specifically, should encourage and even require innovation and research. Officials should expect the chief and the agency to be involved in finding methods to perform their task and duties more efficiently and effectively. The chief and the agency should be encouraged to belong to professional organizations, build research partnerships with universities, and to keep informed of the latest trends in policing. By constantly seeking to enhance how the agency delivers its services, it can build better relationships with the community and enhance the safety, service, and quality of life for everyone.

Recommendation 189: Elected and appointed officials should assist in recruiting and retention of qualified personnel.

It is imperative that policing recruit, hire, and retain qualified personnel, especially since so much about policing depends on the people hired and how they interact with the citizens. While the agency has the primary responsibility to perform these tasks, they cannot do it alone. Elected officials must support the agency by assisting in the advertising, support, and recruiting processes. They should encourage citizens to join the police agency. This would help efforts to increase diversity, encourage change, build better relationships between the agency and the communities being served, and support the agency and the community. Too many times elected officials criticize the chief and agency regarding hiring and diversity. But in most cases, they do little to help, and in some cases make comments and take actions that are counterproductive.

Everyone, especially elected officials have an obligation to help identify, recruit, and retain good, quality personnel of diverse backgrounds. Elected officials can also help by supporting the agency, and providing reasonable equipment, benefits, and work conditions. These items directly impact the ability of the agency to be competitive in its recruiting and retention efforts. And it must be remembered that the agency is not just competing with other police agencies, as they are also competing with the private sector for high quality people. All of this translates to better service to the citizens.

Recommendation 190: Elected officials and candidates should not solicit or accept political endorsements from police employee unions.

In many areas, having the endorsement of various unions, especially the police union, can be a very big support mechanism for any candidate or incumbent. Other unions have some clout like the firefighters' and teachers' unions, but the police unions are oftentimes the most highly sought-after endorsement. This creates many problems including the perception of favoritism; politicians making decisions based on endorsements instead of what is best for the community; and resentment or confusion among the citizens. It can cause resentment among other city departments if the police are perceived as being treated better, especially during contract discussions. The public can perceive the decisions of the elected officials as being influenced by the political support of a police union, even when this is not true. In an effort to keep policing as far removed from the political process and its influences, it is best that candidates and incumbents do not accept or solicit endorsements from police unions.

Chapter 25

Unions

Some states and agencies have unions that represent employees through collective bargaining agreements (contracts), while others do not. Unions originally came into existence to protect employees from the improper (real and perceived) actions of some employers. Unions have a role in policing just as they do in other work environments. There are also a lot of negative perceptions about police unions, and some of it is warranted. While they can protect union members from unfair actions and practices, they can interfere with the proper and necessary discipline of officers and beneficial changes to policing. In some cases, unions have slowed or stopped the adoption of beneficial equipment such as body-worn cameras. But unions can also improve the internal work conditions and can actually enhance the service delivery aspect of a police agency. Recently, some unions have pushed for better equipment, training, and resources to improve the wellness of officers. As with many issues, unions vary from location to location. But if an agency and community have unions, everyone should learn to work together for the mutual benefit of everyone involved.

Recommendation 191: Unions must protect the rights of their members while preserving the core philosophies of policing. They must also do more to support those officers who act appropriately.

The primary mission of unions is to protect the interests of their members. These interests include fair treatment, reasonable pay, and safe work environments. These are good things. Understanding that union members pay dues and are therefore entitled to certain services including representation when accused of improper conduct, this representation cannot be done in a vacuum. The union exists to serve and protect members of the policing profession. There are certain expectations regarding the conduct, behavior, and actions of police personnel. These expectations, as well as other agency policies and procedures, exist to ensure proper delivery of services in a safe manner. Unions should support this. Unions should look to support compliance with rules and regulations, policies and procedures as they help guide officers to legally, ethically, professionally, fairly, and impartially perform their tasks in a safe manner. By having each union member/police officer perform as expected, they are actually protecting that individual member and all other members who might be impacted by the improper actions of a member. Removing officers who continually violate rules or commit serious violations is good for the majority of officers, who most likely are also members of the union.

Unions have a difficult task in that they should and must balance the protection of the individual against the protection of all the members. Many unions do a very good job of this as some have not expended optional resources on defending or representing a member when the member has obviously violated various regulations or policies. But, by virtue of their structure, they have an obligation to represent the member to some degree. They must ensure the agency treats member/officers fairly and within the applicable rules. And the agency should and must comply with its own procedures regarding discipline and other personnel matters. But the police union also operates in the policing profession that has higher expectations. The union must remember that it represents all of its members and this may mean that when they make decisions, they should consider the common good. The best way to protect individual officers is to protect the collective group. Unions should consider the impact of protecting an individual officer versus the potential damage to the entire group of officers/members. The union should perform its duty of protecting union members but within the context of the core philosophies of policing including service to and protection of the citizens in a legal, ethical and professional manner.

Understanding that unions must provide some support to all dues paying members, when the union defends everyone accused of any violation, they weaken the value (perceived and real) of their representation. The public begins to distrust everything the union says because they almost exclusively support the officer. Even in cases where the officer has obviously acted improperly and perhaps illegally, most unions blindly defend the officer. Granted the officer is entitled to representation as they also are innocent until proven guilty. But when the evidence is clear and convincing, staunch defense of the officer by the union reduces believability and support for the officer. This is especially damaging to other union members/officers who have acted properly.

When officers act either as expected or beyond the call of duty, they should be supported or even recognized. This recognition should be by the agency, the community, and the union. When the public only hears from the union when it is defending an officer accused of some rule or law violation, the power of the union's voice is weakened. Most union efforts are spent on defending officers who are accused of wrongdoing. Unions should increase the time and resources spent on supporting the vast majority of officers who serve with distinction. This might be solitary efforts of the union or joint efforts with other entities such as the agency itself. The unions should find ways to positively support and recognize officers as this will hopefully balance the perception many citizens have of police unions and will also help the perception of officers, the agency, and the profession.

Recommendation 192: Unions should participate with management in improving work conditions and the overall work environment. They should not hinder innovations that could enhance officer safety, the work environment, or community safety.

The agency and the union have shared goals and responsibilities regarding many aspects of policing and the work environment. They should work together in an ongoing effort and format, not just when issues arise or when contract negotiations occur. The shared responsibility of protecting the safety, health, and well-being of the member/officers is a constant obligation. One method to accomplish this shared responsibility is to work together in an organized formal manner. Many agencies and unions have created a process wherein union representatives and management meet on a regular basis to discuss issues of mutual concern. During these regular meetings, participants can bring up various issues and concerns. This might include items that are impacting the union members, possible changes to policies or work conditions, or items that either entity might suggest to improve the overall work environment. The intent is to have both entities meet regularly to talk about issues and possibly resolve concerns before they become issues of contention. By having open conversations about issues, it is possible that situations can be enhanced or changed before problems arise. The union and agency management share common goals that should enable them to work together for the good of members, officers, and citizens.

While it seems hard to believe that a union that represents its members would actually hinder actions that would increase officer safety, it sometimes happens. A prime example involves body-worn cameras. In some areas, unions have slowed, delayed, and even stopped the adoption of body-worn cameras. They argue it is a change to work conditions and therefore must be subjected to collective bargaining and negotiation between the union and agency.[1] In some cases, the union has demanded that officers who wear body cameras must be compensated more for this task. This certainly seems extreme in that body cameras help to protect officers from malicious, false, or inaccurate accusations. By demanding something in return for a change (i.e., more control over certain items, increased pay), a quid pro quo in effect, they slow, stop, restrict, or increase the cost of enhancements such as BWC. The use of body-worn cameras helps police officers and union members because the videos overwhelming show that the vast majority of officers perform their tasks legally, ethically, and professionally. All of which is good for the officers and the community.

It is appropriate for unions to protect their members and ensure they are fairly compensated, not overloaded, are properly equipped, and are treated appropriately. But remembering that some changes can improve the work conditions, the union should embrace, support, encourage, and even suggest various changes without demanding additional compensation or trade-offs in the collective bargaining process or agreement. In reality, because each local union belongs to their own group of police unions, they have the opportunity to learn of many different methods, policies, and procedures that they could bring to their own agency to help improve the safety, and work conditions of their members.

Recommendation 193: Police unions should not appear to represent the agency, and should not be involved in political contests, elections, or processes.

When unions make various public statements, some community members (and members of the media) believe or perceive that the statement is actually being made by the police agency itself. Some community members do not understand that the police union is a separate and distinct entity from the police agency. So when the union makes statements and does not clearly identify the statement as belonging to the union, it can be confusing and misleading. The union statement may even contradict official statements by the agency. This can be misinterpreted and may cause citizens to lose faith in the agency or the profession. In some cases, the citizens may even blame the agency for the comments when they did not make them and generally do not have the ability to control or impact union statements. To avoid any confusion, all statements by the union should clearly identify that it is a statement by the union and not that of the police agency.

Understanding that the union is an independent entity, and has the ability to be involved in various activities, police unions should not be involved in political contests, elections, or processes. This recommendation will not be received well by most unions as they enjoy and seek out political power. When unions have political power, clout, or influence, they can sometimes accomplish more for their union members. Unions often times look to support or oppose a political candidate in order to curry favor or attain leverage over them for future support or consideration. In many cases, having the support or endorsement of the police union (just like the firefighters' or teachers' unions) can be a powerful advantage to any political candidate or elected official. The problem is that while it can be an advantage, it can also be a disadvantage among those who are not happy with the police.

Endorsing political candidates is a double-edged sword. If the endorsed candidate wins, there might be some benefit to the union and its members. If the endorsed candidate loses, then there very well may be repercussions that negatively impact the union members/police officers. In some cases, these repercussions may be inappropriately directed to the police agency itself. Also since many people cannot distinguish between the police union and the police agency, they may mistakenly believe that a union endorsement is an endorsement by the agency. And, in many jurisdictions, especially towns and cities, the majority of union members/police officers do not live in the jurisdiction where the candidate is running and therefore cannot vote. While not being involved in the political process could adversely impact the power (real and perceived) of the union, it would result in better relationships with all elected officials which would be of benefit to the members, officers, agency, and community. Candidly, given the current situation, police endorsement of a candidate may not be as beneficial or desired as it once was.

Chapter 26

Media

The media has a large role in how policing is perceived and in influencing public views regarding policing. The general role of the media in American society is important and protected. It is so important it is one of the protections enumerated in the First Amendment of the U.S. Constitution.[1] Because of its role and prominent place in a democratic society, it also has a responsibility to society and the citizens. The media has tremendous power, impact, and influence in America. In today's busy society, many people only hear headlines and don't take the time to get the full information. They make snap decisions about issues based on little snippets of information. If they do take time to get additional information, they should be able to have accurate and complete information so they actually understand the facts, issues, and circumstances so they can make an intelligent informed decision on the issues. Today, various media outlets are known as leaning toward one political philosophy or another. Some are known to be more conservative while others are known to be more liberal. The reality is that the media's role in society is to completely, accurately, and impartially report what is happening or has happened, and then let the citizens make informed intelligent decisions. What one hears about an issue or incident should not depend on what the source is.

The media should adhere to the ethics of their profession. While there are numerous codes and statements, according to the Ethical Journalism Network, there are Five Principles of Ethical Journalism[2] which represent five common themes. These are:

1. Truth and Accuracy
2. Independence
3. Fairness and Impartiality

4. Humanity
5. Accountability

These common themes serve as an important guide for the media which has such an important role in a democratic society. By adhering to these ethical principles, many concerns about the media can be minimized.

Recommendation 194: The media should accurately and completely report police-related issues. This includes (1) avoiding sensational headlines; (2) only using current information, images, and videos; (3) ensuring the information they disseminate is accurate and complete; and (4) accurately reporting what police personnel say.

While this may seem a no-brainer, and will no doubt be received negatively by many news outlets, there is a need for this recommendation. It is also the first of the Five Principles as itemized above, Truth and Accuracy. The public expects to be informed of government (especially police) activities. Informing the public of governmental actions is the basic role of the media. But the public is owed accurate and complete information. They should and must be able to hear, read, or see a media story and then have a good understanding of what actually happened. Oftentimes, the media reports partial information that is technically accurate, but without the complete information, it allows or in some cases directly leads the public to understand or perceive an incident in a way that is not correct. The media should be providing complete and accurate information so citizens can make up their own minds about issues. The media should not be presenting incomplete, inaccurate, biased information, or disinformation. Doing so either negligently or intentionally pushes a viewpoint or agenda which is not consistent with concepts such as original constitutional intent, ethical reporting, truthfulness, or service to the citizens. If the public is to make an informed decision about police-related incidents, activities, and issues, they need to have complete and accurate information. Partial or biased information is a disservice to the citizens and everyone involved or concerned.

It is understood that the media competes for readers, viewers, and listeners. And in an effort to increase customers and revenue, media often resorts to sensational headlines that try to catch the attention of potential customers. In current times, this might be referred to as "clickbait," where sensational headlines are used just to get people to click on the item thereby increasing pay to the site or author. But sensational headlines, that may grab attention, often give incomplete information to the citizens. Some citizens only read or glance at the headlines and do not see, listen, or read the entire article. In many cases, once the full article is read, only then is it determined that the attention-grabbing headline is only partially correct. The concern with this tactic is many citizens do not get the full and accurate story and all of its details, which leaves them with either an incomplete or inaccurate understanding of the incident. They may make decisions or take actions based on that incomplete information. This is not good for anyone and really reduces the credibility of the media.

Oftentimes, media outlets will use old information, pictures, or video to get the attention of potential customers. Using old videos or pictures of burning buildings or cars, or from other incidents is deceptive and serves no valid purpose that is consistent with the constitutional and intended role of media. The only benefit of using images from past incidents is to grab attention and possibly to build up emotion or excitement. Some media outlets have used pictures from years or decades earlier and from incidents that were not even related to what the current story is about. Once again, this can mislead customers causing them to have opinions based on inaccurate information. Current pictures of an incident or situation with full accurate information should be used and would enhance the story.

Because of the role of media in America, and the level of reliance that most citizens have on media, it is important that the media only disseminate information that is accurate and complete. Media has an obligation to ensure that the information it disseminates is true or at least as true and accurate as can be determined when the story is released. Oftentimes media outlets will get comments from citizens at an incident and then broadcast or print those comments as if they are true. Some outlets make no effort to ascertain the factual nature of what they are reporting. Many media sources are responsible and do a good job of verifying information and not disseminating information that appears false on its face. However, like policing, it is the individuals and entities that are irresponsible that cause the problems, issues, and concerns.

When responding to the scene of an incident, the media should ensure people they are interviewing were actually there and saw what they say they saw. And some of the comments are blatantly false, with some being outright lies. The problem is that some citizens believe these lies or inaccuracies and then take actions based on incorrect information supplied by the media. This can and has resulted in community discontent, protests, or civil disturbances. Sometimes elected and appointed officials believe this information and then begin to make statements or comments, or take action based on inaccurate information. In these situations, the media has some responsibility for causing disturbances based on their stories and reporting. The media must ensure that any citizen comments or other information it prints or broadcasts is accurate and complete.

Accurately reporting what police personnel say should be a standard ethical requirement. But unfortunately it is not as there are multiple examples of various media outlets inaccurately reporting what police personnel say.

Sometimes this happens by mistake, but too often it happens intentionally and repeatedly. This gives the public inaccurate information and negatively impacts the working relationships between police and the media, especially those specific outlets that continuously misquote or inaccurately report what was said. Many agencies and police personnel have resorted to recording their interactions with the media to have proof of what was actually said. Some officials only respond to media requests via email so there is an exact written record of what was said. This is truly unfortunate. It not only hurts working relationships but it causes confusion, reduces police trust and cooperation with the media, and misinforms the community.

Recommendation 195: The police and media should understand the role and needs of each other, and strive to build a positive working relationship. This includes working together to draft media-related policies and procedures.

Police should recognize the role of the media in a democratic society. They should work to build a viable working relationship that allows the media to have what information they need (as long as allowable under law and does not compromise an active investigation or safety) in a reasonable time frame. Building such a relationship can be of assistance to the police in that the media can get more information out to the public more quickly. This can be information about significant events or incidents, soliciting help in identifying or locating people, and general information to enhance the overall safety of the community.

The media should recognize the role of the police in a democratic society. The media should reach out to the police and attempt to build sound working relationships. They should understand what information the police can and cannot release. They should assist the police when it would help with community safety. They should be accurate and complete in their reporting. By working together, reasonable mutual trust can be built. By understanding each other's roles and operational parameters, the media and the police can perform their roles in society more efficiently and more effectively. This not only helps both the media and the police, but more importantly it helps with accurate and complete information to the public.

Police agencies have a mission that involves keeping the community safe. Part of that mission is to provide useful information to the community. This includes information about crimes, crashes, and other incidents that have an impact on community safety. The media has a role to provide accurate and complete information to the citizens. Both entities have mutual roles that sometimes overlap, and they should work together to provide useful, accurate, and complete information to the public.

Both entities should establish a process of communication wherein good information can be disseminated to the public. They should work together to establish policies and procedures that facilitate the dissemination of accurate information. This would include access to appropriate police personnel at incident scenes and during regular business operations, as well as identifying what information will be released and what cannot. Some of the information that can be released would be impacted by state law in many instances. But by meeting and discussing issues of mutual concern, media can have more access and more information, while the police can better understand the needs of the media and can have additional avenues to disseminate valuable and accurate information to the community. Both groups should meet at least annually to discuss any issues or concerns, and to work toward a better working relationship for the benefit of everyone.

Recommendation 196: Media should not broadcast certain police activities, and should not interfere with or place themselves in the middle of active investigations.

Some will revolt at this recommendation as they may believe it is meant to shield illegal activities. Nothing could be further from the truth. The media should record and/or broadcast actions of the police when broadcasting those actions does not interfere with the lawful activities of the police; compromise active investigations or responses; or jeopardize officer, citizen, or general public safety. The specific situations discussed here are hostage, barricade, or active shooter situations where the police are moving into positions or are about to take action to rescue or stop threatening situations. By broadcasting every move the police make to tactically end a dangerous situation, the active shooter, barricaded subject, or hostage taker could be informed of the actions. This could result in citizen or officer injuries. The reality is that this has happened on numerous occasions over the years: media was live broadcasting the movements of police officers as they approached the residence where an armed subject was barricaded. This compromised the safety of the officers and the barricaded subject.

New and various technologies substantially increase the ability of the media to live broadcast police activities. This includes camera equipped helicopters, telescoping masts on media vehicles, and drones. Each of these technologies provides additional capabilities to broadcast live and could interfere with police efforts to resolve situations.

While the media has a role as previously discussed, they have a responsibility to not increase risk or danger to anyone. The presence of the media should not become the story or contribute to the story. However, when the police are taking "public" action such as during protests, arrests, and civil disturbances, the media should be present, recording and even live broadcasting. They just should not broadcast tactical movements when such broadcasting could jeopardize the safety of the officers, the citizen involved, or any other citizen.

Notwithstanding the important role the media plays in a democratic society, the media should not place themselves in active investigations or situations. Many times, various media outlets and/or personnel have become actively involved in dynamic situations. Examples of these include calling subjects that are barricaded or holding hostages, or actively involved in resisting police efforts to maintain public safety. In some cases, the media has, either inadvertently or intentionally tied up phone lines while police negotiators are attempting to peacefully resolve situations. Some media outlets have even allowed subjects who have killed citizens and police, and were currently barricaded, to be broadcast live. Recently, the media has been very active in civil disturbances and, in some cases, their presence has ignited or enhanced violence and destruction as some people "play to" or "act out" for the cameras.

These actions substantially increase the danger to police, the subject, and citizens in general. They also hinder the ability of the police to peacefully resolve the situation. Resolving the situation safely is much more important and more valuable to society than getting news out. In those very rare cases, when media exposure would be beneficial to resolving the situation, the police can, will, and have sought out media assistance. The media has an important role, but they also have a moral, ethical, and legal responsibility to not aggravate a situation, especially when people's lives are at stake.

Recommendation 197: The media should respect the privacy of citizens.

While the media has the role of informing the public about various events, they do not have carte blanche to invade the lives of people. Some people put themselves in the public spotlight and therefore assume some risk in having media attention. But most people do not. And even some of those who are in the public spotlight still have the right to some degree of privacy and the right to not be harassed. Oftentimes, media personnel are seen chasing after people who have been charged with crimes, or might only be under investigation. These people are still innocent until proven guilty. And many times, the media seeks out comment from the family or friends of people who have wondered into the public spotlight. It is not uncommon to see people ask for privacy as they deal with some kind of issue, whether it be a criminal charge, an investigation of some type, or even the death of a loved one. As they deal with whatever difficult situation they are facing, they are forced to ask for people, especially the media to respect their privacy and leave them alone. This is truly unacceptable.

It is not uncommon to have multiple media outlets trying to talk with family members, friends, or coworkers about someone else. Every time there is an active shooter, the media floods the areas where the shooter worked, lived, went to school, and in some cases, where they shopped for various items. It is common for media personnel to try to interview the family members of persons who have died from any number of causes. And it is almost universal that the media will try to talk with the family of a police officer who has been recently killed in the line of duty. This is disgusting, insensitive, immoral, and lacking of all compassion. It is also inconsistent with the previously mentioned Ethical Principle of Humanity.

Just because the media has some positive roles in society does not enable or entitle them to be inhumane, to trespass on private property, or to violate the privacy of others. In many situations when a police officer has been shot, and especially when they have been killed, a police agency has had to post an officer at the residence of the fallen officer to stop the media from bothering the family during this devastating time. Whether it is the family of an officer, or of a citizen, the media should be respectful, compassionate, and decent. In most cases, getting the opinion or feelings of family members or friends is simply not newsworthy and it is not of valid public interest. Should they want to make their feelings, views, or opinions known, they can always reach out to the media.

Chapter 27

Citizens

American citizens have various rights when it comes to governmental actions. This is especially true regarding policing and interactions with police. These are critically important with many rights being specifically enumerated in the U.S. Constitution. These rights are further reinforced in state constitutions and in numerous U.S. Supreme Court decisions. All of these rights apply to the citizens and regulate governmental, especially police, actions. It is imperative that these rights be respected and protected by the police.

But citizens also have responsibilities in a democratic society. These include compliance with laws and lawful directions. It is expected that citizens will abide by the laws, ordinances, and regulations of towns, cities, counties, states, and the federal government. Failure to comply with these laws sets in motion a possible interaction with police who are charged with maintaining public safety by enforcing the various laws of the jurisdiction. In every police-citizen encounter, there are at least two people involved—a citizen and a police officer. In some situations, there are more people involved and this might be more police officers, more citizens, and/or any number of bystanders. But in the basic police-citizen encounter, both the officer and the citizen have a role and obligation to ensure the interaction is legal, ethical, professional, and calm. The vast majority of negative interactions between police and citizens could be avoided by appropriate actions and demeanor on the part of the citizen. If the citizen complied with the laws and expectations of society, most citizen-police interactions would never occur. And once an interaction does occur, if the citizen would simply comply with the directions of the police, most interactions would be uneventful. Certainly there are times when the officer's actions have escalated the situation, but on a number or percentage basis, these are very few.

It is understood that the police have the primary responsibility to ensure a proper interaction. But it is not an exclusive responsibility as the citizen shares some responsibility. It is also understood that a citizen's actions can be less civil and courteous than that of an officer. But that does not mean it should be and it doesn't mean that a citizen's actions will not impact (and possibly adversely) the interaction. Police have a lawful duty, obligation, and responsibility to enforce the laws. Citizens have a duty to comply with those laws. The reality is that society, government, and police depend on voluntary compliance with laws and officer directions to maintain order and public safety. It is those times when citizens violate laws (actually or perceived) or fail to comply with the lawful directions of police officers that situations turn problematic.

Recommendation 198: Citizens should comply with laws, regulations, and the lawful directions of police personnel.

Living in a democratic society means that everyone agrees to comply with and be bound by the laws of society to protect individuals and the group of citizens. Individual rights still exist and are extremely important. But they are balanced against the rights and safety of the community. The primary example of this balance involves free speech. While most free speech is protected, not all speech is allowed. Defamation, inciting a riot, threatening speech, and yelling fire in a crowded theater (when no fire actually exists) are all limitations and appropriately prohibited. Laws exist for the protection of everyone, collectively and individually. Voluntary compliance is greatly preferred, is actually expected, reduces crime and disorder, and enhances safety and the overall quality of life.

No one likes to be told what to do and everyone generally thinks that their own actions are safe and acceptable. Almost everyone thinks they are a good driver. The reality is that not everyone does behave safely, acceptably, or in compliance with laws and the expectation of society. This is where government, generally in the form of police officers, enters the situation. Police officers are the ones that have been generally tasked with telling people what they can and cannot do. They tell people "you can't drive that way, park there, take those items from others, and you cannot hit that person." These are all good things and help preserve societal order and safety. But most people just don't like to be told what to do. This immediately causes confrontations between police and citizens.

But compliance with laws and the lawful directions of police officers significantly reduces the number, type, and outcomes of these confrontations or interactions. If everyone is compliant with laws and directions, there would be significantly fewer police-citizen interactions especially those associated with actual or suspected law violations. Compliance with laws and lawful directions is not only legally required, it is good practice. Failure to comply can result in traffic citations, criminal charges, escalating a situation, and increasing danger directly to the specific citizen, other citizens, and the officer. Compliance does not mean giving up any rights. It is the general expectation of compliance that allows everyone to enjoy the rights, privileges, and benefits of society safely.

It is understood that in some circumstances the officer may be wrong (either in reality or as perceived) or even overbearing. The citizen may believe they did nothing wrong. But just because the citizen may believe they did nothing wrong does not mean they did not, and it does not give them the right to not comply with otherwise lawful directions of the officer. From a practical standpoint, challenging the directions of the officer will most likely only escalate the situation. In most cases, the officer believes that they are correct and performing lawfully. And in reality, the officer is acting lawfully in the vast majority of interactions. Based on these two factors (officer belief and reality), if the citizen fails to comply, the officer generally takes actions that are necessary to gain compliance. Hopefully this includes de-escalation, verbalization, and explanation. But depending on the citizen's actions and either compliance or continued noncompliance, the situation may escalate to an arrest and/or the use of force. If the citizen uses force to resist the officer, the officer will legally be justified in using that amount of force which is reasonably necessary to overcome the resistance. The officer would most likely request assistance from other officers who will respond quickly. Upon arrival, the additional officers will attempt to overcome the resistance they perceive. They will not stop and ask the citizen why they are resisting as this could result in additional injuries. And in many cases this would be unnecessary had the citizen merely complied with the law and then subsequent directions.

In some cases, the citizen believes that all police are bad and that they will hurt the citizen if given the chance. This causes the citizen to be noncompliant or actively resist the officer. This is not a reasonable response. If the officer actually was going to hurt the citizen for no reason, the citizen's resistance just gave the officer the actual reason to take additional steps or actions possibly including the use of force. The best course of action is compliance with the laws of society and the lawful directions of police personnel. If the citizen feels the officer did not act properly, the citizen can file a complaint in any number of ways. But arguing with or resisting the officer on the street will generally not end well for the citizen.

Recommendation 199: Citizens have a right to complain about policing and police activities. They also have the right to record police activity.

If a citizen feels that they were not treated properly, that they were ticketed or charged improperly, or that they observed police activity that they believe is improper, they have a right to complain. And they should complain if they witness actions they believe are improper. As part of society, they also have an obligation to complain. The reality is that most professional police chiefs welcome questions or complaints about the agency and its personnel. The agency should acknowledge, accept, and investigate all complaints, questions, and concerns as appropriate to the issue voiced. If during a police-citizen interaction, the involved citizen feels they are being mistreated, they should advise the officer present of the concerns, but should still comply with the directions of the officers. Actively resisting the officer is not appropriate and will likely result in an avoidable escalation of the situation. Then later the citizen should voice the concerns or even file a complaint with the agency. But the situation will usually not be adjusted at that moment, and agencies should not void tickets or drop charges simply based on a complaint being voiced or filed.

Today, most officers understand that they will be recorded as they perform their tasks. And most officers are accepting of this situation as they know they are acting legally, ethically, professionally, fairly, and impartially. However, citizens must perform the recording in a manner that does not interfere with police activities, invade the personal space of officers, or endanger themselves, others, or officers. Citizens cannot pose a risk to anyone or trespass on property in an effort to record police activity. They also cannot cross police lines or barricades to film any activity.

Regarding the personal space of officers and potential interference with police activity, citizens should stay at least ten feet away from officers, especially if they are investigating an incident or are actually involved in a physical arrest. This is to protect the officers and all involved citizens, including the bystander who is attempting to record the situation. In today's environment, people have attacked officers or tried to stop them from making arrests. Therefore, when other citizens get too close to officers engaged in situations, the officers rightfully have concern for their safety. Officers simply do not know if a person approaching quickly or too closely is there to harm them, assist the person being detained, or simply to record the activity. The ten foot distance is a safety buffer for all concerned. Depending on the situation, the distance may be increased for the protection of everyone.

Recommendation 200: Citizens have a responsibility to help de-escalate situations.

While police have the primary responsibility and role to de-escalate, it is not an exclusive role. Yes, on occasion police have escalated (properly or improperly) a situation, and these situations are fully investigated and appropriate actions taken. Many situations escalate beyond a momentary interaction because of the actions, behaviors, or perceptions of citizens. This includes pedestrian encounters, traffic stops, disturbance calls, and other types of police activity.

Most situations that escalate from peaceful protests to disturbances or riots occur due to inappropriate citizen actions. As previously mentioned, citizens do not have the right to destroy property (including paint, graffiti, vandalism, arson), interfere with the movement of others (traffic, pedestrians), or attack people (citizens or officers). These actions change a peaceful protest into a disturbance or riot and cannot be allowed to happen.

Citizens have an obligation to help keep peaceful protests peaceful. They have an obligation to help de-escalate situations. They can do so by identifying the violent and destructive persons hiding in the peaceful crowd. They can separate themselves from those who are seeking to commit violence or destruction. By being silent, hiding or otherwise assisting the criminals among them, they jeopardize the peaceful protest, the potency of their message, and risk injury to themselves, others, and the police. Peaceful protesters should not tolerate, condone, or in any way support or enable criminals to operate or to jeopardize them or the peaceful protest in which they are involved.

Conclusion

This book started in 2020 as much of America was in distress. COVID-19 was growing and taking a toll. A toll in human sickness, suffering, and death. A toll on the economic stability of the country, and most definitely a large economic toll on virtually every person. It strained personal relations and led to divisiveness over government actions regarding all things COVID-19. It negatively impacted the mental health of the country and its citizens.

The year 2020 also saw a continuation of the long-term historical and current issues surrounding race, equality, and fairness in America. Although these struggles, sufferings, and issues are not uniquely American, there is little solace that other countries and societies share these struggles and issues. Perceptions and realities caused considerable discord in America. Some of this was due to governmental actions surrounding issues such as housing, economics, education, and politics. One of the most visible governmental actions, that of regulating individual and societal behavior, generally by way of the police enforcing the laws and trying to maintain peace, law, and order, exploded.

The use of force by police, which sometimes resulted in injuries or deaths, caused a near-universal desire for change. America witnessed police using force, sometimes deadly force. In most cases it was legally justified, and also necessary to prevent harm to other citizens or officers. In a very few horrific situations, the force used was inappropriate, unnecessary, and not consistent with law or police and community expectations. This led to outrage, which in some cases has lingered in America for years or decades. Understanding that any use of force by police is not pretty, some of these scenes were devastating. It was devastating to American support, perceptions, and ideals. It was also devastating to the police profession in many ways. The widespread outcry for change was loud. It was heard. Perhaps it was heard more than in any other time in the past. Changes began to occur with agency's having their budgets cut, some in considerable dollar amounts and percentages. Many states and communities began to implement various reforms directed at various aspects of policing. Some of the reforms bear resemblance to the recommendations contained in this book. Some reforms are needed. But what is really needed is meaningful systemic action to enhance policing. Re-focusing policing on its core philosophies and ideals. Making changes based on thoughtful, inclusive discussions. All stakeholders need to have a voice, and all need to be heard.

To their credit, many agencies have already implemented many of these recommendations in one form or another. To those that have, they are setting the professional tone of how police agencies should act. But they should also seek out their community and have more discussions regarding opportunities for enhancement. Because there are many still available.

To those agencies who do not have suitable policies that are consistent with these and other professional recommendations and standards, they need to change. They need to immediately engage in conversations with their communities and examine how policy, practice, training, and supervision can improve how they provide police services. There is no excuse for outdated policies, practices, culture, or attitudes. Police agencies exist to serve the citizens and to do so professionally, legally, ethically, fairly, and impartially.

As 2021 began, there were some changes. Some reforms have been implemented on paper. Some budget cuts have been made and some actions have been taken. These will have some positive effects and some negative effects. Society continues to see extreme divisiveness, especially over politics and the recent presidential election. The levels of intolerance and violence have increased. This aggravates other parts of American life. Even though vaccines exist and are being distributed, COVID-19 has a massive impact on daily life. People are tired of living under the impacts of coronavirus. People are divided over the virus, wearing masks, and various restrictions that exist due to this ever-more deadly disease. And 2021 saw a resurgence in Covid-19 with the Delta variant striking powerfully.

As mentioned in the Introduction to this book, all these things impact policing. Policing does not happen in a vacuum. But policing continues every day. While most police-citizen interactions go well, the stress of daily life, compounded by the major issues of 2020 and 2021, increase the anger, danger, and violence now facing police. This has also led to violent encounters between the police and the citizens in some situations. It has caused some people to be less compliant with laws and lawful orders, and to be more confrontational and even violent toward the police. Unfortunately, this lack of compliance has led to the need for police to use force in some situations. And once again, these incidents are leading to community unrest long before all the facts are known. In many of these situations, the immediate perception and community reaction is that the police have wrongfully used force.

This immediate, uninformed reaction further exacerbates the overall issues of policing in America. This clearly points out the need for thoughtful, inclusive discussion as to how policing can be reengineered in a meaningful way.

It must be remembered that the vast majority of the actions by police, and interactions between police and citizens occur without incident. Much of this success is directly due to the manner in which the officer performs their tasks. A lot of credit is also due to those citizens who voluntarily comply with the law and officer requests. There are generally three factors which influence a police-citizen interaction:

1. Citizen actions, behaviors, expectations, and perceptions
2. Officer actions, behaviors, expectations, and perceptions
3. Agency practices and expectations related to hiring, training, supervision, and guidance, including policy

Enhancing policing can impact each of these factors, and can resolve the issues facing policing and society. The expectations and perceptions of each person are more personal, but are shaped on hopes, and experiences. Actions and behaviors are very personal and largely controlled by the individual. If both, officers and citizens, come to agreement about what actions and behaviors are appropriate, then there will be less confrontation, noncompliance, arrests, and problems. Both officers and citizens need to be fully compliant with the laws and expectations of society. Officers bear a greater burden as they have been given great power by society; are employed to perform certain tasks in a certain manner; and are required to act consistent with their authority, the laws and court decisions, and their oath of office. But both have an obligation as members of society.

Agency expectations, policies, and practices have large impacts on how the officers perform their tasks. Agency actions decide who is hired, how they are trained and supervised, and how they perform their tasks. The role of the agency is critical in deciding what kind of policing each community has. The correct culture, foundational beliefs, focus, and attitude must be present if the community is to have the type and manner of policing they should have.

The discussions and recommendations in this book are focused on all of these factors, but especially on what the agency should do to ensure that its officers perform as expected. This book is intended to facilitate the thoughtful, deliberate, inclusive discussion that is needed. It is intended to provide specific recommendations to not only guide discussions, but to also provide specific professional actions that can and should be taken now. Hopefully, discussion will occur, thoughtful decisions will be made, and American policing will be enhanced. If this happens, policing will serve and protect communities more efficiently and effectively, and society will be a much better place for everyone.

Abbreviations

ACLU	American Civil Liberties Union
ACR	Alternative Complaint Resolution
APSA	Airborne Public Safety Association
BWC	Body-Worn Camera
CALEA	Commission on Accreditation for Law Enforcement Agencies
CEO	Chief Executive Officer
CEW	Conducted Energy Weapon
CIT	Crisis Intervention Training
COP	Community-Oriented Policing
COPS	Community-Oriented Policing Service
CPR	Cardio Pulmonary Resuscitation
CPTED	Crime Prevention Through Environmental Design
CSO	Community Service Officer
DoD	Department of Defense
DOJ	Department Of Justice
EBD	Education Based Discipline
EMR	Emergency Medical Responder
EMS	Emergency Medical Service
EOD	Explosive Ordnance Disposal
EWS	Early Warning System
FAA	Federal Aviation Administration
FBI	Federal Bureau of Investigation
FOP	Fraternal Order of Police
FTEP	Field Training and Evaluation Program
FTO	Field Training Officer
GED	General Educational Development
IA	Internal Affairs

IACP	International Association of Chiefs of Police
LAPD	Los Angeles Police Department
LASD	Los Angeles Sheriff's Department
LEAA	Law Enforcement Assistance Administration
LEEP	Law Enforcement Education Program
LGBTQ	Lesbian Gay Bisexual Transgender Queer
LTL	Less Than Lethal
MMA	Mixed Martial Arts
MPH	Miles Per Hour
MVV	Mission, Vision, and Values
NDAA	National Defense Authorization Act
NOBLE	National Organization of Black Law Enforcement Executives
NSA	National Sheriffs' Association
OC	Oleoresin Capsicum
PAL	Police Athletic League
PAT	Physical Abilities Test
PERF	Police Executive Research Forum
PIO	Public Information Officer
PIT	Pursuit/Precision Intervention/Immobilization Technique
POC	Point Of Contact
POP	Problem-Oriented/Solving Policing
PSO	Public Safety Officer
ROR	Release On/Own Recognizance
SKA	Skills, Knowledge, and Abilities
SMI	Serious Mental Illness(es)
SMIP	Senior Management Institute for Police
SOP	Standard Operating Procedure
SWAT	Special Weapons and Tactics
TFO	Tactical Flight Officer
TLE	Traffic Law Enforcement
UAV	Unmanned Aerial Vehicle

List of Recommendations

Recommendation 1: The history of American policing, including local issues and history, should be taught to agency personnel.

Recommendation 2: The Peelian Principles of Policing (nine principles and three core ideas) should be a core foundation of every American police agency.

Recommendation 3: The tasks for which policing, and police agencies are responsible should be revisited by the community and policing professionals.

Recommendation 4: Mental health providers should have primary responsibility for handling mental health incidents.

Recommendation 5: Citizens should not call the police for issues that should be handled by the involved citizens.

Recommendation 6: The laws, regulations, and guidelines regarding the use of force, especially deadly force, should be consistent across all jurisdictions and agencies. The federal government should take the lead by (1) adopting the National Consensus Policy on Use of Force, making it mandatory for all American police agencies; (2) mandating participation in the National Use of Force Database which would be administered by the U.S. DOJ or the National Institute of Justice; and (3) the federal courts must assist in building a viable use of force policy that can apply to all jurisdictions and agencies.

Recommendation 7: The U.S. DOJ should conduct a variety of activities relative to policing and police agencies. This includes encouraging, assisting, educating, reviewing, and mandating police agencies to perform as expected. This would also include technical assistance, training, reviews regarding patterns or practices, other reviews and analyses, and consent decrees as might be warranted.

Recommendation 8: The U.S. DOJ should create and administer a mandatory national database of police officers who have been terminated/dismissed for serious reasons or for those who have been decertified.

Recommendation 9: All agencies should define, articulate, and publish the Mission, Vision, and Values of the agency.

Recommendation 10: All agencies should adopt the Law Enforcement Code of Ethics.

Recommendation 11: Police services must be provided in an unbiased manner, and agencies must conduct relevant training.

Recommendation 12: Legitimacy and Procedural Justice must be a foundation of all policing.

Recommendation 13: Arrest and charging activities should be used only when they are the best choice for everyone (including society) and when prudent and necessary.

Recommendation 14: Refresher training on all these concepts must occur on a regular basis.

Recommendation 15: The agency should identify as a "police" or "police services" agency, not a "law enforcement" agency.

Recommendation 16: Agency culture must reinforce these core foundational beliefs.

Recommendation 17: Agencies should adopt and support the Policy Framework for Improved Community-Police Engagement as outlined by the IACP.

Recommendation 18: All agencies should embrace the concepts and implement the recommendations of the President's Task Force on 21st Century Policing.

Recommendation 19: All police agencies should be accredited, preferably through the national/international accreditation body.

Recommendation 20: Agency policies and procedures should be published online.

Recommendation 21: Each police agency must prepare various reports regarding its activities, actions, outcomes, and conduct for internal use.

Recommendation 22: All police agencies should publish various reports, statistics, and analyses regarding their actions for public information.

Recommendation 23: Crime prevention should be a primary concern, focus, and activity of all police agencies.

Recommendation 24: To assist with the order maintenance/public safety service aspect of policing, agencies should embrace Community-Oriented Policing and Problem-Oriented/Solving Policing. These concepts must be organization-wide philosophies and efforts.

Recommendation 25: Citizens and other entities must be involved in community safety and crime prevention/reduction.

Recommendation 26: The chief (agency CEO) should be experienced in policing, with a background in the art and science of policing. The chief should be educated in many ways, have at least a bachelor's degree and demonstrate extensive leadership qualities.

Recommendation 27: The chief and staff should actively participate in professional organizations.

Recommendation 28: The chief should be an active, visible, and accessible member of the community.

Recommendation 29: The chief must be a reasonable advocate, and the primary spokesperson for the agency and its personnel, especially in times of crisis.

Recommendation 30: The chief must hold themselves, the agency, and its personnel accountable.

Recommendation 31: A variety of police-community boards and committees should exist to increase and enhance communication, trust, participation, and transparency. One such board should be a "Chief's Advisory Board" or similar type of structure to share information and receive feedback. Agency personnel must actively participate in these boards.

Recommendation 32: Citizen participation must be encouraged, solicited, and accepted.

Recommendation 33: The agency must have training and directives in place that discuss, encourage, and properly regulate discretion.

Recommendation 34: Education should be a primary focus of the agency, with community outreach and interaction being stressed.

Recommendation 35: Utilize police and community resources (funds, assets, people) to enhance public safety and the general improvement of the overall quality of life. This specifically includes using a sizeable percentage of asset forfeiture funds for outreach, community, crime prevention, and educational efforts.

Recommendation 36: The agency must be proactive in recruiting. It must have an active recruiting plan with defined goals and objectives, and it must be reviewed and adjusted at least annually.

Recommendation 37: The plan should include the goal of having the agency workforce mirror the community it serves.

Recommendation 38: Agencies should identify desirable characteristics for its personnel. This should include some mix of education, knowledge, service, and life experience. Police agencies should adjust their recruiting messages to reflect the type of people desired, and the type of tasks and activities they will perform.

Recommendation 39: Agencies must ensure that their hiring standards are lawful, relevant, and appropriate.

Recommendation 40: Agencies should not restrict their hiring to only already certified officers.

Recommendation 41: A comprehensive background process must be utilized.

Recommendation 42: If the applicant is or has been a police officer, the agency must expand its background process to review personnel files from current or prior agencies and any relevant databases. To this end, all police agencies should be legally required to provide full assistance to other agencies, specifically regarding the provision of all personnel, performance, and complaint records.

Recommendation 43: A comprehensive battery of examinations should be utilized in the hiring process. This would specifically include a written test, an initial Physical Abilities Test (PAT), at least one board/panel interview, a medical examination, and a psychological examination. Standards should be set, and all applicants should be required to successfully pass each and every aspect of the process.

Recommendation 44: The decision to hire or not hire should be made by the agency.

Recommendation 45: Residency should not be an application, hiring, or employment requirement.

Recommendation 46: The agency should review its overall hiring process and decisions on an annual basis.

Recommendation 47: The federal government should mandate certain topics and hours of training for all basic police academies.

Recommendation 48: The basic police recruit academy should be at least six months long, if not longer.

Recommendation 49: Funding and opportunities for candidates to attend basic police academies should be provided.

Recommendation 50: The basic academy curriculum should be controlled by the state certification body.

Recommendation 51: The passing grade should be raised to 80 percent in all topic areas.

Recommendation 52: Academies should provide more tutoring and assistance to students.

Recommendation 53: Dishonesty, untruthfulness, or cheating of any kind in a training course should be grounds for immediate dismissal.

Recommendation 54: Fitness standards should be relevant to the job, with training being reasonable.

Recommendation 55: An annual review and analysis of academy training should be completed.

Recommendation 56: Academy training should be integrated; scenario based and include additional training in human interaction skills.

Recommendation 57: State certification should require successful completion of a state certification examination. No person should be allowed to function as a police officer unless they have passed an approved basic academy and a state certification examination or process.

Recommendation 58: All agencies should have a Field Training and Evaluation Program.

Recommendation 59: In-service training should be integrated and include legal, ethics, and professional aspects in each topic.

Recommendation 60: The agency should create a multi-year refresher training program. Certain topics should require annual refresher training. This includes legal reviews and updates, the use of force and all related policies, fitness and wellness, de-escalation, and human interaction/interpersonal skills, and professionalism. Other topics should be on a multi-year schedule.

Recommendation 61: Officers should be required to qualify with all weapons and firearms, at least annually, and at a skill level of 80 percent.

Recommendation 62: Officers should train on state-of-the-art decision-making simulators.

Recommendation 63: The agency must have a written remedial training policy.

Recommendation 64: All in-service refresher training should be based on written lesson plans and delivered by qualified personnel. All training should be fully documented.

Recommendation 65: Personnel should receive training relative to their new position and role within six months of being promoted. Immediately upon assignment, they should be provided a mentor to guide them as they start to function in their new position.

Recommendation 66: Various positions may require additional or specific training. Therefore, personnel assigned to new positions should be trained on specific items or aspects. Depending on the tasks, responsibilities, activities, or skill sets, this training would be required prior to assumption of the new tasks, or within six months of being assigned.

Recommendation 67: A set of written directives must exist to guide and detail general behavior and an overall code of conduct for all agency personnel. It must specifically require all personnel abide by applicable directives, laws, regulations, and expectations.

Recommendation 68: A written directive must exist that details the disciplinary process.

Recommendation 69: The disciplinary process should be completed in a timely manner.

Recommendation 70: Discipline must be appropriate when matched to the rule violation. It must be consistent but fair to the agency and individual considering the circumstances.

Recommendation 71: The disciplinary system must be based on progressive actions and have training as a key component.

Recommendation 72: A directive should identify the probable range of disciplinary and corrective actions available for various violations. It should also identify those actions violations, or transgressions that would generally result in termination.

Recommendation 73: Officers should have a pre-disciplinary hearing/meeting prior to the implementation of any significant discipline.

Recommendation 74: A review of the public nature of disciplinary records should be conducted.

Recommendation 75: A disciplinary notice should be sent to the state certification body regarding all discipline.

Recommendation 76: Annual disciplinary summaries should be published.

Recommendation 77: Written directives should detail a comprehensive process and procedures for handling complaints.

Recommendation 78: All complaints should be investigated, even anonymous complaints.

Recommendation 79: The agency should utilize proactive accountability measures.

Recommendation 80: The agency must have trained investigators available to handle serious complaints.

Recommendation 81: The complainant should be kept informed of the status of the complaint, including when the investigation is complete, and as to the outcome as allowed by law. Applicable laws should allow the complainant to be advised of the outcome of the complaint and the investigation.

Recommendation 82: Knowingly false complaints should result in appropriate charges.

Recommendation 83: The agency should ensure that investigations are completed in a timely manner.

Recommendation 84: The complaint investigation process should have certain notification characteristics. These include (1) the chief should immediately be made aware of all serious complaints, (2) the chief should be kept informed of the status of said investigations, (3) the chief or a reasonable designee should be made aware of the findings of all complaints, and (4) the commander of the internal investigations component must have direct access to the chief.

Recommendation 85: An annual statistical report should be prepared and published for public knowledge.

Recommendation 86: An annual review of all complaints should be written and submitted to the chief.

Recommendation 87: A mandatory physical fitness program should exist.

Recommendation 88: Counseling services and peer support should exist for all personnel.

Recommendation 89: An Early Warning System (EWS) should exist.

Recommendation 90: The agency should utilize periodic psychological examinations or evaluations.

Recommendation 91: Service and public safety should be the primary focus of all components and personnel.

Recommendation 92: Identify repeat call locations and work to resolve the underlying issues.

Recommendation 93: All sworn personnel and all communications technicians should be Crisis Intervention Trained.

Recommendation 94: All personnel should be trained in de-escalation techniques, and de-escalation should be a universal philosophy of the agency.

Recommendation 95: Patrol personnel should have at least 40 percent non-committed time.

Recommendation 96: Agencies should conduct periodic analyses regarding staffing, allocation, and deployment.

Recommendation 97: Traffic law enforcement should be performed by sworn personnel for the enhancement of public and community safety.

Recommendation 98: The agency must have a comprehensive, overall Use of Force policy that includes: (1) stressing, requiring, and specifically stating that only that amount of force which is minimally necessary to accomplish the lawful task is to be used; and (2) stating that the sanctity or reverence of life is paramount.

Recommendation 99: Personnel should be properly trained in all tools, tactics, techniques, and weapons in which they are authorized to use.

Recommendation 100: All uses of force should be fully documented. This includes any use of force and when force, or higher levels of force, could have been used, but wasn't. There should exist a standardized form that is used by the agency to document all circumstances and situations regarding the use of force.

Recommendation 101: A supervisor should immediately be made aware of any significant use of force.

Recommendation 102: Each use of force should be reviewed by the immediate supervisor and the next level of supervision.

Recommendation 103: Each use of force report should be forwarded to a designated component that reviews all use of force reports and activities. The training component should also review all use of force reports.

Recommendation 104: If the use of force was found to be inconsistent with training, necessity, or policy, the matter would be referred to the disciplinary process.

Recommendation 105: In virtually all cases of improper use of force, training should be required as part of any corrective or disciplinary decision.

Recommendation 106: Following a determination of improper use of force, certain supervisory actions should occur.

Recommendation 107: An annual use of force report should be completed and publicly published.

Recommendation 108: Agency policy should severely limit shooting at or from moving vehicles.

Recommendation 109: The agency should recognize that there are numerous mechanisms and tools of deadly force.

Recommendation 110: Officers must minimize injury and the risk of harm to all persons. Therefore, agency policy should require medical aid be provided and that citizens should be placed in positions and locations to minimize the risk of injury.

Recommendation 111: When a use of force results in significant injury, an investigation should commence immediately.

Recommendation 112: Some investigations should be conducted by an outside agency, or a regional multiagency team.

Recommendation 113: The investigation detailed above should be sent to the chief of the agency involved and the specified prosecutor.

Recommendation 114: All aspects of the actual investigation should be recorded.

Recommendation 115: The agency involved should conduct an internal investigation into these serious incidences.

Recommendation 116: The state should decide which agency will conduct any criminal investigation into the citizen's actions.

Recommendation 117: Holds and techniques that focus on the head or neck should be prohibited or extremely regulated.

Recommendation 118: Research on new tools and techniques should continue.

Recommendation 119: The use of Conducted Energy Weapons (CEW) should be expanded.

Recommendation 120: All officers present during the use of force should be required to submit a written report.

Recommendation 121: The agency should have a comprehensive procedure outlining the process when an officer is involved in a critical incident.

Recommendation 122: When an officer is involved in a critical incident, certain processes should exist to assist the officer in recovering from the effects of the incident. These processes include (1) required participation in a psychological evaluation, (2) being placed on administrative duty status pending the preliminary results of the relevant investigations, and (3) participation in a modified training session relevant to the incident prior to returning to full duty status.

Recommendation 123: The agency must have a written, comprehensive policy regarding peaceful, compliant protests.

Recommendation 124: Police agencies should support and assist with peaceful, legally compliant protests. This includes establishing communications and open dialogue with protest leaders.

Recommendation 125: As long as the protest remains peaceful and complaint, solid impact projectiles or tear gas should not be used.

Recommendation 126: The agency should exercise care and restraint in setting time limits and implementing curfews.

Recommendation 127: The agency must create policies and procedures regarding any recordings made during peaceful, compliant protests. Generally, the agency should record all protests including police actions and responses.

Recommendation 128: The agency should maintain a contemporaneous log.

Recommendation 129: Officers should wear visible identification.

Recommendation 130: The agency should carefully consider officer apparel for peaceful protests.

Recommendation 131: Agencies should have detailed policies and procedures regarding response options to these types of situations.

Recommendation 132: Significant policies, such as the use of force policies should be included in the response to disorder plan

Recommendation 133: Agency policy should require constant and continuous use of cameras.

Recommendation 134: Agency personnel should be uniformed and equipped consistent with the nature of the event.

Recommendation 135: Solid impact projectiles generally should not be used against the crowd as a whole except in extreme situations.

Recommendation 136: Tear gas should be allowed and regulated by policy.

Recommendation 137: Detailed directives should control the use of other devices.

Recommendation 138: Agency plans should provide dispersal routes.

Recommendation 139: The agency should clearly announce all changes.

Recommendation 140: A comprehensive after-action report should be completed and reviewed by the agency and other relevant entities.

Recommendation 141: Every agency should have comprehensive policies and procedures covering all aspects of vehicle pursuits.

Recommendation 142: All pursuits should be thoroughly documented. This specifically includes pursuits that occurred, when pursuits are quickly terminated, or when pursuits are never started due to policy compliance.

Recommendation 143: Pursuit reports should be reviewed through a prescribed chain of command and by the training component.

Recommendation 144: Agency personnel should be trained in emergency vehicle operations generally, and pursuits specifically.

Recommendation 145: The agency should complete an annual analysis of all pursuits.

Recommendation 146: Agencies should have comprehensive policies and procedures regarding each type of specialized vehicle in their inventory.

Recommendation 147: The use of armored vehicles should be carefully regulated. Such vehicles should be shown to the public.

Recommendation 148: Any surplus military vehicle acquired by the agency should be repainted prior to use.

Recommendation 149: Specialty vehicles should not have firearms affixed to them.

Recommendation 150: Any agency utilizing any type of aircraft or unmanned aerial vehicle must have comprehensive policies and procedures regarding their use.

Recommendation 151: All operators must be appropriately trained and certified.

Recommendation 152: Aircraft and UAV should be equipped with video capabilities.

Recommendation 153: The public should have knowledge of these resources.

Recommendation 154: Comprehensive policies and procedures must exist that cover all aspects of the police cameras. This policy must specifically require full compliance by all personnel.

Recommendation 155: Initial and periodic refresher training must be mandated regarding the operation of all cameras especially BWC.

Recommendation 156: All patrol personnel should be issued body-worn cameras and be required to use them pursuant to policy.

Recommendation 157: All police personnel should be required to wear and use body-worn cameras anytime they are making arrests, serving search warrants, conducting any type of enforcement actions, or involved in certain other activities.

Recommendation 158: Body-worn cameras should be tested at the start of each shift.

Recommendation 159: Policy should specify how and where the body-worn camera is to be worn.

Recommendation 160: Camera systems, especially body-worn cameras should be synchronized.

Recommendation 161: Videos should be randomly reviewed.

Recommendation 162: State laws regarding police-related video should be reviewed.

Recommendation 163: The agency should have comprehensive policies identifying and regulating all authorized uniforms.

Recommendation 164: The agency should supply all uniforms and accessories.

Recommendation 165: The agency should designate which uniform version will be worn for various events.

Recommendation 166: The agency should provide body armor to every sworn person and have a policy that mandates its use.

Recommendation 167: The agency must mandate that all uniforms have the officer's identification clearly readable.

Recommendation 168: Agency policy should require periodic inspections of personnel, uniforms, and equipment.

Recommendation 169: Comprehensive policies and procedures must exist regarding all aspects of firearms use.

Recommendation 170: All personnel authorized to carry a firearm must be trained. This includes initial training, periodic refresher training, and remedial training.

Recommendation 171: Agency directives should specify several aspects regarding firearms and ammunition. This should include (1) what firearms and ammunition are authorized for official use; (2) specific documentation of all firearms that are authorized, issued, or carried; and (3) maintaining the ballistics of all firearms authorized, issued, or carried.

Recommendation 172: The agency should provide the primary firearm.

Recommendation 173: The agency must have a policy regarding the carrying of a secondary or backup firearm.

Recommendation 174: The agency should mandate safe storage of all agency weapons, especially firearms.

Recommendation 175: Comprehensive policies and procedures must exist regulating all aspects of the use of shotguns and rifles.

Recommendation 176: Officer-made adjustments to firearms should be prohibited or greatly restricted.

Recommendation 177: Agency policy must address sights, scopes, and optics.

Recommendation 178: The agency must have a comprehensive directive that regulates non-training discharges of a firearm. This should require that any non-training discharge of a firearm be immediately reported, and that all such discharges must be fully investigated and documented.

Recommendation 179: Agencies must have comprehensive policies and procedures regarding all less than lethal weapons authorized by the agency.

Recommendation 180: A written directive must detail, regulate, and require training regarding less than lethal weapons. This directive must require (1) initial and periodic refresher training, and (2) that should an officer fail to successfully complete any relevant training, the specific tool should be removed from the officer.

Recommendation 181: Agency directives must regulate and mandate the carrying of less than lethal weapons. The directive should specifically require that (1) all uniformed personnel carry at least two different types of less than lethal weapons, and (2) detectives and non-undercover plainclothes personnel carry at least one type of less than lethal tool.

Recommendation 182: If a specific less than lethal tool is ineffective, then other tools or techniques must be considered.

Recommendation 183: Any and all uses of less than lethal tools should be thoroughly documented.

Recommendation 184: Elected and appointed officials should make decisions that are the best for the community and its citizens. They should not make decisions or comments based on the heat, pressure, or sudden public opinion of the moment.

Recommendation 185: Elected and appointed officials, including city councils should gather all the facts and information possible.

Recommendation 186: Police chiefs should be insulated from the political process as much as possible.

Recommendation 187: Elected and appointed officials should strive to understand policing.

Recommendation 188: Elected and appointed officials should support continued enhancements and innovation in policing.

Recommendation 189: Elected and appointed officials should assist in recruiting and retention of qualified personnel.

Recommendation 190: Elected officials and candidates should not solicit or accept political endorsements from police employee unions.

Recommendation 191: Unions must protect the rights of their members while preserving the core philosophies of policing. They must also do more to support those officers who act appropriately.

Recommendation 192: Unions should participate with management in improving work conditions and the overall work environment. They should not hinder innovations that could enhance officer safety, the work environment, or community safety.

Recommendation 193: Police unions should not appear to represent the agency and should not be involved in political contests, elections, or processes.

Recommendation 194: The media should accurately and completely report police-related issues. This includes (1) avoiding sensational headlines; (2) only using current information, images, and videos; (3) ensuring the information they disseminate is accurate and complete; and (4) accurately reporting what police personnel say.

Recommendation 195: The police and media should understand the role and needs of each other and strive to build a positive working relationship. This includes working together to draft media-related policies and procedures.

Recommendation 196: Media should not broadcast certain police activities and should not interfere with or place themselves in the middle of active investigations.

Recommendation 197: The media should respect the privacy of citizens.

Recommendation 198: Citizens should comply with laws and regulations and the lawful directions of police personnel.

Recommendation 199: Citizens have a right to complain about policing and police activities. They also have a right to video record police activity.

Recommendation 200: Citizens have a responsibility to help de-escalate situations.

Notes

PREFACE

1. (World Health Organization 2020)
2. (WORLDOMETER 2020)
3. (Lopez 2020)
4. (Lopez 2020)

CHAPTER 1

1. (Britannica 2021)
2. (Office of Justice Programs n.d.)
3. (Scott n.d.)
4. (Potter 2013)
5. (Sage Publications n.d.)
6. (Potter 2013)
7. (United States of America 2020)
8. (Lyman 1964)
9. (Law Enforcement Action Partnership n.d.)

CHAPTER 2

1. (Torrey, et al. 2016)
2. (Collision Reporting Centre 2015)
3. (Centers for Disease Control and Prevention n.d.)
4. (Centers for Disease Control and Prevention n.d.)

CHAPTER 3

1. (Stamper 2016)
2. (International Association of Chiefs of Police 2017)
3. (Federal Bureau of Investigation 2019)
4. (Jackman 2021)
5. (Tennessee v. Garner 1985)
6. (Graham v. Conner 1989)
7. (Congress, Violent Crime Control and Law Enforcement Act of 1994)
8. (Congress, Civil Action for Deprivation of Rights 1979)
9. (International Association of Directors of Law Enforcement Standards and Training n.d.)

CHAPTER 4

1. (International Association of Chiefs of Police n.d.)
2. (IMDb 2020)
3. (Eberhardt 2019)
4. (Gladwell 2007)
5. (Kahneman 2011)
6. (Commission on Accreditation for Law Enforcement Agencies, Inc. 2020)
7. (Fridell 2017)
8. (Bratton 2021)
9. (Tyler 1990)
10. (Fair and Impartial Policing 2020)
11. (Tyler 1990)
12. (Ramsey 2015)
13. (Wood 2020)

CHAPTER 5

1. (International Association of Chiefs of Police 2020)
2. (President's Task Force on 21st Century Policing 2015)
3. (President's Task Force on 21st Century Policing 2015)
4. (President's Task Force on 21st Century Policing 2015)
5. (National Advisory Commission on Criminal Justice Standards and Goals 1973)
6. (Commission on Accreditation for Law Enforcement Agencies, Inc. 2020)
7. (CALEA 2020)
8. (Commission on Accreditation For Law Enforcement Agencies 2020)
9. (Trump 2020)
10. (McMahon, et al. 2006)

11. (Fridell 2017)
12. (Merriam-Webster 2020)

CHAPTER 6

1. (International CPTED Association n.d.)

CHAPTER 8

1. (COPS/IACP 2009)
2. (International Association of Chiefs of Police 2007)
3. (Carter 1989)
4. (National Advisory Commission on Criminal Justice Standards and Goals 1973)
5. (Cunningham, Higher Education and its Impact on Discipline n.d.)
6. (Venteicher 2020)
7. (Cunningham, Reducing Recruit Attrition in Tampa: Practical Research Applied 1988)
8. (Leonard 1974)
9. (Hyland 2019)
10. (Cunningham, Reducing Recruit Attrition in Tampa: Practical Research Applied 1988)

CHAPTER 9

1. (Reaves, State and Local Law Enforcement Training Academies, 2013 2016)
2. (Reaves, State and Local Law Enforcement Training Academies, 2013 2016)
3. (Reaves, State and Local Law Enforcement Training Academies, 2013 2016)
4. (Reaves, State and Local Law Enforcement Training Academies, 2013 2016)
5. (Reaves, State and Local Law Enforcement Training Academies, 2013 2016)
6. (The Institute for Criminal Justice Training Reform 2019)
7. (The Institute for Criminal Justice Training Reform 2019)
8. (The Institute for Criminal Justice Training Reform 2019)
9. (Plant 2005)

CHAPTER 10

1. (Los Angeles Police Department n.d.)
2. (Stephens 2011)

3. (Shane 2012)
4. (Brady v. Maryland 1963)
5. (Giglio v. United States 1972)

CHAPTER 11

1. (Garrity v. New Jersey 1967)

CHAPTER 13

1. (Reaves, Local Police Departments 2013 2015)
2. (Blincoe 2015)

CHAPTER 14

1. (National Police Foundation 2016)
2. (American Red Cross 2020)

CHAPTER 15

1. (Bernstein 2020)

CHAPTER 17

1. (International Association of Chiefs of Police 2019)
2. (Criss 2019)
3. (Reeves 2017)
4. (Reeves 2017)
5. (Reeves 2017)
6. (Reeves 2017)
7. (Reeves 2017)
8. (Reeves 2017)
9. (International Association of Chiefs of Police 2019)
10. (Commission on Accreditation for Law Enforcement Agencies, Inc. 2020)
11. (Commission on Accreditation for Law Enforcement Agencies, Inc. 2020)

CHAPTER 18

1. (Defense Logistics Agency n.d.)

2. (Defense Logistics Agency n.d.)
3. (Defense Logistics Agency n.d.)
4. (National Police Foundation 2016)
5. (National Police Foundation 2016)
6. (National Police Foundation 2016)

CHAPTER 19

1. (International Association of Chiefs of Police n.d.)
2. (Airborne Public Safety Association n.d.)

CHAPTER 20

1. (Yokum 2017)
2. (Farrar 2016)

CHAPTER 21

1. (Pure History 2012)
2. (Criminal Justice Testing and Evaluation Consortium n.d.)

CHAPTER 22

1. (Smith and Mather 2017)
2. (Bartholomew 2017)
3. (Vercammen 2017)
4. (Crime Museum n.d.)

CHAPTER 25

1. (Boston Police Patrolman's Association vs. City of Boston 2016)

CHAPTER 26

1. (United States of America 2020)
2. (Ethical Journalism Network n.d.)

Bibliography

Airborne Public Safety Association. n.d. "To Serve, Save and Protect from the Air." Accessed November 2020. https://publicsafetyaviation.org.

American Red Cross. 2020. "Emergency Medical Response (EMR)." redcross.org. Accessed December 1, 2020. https://www.redcross.org/take-a-class/emergency -medical-response.

Bartholomew, Dana. 2017. "How the North Hollywood Shootout Changed Policing." Police1.com. March 1. Accessed 2021. https://www.police1.com/police-prod-ucts/body-armor/articles/how-the-north-hollywood-shootour-changed-policing -9eDfyRUJOR0FiYNt/.

Bernstein, Maxine. 2020. "Portland Police Barred from Collecting Audio, Video of Protesters - Except in Relation to Criminal Inquiries." oregonlive.com. July 30. Accessed August 2020. https://www.oregon;ive.com/crime/2020/07/judge -bars-police-from-collecting-audio-video-footage-of-protesters-except-in-relation -to-criminal-inquiries.

Blincoe, L.J., T.R. Miller, E. Zaloshnja, and B.A. Lawrence. 2015. *The Economic and Societal Impact of Motor Vehicle Crashes, 2010 (Revised)*. National Highway Traffic Safety Administration, USDOT.

Boston Police Patrolman's Association vs. City of Boston. 2016. 16-2670-B (Superior Court, September 9).

Brady v. Maryland. 1963. 373 U.S. 83, 87 (U.S. Supreme Court, May 13).

Bratton, Bill. 2021. "Implicit Bias." In *The Profession: A Memoir of Community, Race, and the Arc of Policing in America*, edited by Bill Bratton and Peter Knobler, 512. Penguin Press.

Britannica. 2021. "The History of Policing in the West." Brittanica.com. Accessed February 7, 2021. https://www.Brittanica.com/topic/police/The-history-of-policing -in-the-west.

CALEA. 2020. "CALEA-Annual-Reports." CALEA.org. June. Accessed 2021. https://www.calea.org/CALEA-Annual-Reports/2020-Annual-Report.

Carter, David, Allen D. Sapp, and Darryl W. Stephens. 1989. *The State of Police Education: Policy Direction for the 21st Century.* Washington, DC: Police Executive Research Forum.

Centers for Disease Control and Prevention. n.d. *Automated Red-Light Enforcement.* CDC.

———. n.d. *Automated Speed Camera Enforcement.* CDC.

Collision Reporting Centre. 2015. "Collision Reporting Centre.com." Accessed April 12, 2021. https://www.collision-reporting-centre.com.

Commission on Accreditation for Law Enforcement Agencies. 2020. "Perpetual Action for Public Safety and Criminal Justice." calea.org. Accessed October 2020. https://www.calea.org/sites/default/files/News.

Commission on Accreditation for Law Enforcement Agencies, Inc. 2020. *Standards for Law Enforcement Agencies.* Fairfax, VA: CALEA.

Congress, U.S. 1979. "Civil Action for Deprivation of Rights." U.S. Government Printing Office.

———. 1994. "Violent Crime Control and Law Enforcement Act of 1994." U.S. Government Printing Office.

COPS/IACP. 2009. *Law Enforcement Recruitment Toolkit.* Washington, DC: DOJ/ COPS.

Crime Museum. n.d. "North Hollywood Shootout." crimemuseum.org. Accessed December 14, 2020. https://www.crimemuseum.org/crime-library/robberies/north -hollywood-shootout.

Criminal Justice Testing and Evaluation Consortium. n.d. "Saves!" Accessed January 3, 2021. https://www.policearmor.org/saves.html.

Criss, Doug. 2019. "25 Years Ago Today, America Stopped to Watch the Cops Chase O.J. in a White Ford Bronco." cnn.com. June 17. Accessed December 2020. https:// www.cnn.com/2019/06/17us/oj-simpson-car-chase-anniversary-trnd.index.html.

Cunningham, Scott A. 2003. "Higher Education and Its Impact on Discipline." 110th Annual IACP Conference.

———. 1988. "Reducing Recruit Attrition in Tampa: Practical Research Applied." Southern Criminal Justice Association.

Defense Logistics Agency. n.d. "1033 Program FAQs." Accessed December 31, 2020. https://www.dla.mil/DispositionServices/Offers/Reutilization/LawEnforcement/ Program FAQs.aspx.

Eberhardt, Jennifer L. 2019. *Biased: Uncovering the Hidden Prejudice that Shapes What We See, Think, and Do.* New York, NY: Viking.

Ethical Journalism Network. n.d. "The 5 Principles of Ethical Journalism." ethical journalismnetwork.org. Accessed August 7, 2020. https://ethicaljournalismnet-work.org/who-we-are/5-principles-of-journalism.

Fair and Impartial Policing. 2020. "Procedural Justice." Middle Managers Training Curriculum.

Farrar, Tony. 2016. "Body-Worn Camera Study by Executive Fellow Chief Tony Farrar Is Published in Scientific Journal." policefoundation.org. Accessed October 13, 2020. https://www.policefoundation.org/body-worn-camera-study-by-execu-tive-fellow-chief-tony-farrar-is-published-in-scientific-journal.

Federal Bureau of Investigation. 2019. "National Use-of-Force Data Collection." fbi .gov. Accessed May 2020. https://www.fbi.gov/services/cjis/ucr/use-of-force.

Fridell, Lorie A. 2017. *Producing Bias Free Policing: A Science-Based Approach.* Springer.

Garrity v. New Jersey. 1967. 385 U.S. 493 (U.S. Supreme Court, January 16).

Giglio v. United States. 1972. 405 U.S. 150 (U.S. Supreme Court, February 24).

Gladwell, Malcolm. 2007. *Blink: The Power of Thinking without Thinking.* New York, NY: Back Bay Books.

Graham v. Conner. 1989. 490 U.S. 386 (U.S. Supreme Court, May 15).

Hyland, Shelley S., and Elizabeth Davis. 2019. *Local Police Departments, 2016: Personnel.* Bureau of Justice Statistics, U.S. DOJ.

IMDb. 2020. "All in the family." IMDb.com. Accessed 2020. https://www.imdb.com /Title/TT0066626/2020.

International Association of Chiefs of Police. 2007. *A Symbol of Fairness and Neutrality: Policing Diverse Communities in the 21st Century.* Arlington, TX: IACP, 10.

———. n.d. "Aviation Committee." Accessed November 2020. https://www.theiacp .org/working-group/committee/avaiation-committee.

———. 2020. *IACP Policy Framework for Improved Community-Police Engagement.* IACP.

———. n.d. "Law Enforcement Code of Ethics." Theiacp.org. Accessed March 2020. https://www.theiacp.org/resources/law-enforcement-code-of-ethics.

———. 2017. *National Consensus Policy on Use of Force.* IACP.

———. 2019. "Vehicular Pursuits." theiacp.org. December. Accessed November 2020. https://www.theiacp.org/sites/default/files/2019-12/vehicular%20Pursuits %20.

International Association of Directors of Law Enforcement Standards and Training. n.d. "NDI." iadlest.org. www.iadlest.org/About-NDI.

International CPTED Association. n.d. "International CPTED Association." Accessed June 2020. https://www.cpted.net.

Jackman, Tom. 2021. "'WashingtonPost.com.' For a Second Year, Most U.S. Police Departments Decline to Share Information on Their Use of Force." June 9. Accessed June 9, 2021. https://www.washingtonpost.com/nation/2021/06/09/ police-use-of-force-data/.

Kahneman, Daniel. 2011. *Thinking, Fast and Slow.* New York, NY: FSG.

Law Enforcement Action Partnership. n.d. "Sir Robert Peel's Policing Principles." *Law Enforcement Action Partnership.* Accessed April 2020. https://lawenforcem entactionpartnership.org/peel-policing-principles.

Leonard, V.A., and Harry More. 1974. *Police Organization and Management.* Mineola, NY: Foundation Press.

Lopez, German. 2020. "The Rise in Murders in the U.S. Explained." *VOX,* December 2.

Los Angeles Police Department. n.d. "Internal Affairs Group." Accessed December 21, 2020. https://www.lapdonline.org/internal_affairs_group.

Lyman, J.L. 1964. "The Metropolitan Police Act of 1829." *Journal of Criminal Law and Criminology* 55: 141–154.

McMahon, Joyce, Joel Garner, Ronald Davis, and Amanda Kraus. 2006. *How to Correctly Collect and Analyze Racial Profiling Data: Your Reputation Depends on It!* Washington, DC: U.S. DOJ/COPS.

Merriam-Webster. 2020. Merriam-Webster Dictionary.

National Advisory Commission on Criminal Justice Standards and Goals. 1973. *Police.* Washington, DC: U.S. GPO.

———. 1973. *Report on Police.* Washington, DC: U.S. GPO.

National Police Foundation. 2016. *Defense Logistics Agency 1033 Program: Analysis of 2019–2020 Transfers to States Law Enforcement Use.* Arlington, TX: National Police Foundation.

———. 2016. "Use-Of-Force Infographic." police foundation.org. Accessed August 2020. https://www.policefoundation.org/general-resources/use-of-force-infographic.

Office of Justice Programs. n.d. "History of the NYPD." www.ojp.gov. Accessed December 17, 2020. https://www.ojp.gove/pdffiles1/Digitization/145539NCJRS.pdf.

Plant, A.E., M.B. Peruche, and D.A. Butz. 2005. "Eliminating Automatic Racial Bias: Making Race Non-Diagnostic for Responses to Criminal Suspects." *Journal of Experimental Social Psychology* 41 (2): 141–156.

Potter, Gary. 2013. "The History of Policing in the United States, Part 1." *Police Studies Online.* June 25. Accessed May 15, 2020. https://plsonline.eku.edu/inside-look/history-policing-united-states-part-1.

President's Task Force on 21st Century Policing. 2015. *Final Report of the President's Task Force on 21st Century Policing.* Washington, DC: Office of Community Oriented Policing Services.

Pure History. 2012. "History of the New York City Police Department." purehistory.org. May 11. Accessed August 23, 2020. http://www.purehistory.org/law-enforce-ment-in-the-US/History-of-the-New-York-City-Police-Department.

Ramsey, Charles. 2015. *And Justice for All: Dignity and Respect.* Philadelphia, PA: Tedx presentation June 15.

Reaves, Brian A. 2015. *Local Police Departments 2013.* Washington, DC: Bureau of Justice Statistics, U.S. DOJ.

———. 2017. *Police Vehicle Pursuits 2012–2013.* Washington, DC: Bureau of Justice Statistics, U.S. DOJ.

———. 2016. *State and Local Law Enforcement Training Academies, 2013.* Washington, DC: Bureau of Justice Statistics, U.S. DOJ, 4.

———. 2016. *State and Local Law Enforcement Training Academies, 2013.* Washington, DC: Bureau of Justice Statistics, U.S. DOJ, 12.

Sage Publications. n.d. "The History of the Police." sagepub.com. http://www.sage-pub.com/sites/default/files/upm-binaries/50819ch.1.pdf.

Scott, Roger. n.d. "Roots: A Historical Perspective of the Office of the Sherriff." Sherriffs.org. Accessed 2021. https://www.sherrifs.org/about-nsa/history roots.

Shane, Jon M. 2012. "Disciplinary Matrix: An Emerging Concept." *Police Quarterly* (Sage) 15 (62).

Smith, Doug, and Kate Mather. 2017. "20 Years Ago, a Dramatic North Hollywood Shootout Changed the Course of the LAPD and Policing at Large." latimes.com.

February 28. Accessed 2021. https://www.latimes.com/local/lanow/la-me-in-north-hollywood-shootout-revisited-20170228-htmlstory.html.

Stamper, Norm. 2016. *To Protect and Serve: How to Fix Americas Police.* NY: Nation Books.

Stephens, Darrell W. 2011. "Police Discipline: A Case Study for Change." *New Perspectives in Policing*, June: 12.

Tennessee v. Garner. 1985. 471 U.S. 1 (U.S. Supreme Court, March 27).

Thomas Whetstone, 2021. "The History of Policing." Britannica.com. Accessed February 7, 2021. https://www.Britannica.com/topic/police/The-history-of-policing-in-the-West.

The Institute for Criminal Justice Training Reform. 2019. "37 States Allow Untrained Police." Accessed December 19, 2020. https://www.trainingreform.org/untrained-police.

Torrey, E.F., A.D. Kennard, D.F. Eslinger, H.R. Lamb, and J. Pavle. 2016. "Serious Mental Illness (SMI) Prevalence in Jails and Prisons." Treatment Advocacy Center. September. Accessed April 2020. https://treatmentadvocacycenter.org/storage/documents/backgrounders/smi-in-jails-and-prisons.

Trump, Donald J. 2020. "Executive Order 13929 Safe Policing for Safe Communities." *Federal Register, Presidential Documents* 85 (119). Washington, June 19.

Tyler, T.R. 1990. *Why People Obey the Law.* Boston, MA: Yale University Press.

United States of America. 2020. "America's Founding Documents: The Bill of Rights: A Transcription." *National Archives.* Accessed April 10, 2020. https://archives.gov/founding-docs/bill-of-rights-transcript.

Venteicher, Wes. 2020. "California Police Officers Would Have to Be 25 or Get Bachelor's Degree under New Proposal." sacbee.com. December 7. Accessed December 7, 2020. https://www.sacbee.com/new/california/article247622645.html.

Vercammen, Paul. 2017. "20 Years Ago, Gunbattle Terrorized North Hollywood - and Shocked America." ccn.com. February 28. Accessed 2021. https://www.cnn.com/2017/02/28/us/north-hollywood-bank-shootout-anniversary/index.hml.

Wood, George, T.R. Tyler, and V. Papachristos. 2020. "Procedural Justice Training Reduces Police Use of Force and Complaints against Officers." *Proceedings of the National Academy of Sciences of the United States of America*, 117: 9815–9821.

World Health Organization. 2020. "WHO Coronavirus disease (COVID-19) Dashboard." Accessed January 1, 2021. https://covid19.who.int.

WORLDOMETER. 2020. "United States Coronavirus Cases." Accessed January 1, 2021. https://www.worldometers.info/coronavirus/country/us/.

Yokum, David, A. Revishankar, and A. Coppock. 2017. "Evaluating the Effects of Police Body-Worn Cameras: A Randomized Controlled Trial." thelab@dc.gov.

Index

About the Author

Scott Cunningham is a thirty-eight-year police professional. He has served as an officer with six different agencies, including college, small town, medium-sized cities, and large urban departments. He has been certified as a police officer in Indiana, Florida, and North Carolina. For over eleven years, Chief Cunningham served as the chief of police for three agencies in North Carolina. He holds an active North Carolina certification as a police officer. He also holds multiple degrees including a Bachelor's degree in Forensic Studies and History from Indiana University, a Master's in Public Administration from Golden Gate University, and a PhD in Adult Education and Organizational Management from the University of South Florida. He attended the Administrative Officers Course at the Southern Police Institute of the University of Louisville, and the Senior Executives in State and Local Government course at Harvard University.

Chief Cunningham has served on various community boards and professional committees, commissions, and organizations. He spent eight years on the Criminal Justice Education and Standards Commission for the State of North Carolina, and has held various positions with the North Carolina Association of Chiefs of Police, and the International Association of Chiefs of Police. He is also a team leader/assessor for the Commission on Accreditation for Law Enforcement Agencies, and an Executive Trainer for Fair and Impartial Policing.

Throughout his career, he has taught at police agencies, police academies, and universities, including the Criminology Department of Texas State University. He has authored numerous articles and studies on topics such as educational benefits in policing, leadership, policy development, pursuits, and ethics.